THIEF IN THE NIGHT

The Problem. In the first half of the nineteenth century there was world-wide and fervent expectation that during the 1840's the return of Christ would take place. The story made the headlines and even reached the Congress of the United States. From China and the Middle East to Europe and America, men of conflicting ideas shared in the expectancy. Scoffers were many but the enthusiasm was tremendous, and *all agreed on the time*. Why? And what became of the story? *Did* anything happen or was it all a dream?

The Solution. Patiently, and with exemplary thoroughness, William Sears set out to solve this mystery. In *Thief in the Night* he presents his fully detailed "conduct of the case" in an easy style which enthuses the reader with the excitement of the chase. The solution to which all the clues lead comes as a tremendous challenge.

This is a mystery story with a difference: *the mystery is a real one*, and of vital importance to every human being. The author presents the evidence in *The Case of the Missing Millennium* in such a way that you can solve it for yourself.

BY THE SAME AUTHOR

BOOKS

The Flame (George Ronald)—with Robert Quigley
God Loves Laughter (George Ronald)
Release The Sun (Bahá'í Publishing Trust, Wilmette)
The Wine of Astonishment (George Ronald)
The Prisoner and the Kings (General Publishing Co. Ltd.,
Toronto)

PLAYS

Dad Cashes In (Award-winning play)
The Cardigan Kid
The Black Harvest
Gillis Is Dead
The Hour
The Undoing of Albert O'Donnel
The Soft-Boiled Egg (Sixth Yearbook of Best Plays)

FILM SCENARIOS

Dilemma in Donegal (With Robert Quigley)

TELEVISION

In The Park (Weekly Comedy, with Paul Ritts) CBS
The Bill Sears Show (Award-winning daily sports show)
WCAU-TV

THIEF IN THE
NIGHT

or

The Strange Case of the Missing Millennium

by

WILLIAM SEARS

GEORGE RONALD
OXFORD

Published by George Ronald
46 High Street, Kidlington,
Oxford, England
ALL RIGHTS RESERVED
First edition 1961
Eleventh reprint 1980
First cased edition 1980

ISBN 0 85398 096 9 (cased)
ISBN 0 85398 008 x (paper)

PRINTED IN GREAT BRITAIN BY
RICHARD CLAY (THE CHAUCER PRESS), LTD.,
BUNGAY, SUFFOLK

But the day of the Lord will come as a thief in the night; in the which the heavens shall pass away with a great noise, and the elements shall melt with fervent heat, the earth also and the works that are therein shall be burnt up.

II *Peter* iii. 10

CONTENTS

vii

FOREWORD

I admit that the headline intrigued me. Quickly I glanced at the front pages of two other newspapers.

SCIENCE PROVES SOUL IMMORTAL

CONTINENT OF ATLANTIS RISES IN
SEA OFF PORTUGAL

I looked across the television news desk at the editor.
'Anything else?'
He pointed.

MEDICAL DISCOVERY ENDS ALL DISEASE

HITLER FOUND ALIVE IN VIENNA

I nodded. 'It's the end of the world, all right.'
He handed me the magazine in which these headlines were printed.
'Take it along and read it.'
I went back to my desk in the Sports Department, opened the magazine, and began to study it carefully. It was a shot in the arm. Only this morning I had felt like a detective who was trying to solve a crime one hundred years after the deed had been committed. Until this moment, the trail had been very cold. At least this article encouraged me to go on with my search. Apparently thousands of people were still as keenly interested in solving the mystery as I was, even after more than a century.

I took a folder out of my filing cabinet and with a soft black pencil wrote on it: *The Strange Case of the Missing Millennium*.

The magazine article consisted of sample headlines from newspapers all over the country. Editors had been asked to submit to the magazine some imaginary headlines, headlines which, the editor felt, would be capable of arousing the greatest possible excitement.

They had chosen some dandies:

SCHOLARS PROVE SHAKESPEARE REALLY MARLOWE

NO MORE WINTER EVER

HOLY GRAIL FOUND IN WALES

CONAN DOYLE CONTACTS EARTH

SANTA CLAUS NO MYTH

I chuckled. The morning that all these headlines were printed would certainly be a day to run for the hills.

There was one particular effort that instantly gripped my attention. According to these hard-boiled newspapermen, this headline, if authentic, would be the most electrifying of all. This one, they said, would really rock the world back on its heels. It consisted of only two words:

CHRIST RETURNS

I had been working on just such a news story for two years. I had accidentally come upon what I considered to be an amusing and puzzling mystery, and had already spent two years trying to solve it. It all began harmlessly enough when someone handed me a book written by a namesake of mine, Clara Endicott Sears. No relative. At least so they told me around Searsport and Vanceborro in Maine. If I had known what lay ahead, I might have burned the book right then and there.

I was working a night-wire for the United Press at the time, so I had a few hours in which to sit and think. In Clara's book I found an entertaining and fascinating story about the people who had eagerly awaited the return of Christ during the nineteenth century.

My big surprise came when I learned that magazines and newspapers in that day had actually printed stories about this spectacular event. Some were told in jest, some in ridicule, and some with deadly seriousness. In the press and on the streets, you could savour every emotion:

CHRIST—COMING OR NOT?

END OF THE WORLD TOMORROW

JESUS AT THE DOOR

TERRIFYING COMET ALARMS EARTH

THE ADVENT: TRUTH OR HOAX?

Everyone enjoys a good suspense story, especially the kind of thrill implied in the threatening words: 'The end of the world!' The prophets of doom had run the gamut, from the literalist who said, 'The world will come to an end on Thursday, November 23rd at seven p.m. beginning in the Ohio Valley and spreading north through Michigan', to the earnest student of Scripture who warned that 'in that day the stars shall fall from heaven and the earth be removed from her place.'

There is no greater suspense story than this. It is filled with terror and magic, and it had been told with fantastic fervour in the 1840s.

Excited reports spread through the United States, Britain, Canada, Europe, Asia, even to Africa and Australia. People throughout those regions were strongly warned to prepare for the sudden appearance of Christ, the results of whose 'coming' promised to be either delightful or disastrous, depending on the teller.

The vast majority of people went on their way with tolerant, amused smiles. They pitied the victims of such fanaticism. Many, however, found it a time fraught with fear and panic.

In pamphlets, on the platform, in the pulpits, and in the press, Bible scholars called upon a non-listening, uninterested world to repent.

'Now is the hour!' they threatened.

Many believed them. Whole families sold their homes and possessions. Others cashed in their bank accounts and gave away their worldly goods to the unbelieving. Some prepared special ascension robes. Tradition states that some went up into the hills on a fatal, chosen day, to await the descent of Christ upon a cloud, only to be greeted by a downpour of rain.

I examined actual legal records in which some of the zealous deeded over their property to the coming Christ. An entire village was prepared for His coming. It was called Heaven (Paradise), and was established as His American residence.

A passionate madness seized people in widely separated sections of the Christian world at that time. Why? Why did they all expect Christ? Why at that particular time?

It was a puzzling, first-class mystery story. It was as though a 'millennial' virus had suddenly infected people in five continents. As I read about the colourful, amusing, and sometimes shocking things that happened in these widely scattered parts of the world, I became curious, and that curiosity was the beginning of this volume.

I can't honestly say whether it was in the Library, the Museum, or by the Cave of Elijah on Mount Carmel that I suddenly found myself engrossed in a fascinating full-time study. The growth of interest had been gradual, but eventually I was determined to find out whether the return of Christ was a myth, a mistake, or the greatest unsolved mystery of our age.

One day in the reference room of one of the endless libraries I haunted during this period, I experienced a sudden, unique thrill, the sort the archaeologist must feel when his pick strikes a wall and he sees it crumble before his eyes, revealing an ancient, exciting new world, at the very moment he was about to abandon his search.

I discovered I was *not* on a wild-goose chase! Among those dusty library shelves I found a fellow-detective, and in his company the excitement of the chase began all over again. Professor E. G. Browne of Pembroke College, Cambridge, had broken the ground before me. He, too, apparently had been fascinated by the same story and had already unravelled a part of it. He wrote likening it to the story of Christ:

'I feel it my duty, as well as pleasure . . . to bring the matter to the notice of my countrymen. . . .'[1]

Later I traced Browne's searching steps in the Holy Land; I read the letter in his own handwriting in which he made plans to come to Israel to meet this great Figure. He admitted that he would not rest until he had settled the matter in his own mind.[2]

I found that a contemporary of Browne's, the renowned Jowett of Balliol College, Oxford, had echoed this feeling. He, too, had chanced upon the story that now lay open before me. He wrote:

'It is too great and too near for this generation to comprehend. The future alone can reveal its import.'[3]

Both Professors Browne and Jowett associated their discovery with the return of Christ They both expressed keen interest in the relevance and import of the story. Now, after several years of careful research and study, I, too, had arrived at this same conclusion. I decided to take up the story where they had left it and to follow it to its end.

The following chapters are the record of my seven years of search; they offer my solution to this intriguing century-old mystery. They suggest that our modern newspapermen are one hundred years too late in wishing that they were able to print the dramatic headline:

CHRIST RETURNS

In fact, our press has been scooped by over a century. You will find here considerable evidence to show that when the newspapers and publications of the 1840s printed their stories headed, *Return of Christ Expected,* they were printing not fancy, but fact, even though they were unaware of the nature of the story at the time, and were totally unable to substantiate its truth in that hour.

If what I have uncovered is the truth, then (according to the testimony of the hard-boiled newspaper editors of the West) it is the most shocking and dramatic story that anyone could possibly tell in print.

But will anyone believe me?

You are now starting where I started a few years ago on *The Strange Case of the Missing Millennium.*

WILLIAM SEARS.

PART ONE

The Unsolved Problem

1. Once to Every Man and Nation

My first step was to investigate that period in history between the years 1830 and 1850. It was a time of strange and troublesome events. Men stared in wonder and uneasiness at the great halo that circled the sun. They looked up fearfully at the night sky where a giant comet with a fiery tail rushed through the darkness. Some said that the comet was racing toward mankind bringing the 'end of the world'.

An interesting account of this period reads:

> 'A converted Jew in Palestine, Joseph Wolff, predicted the Advent (of Christ) for 1847. Harriet Livermore, an eloquent and arresting woman of the time, who figures in Whittier's *Snowbound*, preached the Second Coming everywhere, including the House of Representatives at Washington, where crowds gathered to hear her. Lady Hester Stanhope, a valiant madwoman, niece of William Pitt, who turned her back on London and power and fashion, made her home in Lebanon among the Arabs and Druses, in order to be ready and near to the scene of the Advent. She kept, it was reported, two white Arab steeds in her stable, one for the Messiah, one for herself!'[1]

Another writer stated:

> 'There is a little mosque, we are told, in the Holy Land, where a priest presides, keeping ready the shoes that the Messiah is to wear when he comes to Jerusalem.'[2]

It was said of those days:

'So real was the hope of the Advent, people were actually taking almost violent measures for it. It was the nineteenth century, yet the shooting stars of the year 1833, and the parahelia, or halo-like rings, around the sun in 1843, were objects of the most awesome speculation and discussion. And the tail of the great comet of 1843 measured 108 million miles in length. ... Whole families were engaged in making shrouds against that fateful day.'[3]

Some of the more zealous believers, it is said, donned their 'ascension robes' and prepared to await Christ's descent upon the clouds of heaven.

Their more sceptical, and practical, but equally uninformed neighbours pointed out that clouds did not *descend*, but were vapours that *rose up* from the earth.

Other scholars quoted St. Augustine who had written an entire volume proving that there could not be anyone living on the other side of the earth because it would then be impossible for such people to see Christ when He *came down* in the clouds on the day of His return.

Mathematicians asked: 'Which way is *down*? Furthermore, they said, taking into consideration the curvature of the earth, there would have to be thousands and thousands of 'solo' flights to the earth by Christ before all humanity would be able to see His descent. They poked fun at the literalists in many other ways, saying that obviously this coming *down* on the *clouds* was symbolical.

Still others suggested that perhaps these clouds were not a chariot that Christ rode from heaven, but a mist that arose from earth to obscure man's vision.

However, in spite of scepticism and doubt, designers created special 'ascension robes' in various styles for the great coming event, especially for those who wished to be in fashion on that day. It is said that they were displayed in some of the shop windows in the Eastern parts of the United States. Although this matter of ascension robes has been hotly denied in many quarters, I frequently encountered the story.

The following letter, one among many, makes this point quite evident. The letter was written by Ida M. Wing to Clara Endicott Sears on August 21st, 1921. It reads:

'I have heard my mother tell that when she was a girl she remembers that her mother made a white robe, put her house in order, put lamps in the windows and sat up all night waiting for the end of the world to come.'[4]

When the great comet of 1843 streaked across the heavens, people pointed at it with alarm, saying:

'It is now the hour for Christ's return!'

In that same year, the poet James Russell Lowell wrote:

> 'Once to every man and nation
>   comes the moment to decide,
> Some great cause, God's new Messiah. . . .'[5]

The French poet Lamartine, in a flood of praise, asked of God: Is this not the time for you to reveal yourself?

On May 24th, 1844, in Washington D.C., Mr. Samuel F. B. Morse, the inventor of the telegraph, stepped to the keyboard of his new instrument. He was about to send the first official telegram in history flashing along the wires from Washington to Baltimore. The press had heralded this day as a modern miracle. By this invention, it was said, the world would be united physically in the twinkling of an eye. These lightning-like impulses leaping along the wires would shrink the size of the planet, they said.

In fact, when Congress appropriated $40,000 for Morse to continue his work, he was told that now he could send his "lightnings" to the world. Thus his invention was associated

3

with the words in the *Book of Job*, although at the time it was said partly in jest.

Students of Scripture asked: 'Is this not still another proof that 1844 is indeed the hour for the appearance of Christ? Is it not written in the Book of Job that only *God* can send 'lightnings that they may go and say unto thee *here we are*!'[6] Does it not mean that Christ is here? Did not this same Job promise:

'For I know that my redeemer liveth, and that *he shall stand at the latter day* upon the earth.'[7]

Samuel Morse put his hand to the keyboard of the telegraph and tapped out that first formal message. The words were taken from the *Book of Numbers*:

'What hath God wrought!'[8]

I was curious about that message of Morse in 1844. What *had* God wrought in that day, if anything besides the telegraph? Was there a hidden story? Was it possible to find it? At least this was a beginning.

About this time I came upon the account of a lecture given by the British scientist, Sir Lawrence Bragg, in Carnegie Hall, New York. Sir Lawrence drew a graph of the scientific achievements of man until the period around 1844. He showed that man's advancement up until that time had been very slow, so slow, indeed, that the line of the graph up to 1844 was almost horizontal.

Subsequently, however, and immediately, the line of the graph went almost directly upwards, and has continued to climb ever since.

This *did* interest me. Why? What had caused this new spirit of energy and creation in the world following the year 1844? Why had it begun in that particular period?

4

Had some historical event taken place in 1844 which could account for this new upsurge of knowledge and invention? Was there some happening which the historians had overlooked, or neglected? Did it have anything to do with the coming of the Messiah, the generally talked about return of Christ in that very year?

These were questions to which I now eagerly wanted the answer. *The Case of the Missing Millennium* was at last becoming interesting. I decided to make a thorough check on the exact year of Morse's 1844 message.

2. The Strange Case of the Missing Millennium

I soon discovered that the year 1844 figured more prominently in the calculations of millennial Bible scholars than any other year. Many of these students of Scripture, working independently of each other in separate continents, arrived at almost the identically same time for the return of Christ.

It was the period 1843–5.

Wolff in Asia, Edward Irving in England, Mason in Scotland, Davis in South Carolina, William Miller in Pennsylvania, Leonard H. Kelber in Germany, and many others in various parts of the world believed that this was indeed the 'time of the end'.[1]

These Bible scholars did not all agree on the exact date, nor did they all explain the prophecies in a like manner. However, it was said of them:

> '. . . In America, Europe, and Asia the clear message of the ending of the prophetic time in 1844 was proclaimed with power by many voices.'[2]

Andrew Jackson Davis delivered 157 lectures in New York in 1845. Edgar Allan Poe attended regularly, and heard

Davis foretell the time when travel advertisements would read, 'Through to California in four days!' Davis also foretold the future speed of air travel. He repeatedly lauded the wonder of the new age that was coming, calling it a material heaven that was a preparation for the spiritual kingdom. He said, 'A glorious period is before mankind. . . . Fall in love with the new dispensation.'[3]

William Miller began lecturing in 1831 concerning the return of Christ. He declared that he couldn't help himself, that a voice kept urging him on, saying, 'Go tell the world.' In 1832, he wrote: 'The evidence flows from every quarter . . . Behold the Saviour comes!'[4]

Forman, in his *Story of Prophecy* says, 'The causes for religious stirrings were at that period in the air and ubiquitous'.[5] He points out that Emerson attended a convention on Universal Reform and himself commented on the wide variety of those present, from madmen to philosophers. In Emerson's own words, they were 'madmen, madwomen, men with beards, Dunkers, Uggletonians, Come-Outers, Groaners, Agrarians, Seventh-Day Baptists, Quakers, Abolitionists, Calvinists, Unitarians and Philosophers.'[6]

No wonder Clara Endicott Sears subtitled her book, *A Strange Bit of History*.

Just as 1844 approached, a clergyman of the Church of England, Mourant Brock, made the following statement:

'It is not merely in Great Britain that the expectation of the near return of the Redeemer is entertained, and the voice of warning raised, but also in America, India, and on the continent of Europe. In America about three hundred ministers of the Word are thus preaching this gospel of the kingdom; whilst in this country, about seven hundred of the Church of England are raising the same cry.'[7]

I realized that with over a thousand clergymen in two

6

countries alone preaching the return of Christ at that period, *The Case of the Missing Millennium* became a story well worth investigating further.

W. A. Spicer, in *Our Day in the Light of Prophecy*, wrote:

'Here and there students of the Word saw that the 2300 year period of *Daniel* viii. 14, as explained in the ninth chapter, would end soon . . . and looked to the year 1844 as the time when the judgment would come.'

Speaking of this unique convergence of prophecies upon the year 1844, Spicer wrote:

'Witnesses were raised up in Europe, in Holland, Germany, Russia, and the Scandinavian countries. Joseph Wolff, the missionary to the Levant, preached in Greece, Palestine, Turkey, Afghanistan, and other regions, the coming of the judgment hour.'

This millennial zeal reached its climax in the year 1844. I wanted to know exactly why. What had led all these people to the same year?

I found the answer. This date in history had been chosen primarily because of *three specific promises* made by Christ Himself to His disciples. He gave these three promises, saying that when these three things came to pass, He (Christ) would return to earth. The promises are as follows:

1. His Gospel would be preached everywhere on earth.
2. The 'times of the Gentiles' would be fulfilled, and the Jews would return to Israel (Palestine).
3. All mankind would see the 'abomination of desolation' foretold by Daniel the Prophet.

My next step, therefore, was to take up these *three promises* in order, and to follow this clue to its conclusion.

My plan was simple. I would (1) find each promise made by Christ in the Scriptures, (2) decide exactly what Christ *had* promised to His disciples, (3) determine if these three promises had actually been fulfilled, and (4) if they had been fulfilled, just when and how.

I was no longer dealing with theory: I now had something specific to consider.

3. The First Promise

The *first promise* of Christ was easy to find. He made it to His disciples in direct reply to their questions. They asked Him:

'Tell us, when shall these things be? And what shall be the sign of thy coming, and of the end of the world?'[1]

This verse is found in the twenty-fourth chapter of *Matthew*. Christ then gave His *first promise* to His disciples in the following words:

'But he that shall endure unto the end, the same shall be saved. And this gospel of the Kingdom shall be preached in all the world for a witness . . . then shall the end come.'[2]

This was clear enough. The end would come, and Christ would return, when His Gospel was preached throughout the world.

My next step was to discover when the Gospel of Christ was considered to have been preached throughout the world.

A study of the spread of Christianity made by scholars of the 1840's, convinced them that the message of Christ had, by their day, already encircled the globe. The Gospel was being taught in all the continents. By 1844 it was being taught even in the interior of Africa, not by solitary missionaries, but on an

8

organised scale. A commercial history of East Africa states: 'Christian missions began their activities amongst the African people in 1844.'[3]

Dr. D. L. Leonard, historian of the Mission movement, in his *A Hundred Years of Missions*, says of the spread of the Word of Christ and His Gospel: '. . . for the first time since the apostolic period, (there) occurred an outburst of general missionary zeal and activity.'

He is speaking of the last years of the eighteenth century, leading to the nineteenth century, to 1844, and beyond. 'Beginning in Great Britain, it soon spread to the Continent and across the Atlantic. It was no mere push of fervour, but a mighty tide set in, which from that day to this has been steadily rising and spreading.'

Another account states: 'In 1804 the British and Foreign Bible Society was organised. Students of the prophetic word felt at the time that these agencies were coming in fulfilment of the prophecy.'[4]

This was a direct reference to the prophecy of Christ that He would return when His gospel was preached everywhere in the world.

Before 1804, the Bible had already been printed and circulated in fifty languages. In 1816 the American Bible Society was formed. George Storrs in the newspaper, *Midnight Cry*, on May 4th, 1843, stated that these two societies (British and American) with their innumerable branches were spreading the Gospel of Christ in every part of the world.

G. S. Faber in *Eight Dissertations*, which was completed in the very year of greatest prophetic fervour, 1844, declares: 'The stupendous endeavours of one gigantic community to convey the Scriptures in every language to every part of the globe may well deserve to be considered as an eminent sign even of these eventful times. Unless I be much mistaken, such

9

endeavours are preparatory to the final grand diffusion of Christianity, which is the theme of so many inspired prophets, and which cannot be far distant in the present day.'

M. H. Goyer writes in his book on prophetic fulfilment: 'The British and Foreign Bible Society (for one example) has issued, since its foundation in 1804, over 421 million copies of the Scriptures, in practically every country known throughout the globe.'

In *Our Day in the Light of Prophecy*, Spicer wrote that the Gospel in his day had been spread 'to ninety-five per cent. of the inhabitants of the earth.' He added: 'It was in *1842* that five treaty-ports in China were opened to commerce and to missions—advance steps in the opening of all China to the Gospel. In *1844* Turkey was prevailed upon to recognise the right of the Moslems to become Christians, reversing all Moslem tradition. In *1844* Allen Gardiner established the South American Mission. In *1842* Livingstone's determination was formed to open the African interior.'

Dr. A. T. Pierson in *Modern Mission Century* wrote: 'India, Siam, Burma, China, Japan, Turkey, Africa, Mexico, South America . . . were successively and successfully entered. Within five years, from 1853 to 1858, new facilities were given to the entrance and occupation of seven different countries, together embracing half the world's population.'

There were many additional references which made it clear that the Gospel of Christ, and its teachers, had entered every continent by the year 1844, spreading the Word of Jesus the Christ throughout the world.

This was considered by the students of Scripture to be in exact fulfilment of the words of Christ given in *Mark:*

   'And the gospel must first be published among all nations.'[5]

In this same chapter, Christ warns that when this takes place:

'Take ye heed, watch and pray: for ye know not when the time is.'[6]

When this Gospel is published in all nations, Christ again promises:

'. . . then shall they see the Son of man coming in the clouds with great power and glory.'[7]

The millennial scholars of the 1840's felt that Christ's first promise had been fulfilled. They felt it had been clearly demonstrated that the Gospel of Christ had been 'preached in all the world for a witness' and, therefore, the hour for His coming must now be at hand.

I was convinced myself that the *first promise* of Christ had indeed been fulfilled by the year 1844. There could be no doubt of this.

It was an interesting beginning.

4. The Second Promise

The *second promise* of Christ was just as easy to find. It was in the twenty-first chapter of *Luke*. This promise was also made by Christ in reply to a direct question asked by His disciples. They asked Him:

'. . . When shall these things be? and what sign will there be when these things shall come to pass?'[1]

Christ warned them of false prophets in that day, who would bear His name, then He gave them His *second promise* by which they could be sure of His own return. He said:

'And they shall fall by the edge of the sword, and shall

be led away captive into all nations: and Jerusalem shall be trodden down of the Gentiles, *until the times of the Gentiles be fulfilled.* . . . And then shall they see the Son of man coming in a cloud with power and great glory.'[2]

The meaning of the term 'times of the Gentiles' was familiar and clear to Scriptural scholars. I learned that it denoted that period of time during which Jerusalem would be held in the power of aliens, non-Jews (or Gentiles), and during which the Jews themselves would be excluded from their homeland.

In plain words, Christ promised that He would return to earth when the Jews came back to their homeland following their period of banishment. Thus, in the hour of their return, the 'times of the Gentiles' would be fulfilled.

I made a careful study of Christ's *second promise*. The first part of it said: 'They shall be led away captive into all nations.' I found that within forty years after His crucifixion, this part of His promise began its fulfilment.

Jerusalem was destroyed by the Roman Titus, in A.D. 70, and the Jews were scattered and exiled. The Jews tried to regain their freedom in A.D. 132 under Bar Cochba, but they were crushed by the armies of the Roman Emperor Hadrian. This time Jerusalem was devastated even more completely than it had been by Titus. The site of the city was ploughed under and a new city, named in honour of Hadrian, was built upon the ruins.

The Jews were banished. Many of them, exactly as had been foretold by Christ, fell 'by the edge of the sword.' They fled, scattered, and were 'led away captive into all nations.'

It was permissible for colonists to enter Jerusalem, but it was a crime punishable by death for a Jew to enter.

The Romans were the first aliens (Gentiles) after the time of Christ to tread down the holy city of Jerusalem. The next aliens to seize and hold it captive were the Muslims. They conquered Jerusalem in A.D. 637 and upon the foundation of the Temple of Solomon, they raised the Mosque of Omar. During their period of occupation, Jews were largely excluded from their homeland, the few remaining being proscribed.

This restriction came to an end in the year 1844. Remarkable!

The famous Irish scholar and author, George Townshend writes: '... the strict exclusion of the Jews from their own land enforced by the Muslims for some twelve centuries was at last relaxed by the Edict of Toleration and the "times of the Gentiles" were fulfilled.'[3]

Townshend further points out that this document, the *Edict of Toleration*, was issued by the governing authorities in the year *1844*.

Worth Smith also mentions this Edict in his *Miracle of the Ages*. He points out: 'In the year of A.D. 1844 ... the (Muslims) under the leadership of Turkey were compelled by the Western Powers, notably England, to grant religious toleration to all (nations) within their borders.'

This included the Holy Land, Palestine. I was able to secure and study copies of the original letters and documents which led to the signing of the so-called Edict of Toleration in 1844. The Turkish Government agreed to permit religious freedom and signed the document which guaranteed that 'The Sublime Porte (Constantinople) engages to take effectual measures to prevent henceforward' any further religious intolerance. For the first time in twelve hundred years the Jews were guaranteed the right to return to Israel in freedom and security. The date on this document was March 21st, 1844.

Bickersteth in *A Practical Guide to the Prophecies*, wrote: 'In a letter from Tangiers, date June 20th, 1844, given in the public journals, speaking of the difficulties besetting the kingdom of Morocco, it is stated: "It seems that the Moors

(Muslims) have always had forebodings of this year. For a long time they have been exhorting each other to beware of 1260 (1844) which according to our reckoning is the present year ".'

These millennial scholars found strong confirmation in the New Testament itself that 1844 was the year intended by Christ for the fulfilment of His *second promise* concerning the 'times of the Gentiles.' This confirmation came from the *Book of Revelation*. In chapter eleven it states:

'And the Holy City (Jerusalem) shall they tread under foot for forty and two months.'

. Thus, for the first time in the Scriptures, the exact duration of the 'times of the Gentiles' is given. It will be for forty-two months. In the next verse of Revelation this period of time is given in yet another way. It is said it will last for '1260 days.'

Bible scholars insisted that the end of this period of forty-two months or 1260 days was identical with the year 1844. This fascinated me, so I set down their process of reasoning. They arrived at this conclusion by the following deductions:

1. In the study of biblical prophecy, the period of time called a 'day' becomes a 'year' when calculating the passing of time:
2. This theory was supported by the following prophecies.
A. *Numbers* xiv. 34. 'Even forty days, each day for a year.'
B. *Ezekiel* iv. 6. 'I have appointed thee each day for a year.'

There was general agreement on this formula.
In the compilation *The Story of Prophecy* by Henry James Forman, I found the following: '. . . Biblical prophecy

students, after a scrutiny of the entire problem of Bible chronology, deduce the following conclusions as virtually axiomatic—namely, that (1) In symbolic prophecy a day is the symbol for a year . . .'

On this same subject, F. Hudgings in his *Zionism in Prophecy* writes: 'A solar year, of course, contains a fraction over 365 days, but in computing 'symbolic time' as it is set forth in the Scripture, students of prophecy find that the writers simply divided the year into 12 months of 30 days each. In other words, a time or a year in Scriptural symbology refers to 360 solar years—each day representing a year.'

Further study revealed that it was not such an arbitrary choice on the part of these students of Scripture as might at first appear.

Their measuring rod was taken from the first book of the Bible, *Genesis*. The axiom of 360 days for a *year* or a *time* was derived from the following verses:

1. *Genesis* vii. 11.—The waters of the flood came on the *17th day* of the *second* month.
2. *Genesis* viii. 4—The waters abated and ceased on the *17th day* of the *seventh* month.
3. *Genesis* vii. 24:—The waters prevailed upon the earth *150 days*.

From the *17th day* of the *second month* to the *17th day* of the *seventh* month was exactly *five* months. These five months took exactly *150* days. Therefore, they were *five* months of *30* days each. This, the scholars agreed, would make a year of *360* days, or *12* months of *30* days.

Therefore, a *day* in calculating prophecy was a *year* of 360 days.

By using this accepted formula of a *day* for a *year*, the scholars calculated that the Gentiles would tread the Holy City

(Jerusalem) under foot for 1260 years. Therefore, the prophecy from Revelation could now be read:

'And the Holy City (Jerusalem) shall they tread under foot for 1260 years.'

According to the *second promise* of Christ, these Gentiles (Romans-Muslims) would tread the city underfoot until the hour of His return which would be 1260 years by the measurement of prophecy. During all that time, the Jews would be banished from their own land. But, in the hour of Christ's return, the privilege of going home would be restored to them, and the 'times of the Gentiles' would be ended.

An examination of the calendar of the Muslims, who held the Holy City captive, revealed to these millennial scholars an astonishing thing: The year 1260 of the calendar of the Muslims coincided with the year 1844 of the calendar of the Christians.

The year 1260 given in *Revelation* as the time when the days of the 'Gentiles' would be ended and the Jews would be permitted to return to their homeland, was the same year as that of 1844 when the Muslim rulers were forced to sign the Edict of Toleration permitting the return of the Jews to Israel.

I began to understand the growing enthusiasm of the Bible scholars of the 1840's. Christ had promised that when the 'times of the Gentiles' was fulfilled, He would come back to earth. To these students of Scripture, the *second promise* of Christ was exactly fulfilled, and the date (1844) established without question.

I was inclined to agree. This made me more eager than ever to test the third and final promise.

5. The Third Promise

I found the *third promise* of Christ to be the most interesting of all. It was given in the twenty-fourth chapter of *Matthew*.

This *third promise* was again given in direct answer to the questions of His disciples:

'And as he sat upon the mount of Olives, the disciples came unto him privately, saying, Tell us, when shall these things be? And what shall be the sign of thy coming?'[1]

Christ foretold that 'iniquity shall abound' in that day, and that the 'love of many shall wax cold'; then He makes His *third promise* in these words:

'*When ye therefore shall see the abomination of desolation, spoken of by Daniel the prophet,* stand in the holy place, (whoso readeth, let him understand.)'[2]

The chapters of *Daniel* which deal with this subject are those from eight to twelve inclusive. These chapters (according to the millennial scholars, as well as my own research) foretell not only the *second* coming of Christ, but to my keen interest, His *first* appearance as well.

It was this link between the *first* and the *second* coming of Christ which give to these chapters of *Daniel* such great importance in the study of the subject, and indeed this *third promise* was considered to be the most important of the three.

In these chapters, Daniel prophesies that from the issuing of the decree to rebuild Jerusalem, until the time when the Messiah shall be cut off (crucified) there are appointed 70 weeks. Daniel gives this prophecy in two different ways:

1. As 70 weeks.
2. As 7 weeks, 62 weeks, and one week; during which the Messiah confirms the covenant.

However, both ways total up to 70 weeks or to 490 days. This becomes 490 years in prophecy with a *day* for a *year*.

17

In His *first* coming, it is prophesied that from the issuing of the decree to His *cutting off*, or crucifixion, 490 years will pass. The important thing then was for me to discover at what time the decree had been issued.

I found that there were four decrees to rebuild Jerusalem. They were as follows:

1. Issued by Cyrus in the year 536 B.C. This decree is recorded in the first chapter of *Ezra*. *It went unfulfilled.*
2. Issued by Darius in the year 519 B.C. This decree is recorded in the sixth chapter of *Ezra*. *It also went unfulfilled.* Only the Temple was rebuilt.
3. Issued by Artaxerxes in the seventh year of his reign in the year 457 B.C. This is recorded in the seventh chapter of *Ezra*. *It was fulfilled by the fourth decree.*
4. Issued by the same Artaxerxes in the year 444 B.C. This is recorded in the second chapter of *Nehemiah*. *This decree fulfilled the third.*

Most of the students of Scripture accepted the third decree of Artaxerxes as the one referred to by Daniel. They reasoned that since the fourth decree was merely an extension of the third, and was issued by the same king it was in reality the same decree. Therefore, they favoured the decree issued in 457 B.C.

With this knowledge, it was now possible to state the prophecy of Daniel as follows: From the issuing of the decree of Artaxerxes in the year 457 B.C. until the time of the crucifixion of Jesus the Christ, there would be appointed (or pass) 70 weeks, 490 days—or in prophecy, 490 years.

Many Bible scholars merely subtracted the 457 from the 490. This gave them 33 years. The Messiah (Christ) in His *first* coming would therefore be 33 years of age when He was cut off or slain.

I found that authorities differed widely as to the date of the birth of Christ, as well as to the date of His death. According to the Gospels, His birth took place before the death of Herod. Many historians calculated the death of Herod to have taken place in the month of April in the year 4 B.C. Some said it was the year 5, some 6, some as early as the year 8 B.C. Therefore, some of these scholars maintained that Christ was only 28 or less at the time of His death.

Others give a different year and a different day. However, they all centre around the period foretold by Daniel. Thus with amazing accuracy, Daniel had given the time for the *first* coming of Christ. No wonder Jesus Himself was so emphatic about Daniel's prophecy concerning His *second* coming or return. He told His disciples to 'stand in the holy place' when Daniel's prophecy about the 'abomination of desolation' was fulfilled. In that day He promised:

'. . . they shall see the Son of man coming in the clouds of heaven . . .'[3]

I followed the pattern of the millennial scholars of the 1840's and carefully examined Daniel's prophecy concerning the 'abomination of desolation'. His exact words were:

'How long shall be the vision concerning the daily sacrifice, and the *abomination of desolation*, to give the sanctuary and the host to be trodden under foot? And he said unto me, Unto two thousand and three hundred days; then shall the sanctuary be cleansed.'[4]

Thus Daniel prophesied that two thousand three hundred days (2300) would pass before the sanctuary would be cleansed. Following this time, all things would be made pure again. Before this time, the people would have fallen into a state of 'abomination' without love for God or man; then the

Messiah would appear and restore their Faith and the purity of their belief. This was the general conclusion.

When would this take place? Daniel said it would come to pass in 2300 days. In prophecy, this becomes 2300 years.

Using the same frame of reference for the *second* coming, as was used for the *first* coming (the decree of Artaxerxes), the Bible scholars made the following calculations:

1. The decree was issued in 457. They subtracted 457 from 2300 and arrived at 1843. Thus the year 1843, they said, would mark the beginning of the end of the 'abomination of desolation.'
2. Some scholars pointed out that from the issuing of the decree in 457 until the birth of Christ there were 456 years, not 457; therefore, it was necessary to subtract 456 from 2300. This left the year 1844.

Although many disputes arose as to the exact month, day, and hour, there was a basic agreement among nearly all that Christ's return must take place between the years 1843 and 1845, with the year 1844 as the central point of reference.

One group of Christian scholars worked out Daniel's prophecy in the greatest detail. They even built a special chart to show that Christ would return in the middle of the year 1844.[5]

E. P. Cachemaille, sometime scholar of Cambridge University, in a new edition of H. G. Guinness's book *Light for the Last Days*, maintains that this book had been recognised for over thirty years as a standard work of chronological prophecy. He quotes Guinness as saying the following about Daniel's prophecy: 'The decree (Edict of Toleration) was published in the 1260th year of the (Muslim) calendar. It is dated March 21st, 1844. This date is the first of Nisan in the Jewish year, and is exactly twenty three centuries (2300 years) from the first of Nisan, B.C. 457, the day on which Ezra states that he left Babylon in compliance with the decree given in the seventh year of the reign of Artaxerxes.'

Thus the year 1844 was firmly established in their minds as the year for the fulfilment of the *third promise* of Christ concerning Daniel's prophecy.

I found that *all three* of Christ's promises to His disciples had been fulfilled exactly as He promised.

1. The Gospel had been preached in all the world for a witness.
2. The times of the Gentiles had been fulfilled.
3. The prophecy of Daniel given by Christ as the time to stand in the holy place had come to pass.

Each of these promises had been fulfilled in the year 1844!

6. Other Promises

During my investigation of the *three promises* of Christ, I had come upon several other astonishing prophecies which I decided to record before moving on to the next field of investigation. I have selected only a few of the most interesting.

To me *The Case of the Missing Millennium* had taken on greater stature, not to mention excitement. Together with the Christian scholars of that day, I, too, had found that prophecy after prophecy terminated in the year 1844.

These prophecies spoke of the *Time of the end*, the *Day of Judgement*, the *Last days*, the *Day of Resurrection*, and the *Hour for the Return of Christ*. Yet they spoke of them in a new and provocative manner.

Christ said:

'. . . there shall be wars and rumours of wars . . . And then shall they see the Son of man coming . . .'

Bible scholar Paul K. Dealy in his *Dawn of Knowledge* writes:

'History records the following great wars among the leading nations: (1) About this time a war was in progress between China and England terminating in the loss of Hong Kong to the former. A treaty was signed between them in 1842. (2) The Crimean war—England, France and Turkey against Russia 1854. (3) The atrocious Sepoy mutiny 1857-8. (4) France and Italy against Austria 1859. (5) Civil war of the United States 1861-65. (6) Franco-Prussian war 1870-1. (7) Russian–Turkish war 1877-8. (8) And during the last decade the wars between China and Japan, Turkey and Greece, Spain and the United States, the invasion of China by all the great powers, and the Boer war.'

To this list could be added the two greatest world wars that mankind had ever seen. The Korean war, the war in Indo-China, the Arab–Jewish war, the multiplying minor wars and revolutions within countries, the increasing border skirmishes, the constant 'cold war' and the never-ending newspaper head-lines that threaten man daily with 'rumours of wars.' Certainly the words of Christ aptly fit this day.

In the late 1800's, the conviction became very strong among the American Indians that the Messiah had already appeared and was on earth. Throughout the Western Hemisphere, the great majority of Indians had for centuries been awaiting the appearance of their promised Redeemer.

In the latter part of the nineteenth century, General Miles of the United States Army reported in a St. Paul, Minnesota, newspaper that during his tour of the west, 'I have learned that this belief (in the Messiah) exists among . . . 16 tribes.'

The belief in the coming of this same Messiah was also strongly held in the East. Krishna had foretold the coming of a great World Educator.

G. S. Arundale, Education Commissioner of Indore State,

India, in his introduction to *The Coming World Teacher*, writes: 'So many thousands of people all over the world believe in the near coming of a Great World Teacher, that the existence of this belief is a matter of common knowledge, at least among the educated people.'

Commissioner Arundale expresses the belief that the hope of mankind lies in this direction, and he conveys this message, he says, '. . . to young and old, to Jews, to Christians, to Musselmans, to Buddhists, to Parsees, to Jains, to Hindus.' He adds that 'to many in each of these pathways to God the belief in the near coming of a Great World Teacher has been as a great alchemical power transforming their lives.'

Taylor in his *Reign of Christ on Earth*, states that in Yemen (Temen of the Scriptures) a rabbi told Mr. Wolff, (an ardent believer in the return of Christ in the 1840's) that his tribe did not return to Jerusalem after the Babylonian captivity even when Ezra by special letter invited their princes to return. They feared Daniel's prophecy of the destruction of Jerusalem. 'But,' the rabbi said, 'we do expect the coming of the Messiah.'

The Roman poet Virgil spoke of the Messianic prophecies, saying that they 'point to an age to come, and a new birth of nature, and at the same time link the glorious Kingdom they depict with an exalted Personage who would, they say, reduce all mankind to a single empire.'

The historian Plutarch wrote: 'There will come a time, appointed by fate, when . . . happy men shall have one and the same life, language and government.'

The Greek philosopher Plato foresaw that 'in the end . . . God the author of the primitive order, will appear again and resume the reins of Empire.'

In Hazlitt's *Table Talks*, we read that Martin Luther himself 'expressed the thought that Christ might come in 1558 or 105 years after the conquest of Constantinople by the Turks (in 1453).'

As a matter of fact, I found that this date—the fall of Constantinople to the Turks in 1453—had been mentioned many times in the Messiah prophecies. I was curious to find out the reason for the interest in this date. The substance is this: By 1453 Christianity had been separated into three great divisions: Roman Catholic, Protestant, and Greek Orthodox Catholic. When Constantinople fell to the Turks (Muslims) in 1453, it was said that the prophecy given in the *Book of Revelation* had been fulfilled.

This prophecy concerns the cutting off of one third of the believers in Christ. It foretells that from the slaying (or cutting off) of one-third of men (from the truth) there would be prepared:

'. . . an hour, and a day, and a month, and a year.'[1]

When this time had elapsed, the Messiah would come; Christ would return.

In 1453 the capital of the Eastern Orthodox Catholic Church fell to non-Christians, and students of prophecy took this to be a symbolic fulfilment of the one-third being cut off.

W. Harbert, a Christian scholar, in his *The Coming Battle*, writes: 'The 390 years (of *Rev.* IX. 15) . . . if taken onward (from 1453, the height of the Turkish Empire) will bring us to 1843.' This, he said, was a clear proof that this date foretold the appearance of Christ on earth.

In prophetic measure, millennial scholars calculate that a year would be *360* days, a month *30* days, and a day *1* day. The hour was discounted. This gave a total of 391 days, and not 390 as stated by Harbert. Therefore, they reasoned, that using the axiom of 'a day for a year' the total period of time between the 'cutting off' and the 'return' of Christ would be 391 years.

Constantinople fell in 1453. One-third part of the men of Christ were symbolically cut off with the fall of the centre of their faith to the Muslims; 391 years later they would be restored to truth with Christ's return.

1453 + 391 equals 1844!

Another remarkable prophecy for the year 1844 from an entirely different direction. Intriguing?

7. And Others Still

It was the Turks who brought about the fulfilment of the 1453–1844 prophecy, and it was the Turks also who brought about another fulfilment of the 2300–1844 prophecy from the *Book of Daniel*.

Several authorities maintain that the decree of Artaxerxes was signed in 457 B.C. at the Spring Equinox, the first day of Nisan of the Jewish calendar. The Edict of Toleration which permitted the Jews to return and settle in freedom in Israel was also signed at the Spring Equinox in 1844, again the first day of Nisan of the Jewish calender. Exactly 2300 years had intervened.

This prophecy, as well as that of the 1260 days given in *Revelation*, and the 391 given in the same book, were only a few of the unique and fascinating links between Christianity and Islám in the realm of Messianic prophecy.

The Christian and Muslim calendars both converge on this remarkable year 1844; 1260 years multiplied by 354 days (the number of days in the Muslim lunar year) yields a total of 446,040 days; 446,040 days divided by 365 (the number of days in the Christian solar year) gives a total of 1222 years. The Faith of Islám began in the year 622 of the Christian calendar. 622 + 1222 equals 1844 once again.

The Sunní sect of the Muslims expects the return of the Spirit of Christ in the last days, and associates in prophecy this hour with the year 1260 of their calendar. This is also the year 1844 of the Christian calendar.

The Shí'ih sect of Islám flourishes in the land where Daniel had his vision of the coming of one, in 1844, like unto the Son of man. These Muslims have a prophecy which foretells that the twelfth spiritual ruler of their Faith, who disappeared in the year 260, will return in a thousand years, or in the year 1260—once again the year 1844 of the Christian calendar.

Imám Ja'far, when questioned concerning the year in which the promised One would appear, replied:

'Verily, in the year sixty ('60–1260) His Cause shall be revealed, and His name shall be noised abroad.'[1]

The learned and famous Arab scholar, Muhyi'd-Dín-i-'Arabí collected many prophecies concerning the year of the Advent. Such as:

'In the year _Ghars_ (1260) the earth shall be illumined by His light.'[2]

Another prophecy, attributed to one of the great spiritual leaders of Islám, declares:

'In _Ghars_ (1260) the Tree of Divine Guidance shall be planted.'[2]

All of these prophecies pointed to the same identical year: 1844.

One of the most interesting prophecies of all, came from the Old Testament. It concerned the forthright prophecy, given by Moses, who warned the Jews that if they were not obedient to God, the Lord would punish them 'seven times.'

This prophecy in the book of _Leviticus_ says:

'I will chastise you *seven times* . . .
I will make your cities waste . . .
And I will scatter you among the heathen . . .'[3]

They were not obedient, and the prophecy went into effect. 'Seven times' equals seven years in prophecy. Seven years of 'each day for a year'. This makes a total of 2520 years.

In one book, William Miller writes: 'In the year 677 before Christ; see II *Chron.* xxxiii. 9–13; see also the Bible chronology of that event; this being the first captivity of Judah in Babylon. Then take 677 years which were before Christ, from 2520 years, which include the whole 'seven times' or 'seven years' prophecy, and the remainder will be 1843 years after Christ . . .'

Other scholars maintained that it was 676 years from the first captivity to the birth of Christ, and that consequently the year of fulfilment should be 1844 and not 1843.

Other scholars pointed out that this same prophecy of the 'seven times' was given in the *Book of Daniel*. Certainly, they said, these same 2520 years from the time of Nebuchadnezzar could not be made to come out to precisely this same 1844 period; therefore, the date must be wrong.

The prophecy of Daniel and the 'seven times' clearly states that it will take place when a Holy Messenger of God appears on earth. The prophecy says:

'Behold, a watcher and a holy one came down from heaven; He cried aloud, and said thus . . . let *seven times* pass over him.'[4]

Most of the millennial scholars who dealt with this prophecy felt that it began in 604–602 B.C. when Nebuchadnezzar conquered Jerusalem.

Some of the students of Scripture pointed to a remarkable coincidence. According to the calendar of Iraq, the original land of Nebuchadnezzar, there were 2520 years from 604–602 B.C. to 1844. These were lunar years. Thus the discrepancy between the prophecies of Moses and Daniel was resolved by the astonishing fact that:

1. There were 2520 *solar* years from 676 B.C. to A.D. 1844,
2. There were 2520 *lunar* years from 602 B.C. to A.D. 1844.

Among other miscellaneous evidences, I found the following: 'The Zohar (*c.* 1290), the great textbook of medieval Kabbala' gives the 'year 5600 A.M. = 1840 C.E. (Christian era) . . . when the gates of wisdom will be opened.'

Judah Alkalai writing on Zionism in the nineteenth century regarded the 1840 period as the time for the Messiah. A. H. Silver in *Messianic Speculation in Israel* says, 'The year 1840 was counted on by many as the Messianic year' and the beginning of Redemption.

Simon ben Zemah Duran (1361–1444), author of *A Commentary on the Book of Job*, gives the year 1850 C.E. as the Messianic year.

The Reverend E. Winthrop, Episcopal Minister of St. Paul's Church, Cincinnati, thus describes the coming of Christ in his *Second Advent Lectures* (1843): 'We gather from the prophecies of the Old and New Testaments that . . . Christ may come at any moment. Watch therefore and pray always. It is quite probable that the generation now living (1843), or at least a portion of it, may see our Lord's prophecy completely fulfilled by His second advent in glory.'

8. Lift Up Your Heads

The preceding prophecies are by no means the entire list which led to this year of expectancy in 1844. However, they are sufficient to indicate the reason for the growing excitement and enthusiasm as the year of the expected Advent, 1844, approached.

Quarrels were many during those hectic days; disputes as to the exact meaning of each passage of prophecy broke out frequently; denials of the entire millennial concept were common. The battle raged in press, pamphlet, and pulpit. There is no space to write here of all the astonishing and sometimes amusing arguments which were used. Each school of Bible scholars had its own ideas, based upon its religious background and training.

Looking back upon their research, it is easy to understand, from their viewpoint, their mounting excitement over their discovery. The prophecies did indeed converge with an astonishing focus on the year 1844. There seemed no room for doubt that the hour had at last come upon the earth.

It is therefore also possible to share their feelings of profound disappointment and disillusionment when Christ did not appear *in the clouds of heaven* with all His angels as they expected.

The trumpet did not sound. The dead did not arise from the graves. The stars did not fall from heaven. The sun did not suddenly go dark. The moon did not turn to blood.

As a result, the Adventists who had been so outspoken in their belief that Christ's return was at hand, were now held up to ridicule. Hastily they tried to change their calculations. They revised their mathematical formulas, searching for a possible error in what had been an unquestioned truth.

Their confusion and disenchantment delighted and amused the more orthodox who had ignored the entire episode; 'The earth still spins on its axis, Christ has not come to judge the

29

sheep and the goats, and the end of the world is a myth. It is, as we told you it would be—business as usual.'

It was of little use for the discomforted to point out that this very attitude was another sign of His coming, when men would be 'eating and drinking as in the days of Noe'.

As a detective trying to solve this puzzling century-old mystery, it occurred to me that one of the basic techniques of criminology might well be applied here.

If an overwhelming abundance of evidence points to only *one* possible conclusion, and that conclusion proves to be false, it is never wise to cast aside all the evidence as being wrong. It is always wiser to assume that perhaps the evidence *is* correct, and that another and entirely different interpretation of the facts, or a completely different conclusion might be drawn from this same evidence.

This was the course I decided to pursue.

I have placed a complete list of references at the back of this book so that you can, if you wish, read about these days in more detail. My purpose is not to justify any one of these schools of thought, or to exhaust the search. It is merely to follow the main stream of the story concerning just what happened in 1844.

There could be little doubt as to the authenticity of the prophecies, or of their remarkable fulfilment. Then what had happened? Christ gave three crystal clear promises that He would return when:

1. the Gospel was preached everywhere;
2. the 'times of the Gentiles' was fulfilled;
3. mankind beheld the 'abomination of desolation' spoken of by Daniel.

When these things came to pass, He promised, He would return. He also promised:

'And when these things begin to come to pass, then look up, and lift up your heads; for your redemption draweth nigh.'[1]

It was too late for me to turn back now. If our newspaper editors considered that the most dramatic story which could be told in modern headlines would be *Christ Returns*, imagine how much more exciting it must have been in those days when they had so much evidence that the time was indeed upon them.

I had a hunch that something was missing. Somewhere something had been overlooked. The prophecies for the *second* coming of Christ were a hundredfold more abundant and powerful than they had been for His *first* coming.

In 1844 a new spirit came into literature, music, art, education, medicine and invention. This was the very year on which all the prophecies converged.

Would we have to wait three centuries to learn the truth about His *second* coming, as we had waited to learn the truth about His *first* coming?

Not if I had my way. I had at least a dozen more 'leads' to follow. Perhaps one might bring in the sunlight.

9. The Mystery of the White Stone

When a Missing Persons Bureau begins to look for someone who is lost, it has many basic facts to help narrow down the search. The agents know the exact name as well as the last address of the person whom they are seeking. They are able to talk with relatives. They are given detailed and documented descriptions.

My task was not nearly as simple. I was beginning my search more than one hundred years after the event. I had no personal details and no description of the missing Messiah.

To make things more difficult, I had to wade through a maze of conflicting prophecies. Many of these prophecies had originally pointed to the period round 1844, but when Christ did not come down from heaven in the clouds as expected the prophecies were rearranged to fit events which had been known to have happened: World War I, the great depression, World War II, and a possibly greater conflict yet to come.

There was still a strong feeling of expectation for a Messiah in many parts of the world, but I realised that it would be extremely difficult to identify Him since He was expected to be white in Europe, black in Africa, yellow in the Far East, brown in the Islands, and red among the American Indians.

My task became triply complicated when I learned that He was expected to be Christian in the West, Hindu in India, Buddhist in China, Jewish in Israel, a Muslim among the Arabs, and a Zoroastrian among the Parsees.

Therefore, I was greatly heartened when an additional clue came to my attention. While it did not give me the name of the missing Messiah whom I sought, it told me plainly what His name *would not be*.

As a detective on *The Case of the Missing Millennium*, it was not my job to become involved in the complicated theories which my search revealed, but to stick to one thing, namely, what happened in 1844? Was there a Messiah or not?

For this reason I was pleased with my discovery that this Messiah of 1844 (if such there were), would not be called Krishna, Moses, Buddha, Zoroaster, Christ or Muhammad, nor by any other previously known name.

Christ Himself had warned us in both *Matthew* and *Luke*, in the Chapters which gave His three promises concerning His coming in 1844, to beware of those false prophets who, in that day, bore His own name, Christ.

My clue plainly showed that I must seek someone bearing

a different name. Perhaps He would have the same Christ-spirit, but He would certainly have a different name—unless I had badly misread the evidence.

I found my first reference in the words of the prophet Isaiah:

'and thou shalt be called by a *new* name.'[1]

It was also clear that if the Messiah was to bear a new name, the same would be true of His followers. This meant that I would not find His followers among the people known as Christians, Jews, Muslims, etc., in that period about 1844.

Apparently the same pattern as at the time of the *first* coming of Christ would be repeated. His followers at that time were called by a *new name*, Christians, followers of Christ. They were not called Jews, although it was the Holy Book of the Jews that foretold His coming, and although it was the followers of that Book who so eagerly awaited His appearance.

Isaiah promises clearly that the followers of the Messiah of the last days will bear a different name. He says:

'The Lord God shall . . . call his servants by another name.'[2]

That Isaiah is speaking of *the time of the end* and not of the time of Christ's *first* coming, is confirmed by the New Testament *Book of Revelation* where a *new name* is once again promised for the followers of Christ in the day of His return:

'To him that overcometh will I give to eat of the hidden manna and will give him a white stone, and in the stone a *new name* written, which no man knoweth saving he that receiveth it.'[3]

There can be no question that Isaiah is speaking of this same last day of the 'one fold and one shepherd' when we examine his further words in that chapter. He promises that there shall be prosperity for the Jew in Israel and Jerusalem, and that the sons and daughters shall rejoice in their own land. We know this return of the Jews took place only with the signing of the Edict of Toleration in 1844. Isaiah not only promises a 'new name' in this chapter, but he also foretells:

> 'And they shall call them (His followers) the holy people, the redeemed of the Lord.'[4]

The New Testament gives warning that 'no man knoweth (the *new name*) saving he that receiveth it.' Obviously it was not going to be any easier to accept the *new name* in Christ's *second* coming than it had been in His *first*. Only that small group who had correctly read the prophecies and believed in the Messiah in His *first* coming had accepted the name Jesus of Nazareth as the Christ, and only the passing centuries brought popularity to the name Christian. Apparently it would be the same in His *second* coming. In one and the same chapter of *Revelation* we read:

1. 'I will write upon him (that overcometh) my *new name*.'[5]
2. 'I will confess his (new) name before my Father . . .'[6]
3. 'I will not blot out his (*new*) *name* out of the book of life . . .'[7]
4. 'These things saith he that is holy, he that is true, he that hath the key of David, he that openeth and no man shutteth . . . *I have set before thee an open door,* and no man can shut it: for *thou . . . hast not denied my name.*'[8]
5. 'He that hath an ear, let him hear . . .'[9]

In these words is the promise that in the day of His return, Christ will be the 'holy' and the 'true' Messiah, that He will have the 'key', and that He will 'open the door' to anyone who has 'ears to hear', and who will not deny His *new name*.

I decided to look further behind this 'open door'.

10. The Rich Who Are Poor

The clue of the *new name* required careful study. Christ Himself gives notice that He will come in an unexpected manner, at an unexpected time, and that it will be difficult to recognize Him. He says in the very chapter which promises the *new name:*

> 'Be watchful . . . If therefore thou shalt not watch, I will come upon thee as a thief, and thou shalt not know at what hour I will come upon thee.'[1]

To those who would cling to His old name, denying the *new name*, Christ in that same chapter admonishes:

> 'I know thy works, that thou hast a name that thou livest, and art dead.'[2]

As a Christian, I didn't like the idea of a new name at all. In fact, throughout the early part of my investigation I suffered frequently from the pricking of my conscience. This theory of a *new name*, however clearly it was written in both the Old and the New Testaments, was contrary to everything I had been taught. Still, I had to admit that those words 'If thou shalt not watch, I will come upon thee as a thief' could not be lightly set aside.

My investigation of this clue of the *new name* demonstrated clearly that the followers of Christ had been told in unmistakable terms to cast aside all that they held dear in the hour of His *second* coming, just as they had been forced to do in the day of His *first* coming, if they hoped to recognize Him and receive His *new name*.

The evidence showed distinctly that His return would not be according to the beliefs, standards, or expectations of any man. Each individual was warned to search out the truth for himself, to be among those who 'overcome' the obstacles placed in their path. Each one must look with his own inner eye for the Messiah. It would not be sufficient in the day of Christ's return to go along the old path and call upon Him by His old name, for in the same chapter in which is promised the *new name*, it is also foretold of God

'Thou hast tried them which say they are apostles, and are not, and hast found them liars.'[3]

Later in that same book of *Revelation*, it speaks of the 'great day of God Almighty'. Again Christ warns:

'Behold, I come as a thief.'[4]

Then He comforts those with spiritual insight, saying:

'Blessed is he that watcheth . . .'[5]

I discovered an astonishing fact in two successive chapters of this final book of Christian Scripture. In these two chapters, mankind is repeatedly warned of the *second* coming of Christ, and is cautioned again and again that it will take a spiritual eye and ear to see and to hear this truth. We find these warnings coming rapidly upon each other in the following order:

1. 'I will come unto thee quickly, and will remove thy candlestick out of his place, except thou repent.'
2. 'He that hath an ear, let him hear . . .'
3. 'I will give thee a crown of life.'
4. 'He that hath an ear, let him hear . . .'
5. '. . . I will come unto thee quickly . . .'
6. 'He that hath an ear, let him hear . . .'
7. '. . . hold fast till I come . . .'
8. 'He that hath an ear, let him hear . . .'
9. 'Be watchful . . .'
10. 'If therefore thou shalt not watch, I will come upon thee as a thief . . .'
11. '. . . thou shalt not know at what hour I will come upon thee.'

12. 'He that overcometh, the same shall be clothed in white raiment; and I will not blot out his name out of the book of life.'
13. 'He that hath an ear, let him hear . . .'
14. 'I also will keep thee from the hour of temptation, which shall come upon all the world, to try them that dwell upon the earth.'
15. 'Behold I come quickly . . .'
16. 'I will write upon him my new name.'
17. 'He that hath an ear, let him hear . . .'
18. 'I know thy works, that thou are neither cold nor hot . . .'
19. 'I will spue thee out of my mouth . . .'
20. '. . . thou sayest I am rich . . . and have need of nothing: and knowest not that thou are . . . poor and blind . . .'
21. '. . . be zealous therefore, and repent.'
22. 'Behold I stand at the door . . .'
23. '. . . and if any man hear my voice, and open the door, I will come in.'
24. 'He that hath an ear, let him hear. . . .'[6]

There seemed little doubt that only those who had 'eyes to see' and 'ears to hear' would 'receive' the *new name*, recognize it, and understand it.

In the midst of this outpouring, so filled with the promise of Christ's *second* coming, and so laden with warnings that spiritual faculties would be required to perceive the manner of His coming, the promise of a *new name* is given yet another time.

This time it speaks not only of the *new name*, but of the *new city*, the *new Jerusalem* of that day. In these words, all those things with which man was then familiar would be changed, just as they had been changed in the day of His *first* coming. Unless a man could 'overcome' his preconceived ideas, his prejudices, and empty his cup of 'former things', he would not recognize the *new name* and the new day. If he could set aside all that he possessed and believed in, Christ promised him the following blessing:

> '*Him that overcometh* will I make a pillar in the temple of my God, and he shall go no more out: and *I will write upon him the name of my God*, and *the name of the city of my God*, which is *new Jerusalem*, which cometh down out of heaven from my God: and I will write upon him *my new name*.'[7]

The deeper I went into my search, the more I realized that I had a tiger by the tail and couldn't let go. Instead of gradually diminishing the interest *The Case of the Missing Millennium* steadily gained momentum.

But now my most difficult problem was with myself. I had many mental obstacles to overcome. I had to work overtime at being (in the words of Christ) 'him that overcometh', and I didn't like the taste of it at all. I found the story fascinating, but something inside me rebelled. Long years of training at school, Sunday-school and home rose up within me to do battle. I hoped for the moment that all my research would prove to be nothing more than a fascinating story, but I had a nagging suspicion that the fun was only beginning. I repeated to myself a number of times the words:

> 'He that hath an ear to hear, let him hear.'
> 'He that hath an eye to see, let him see.'

Frankly, it didn't help much. Then I began to laugh at my predicament and to remind myself that I was a detective trying to solve a century-old mystery, and not a Christian trying to defend my beliefs.

11. The Light That Blinds

Although I was now confident that, according to the Bible, the Messiah would have a *new name* in the day of His coming, it still did not satisfy me. As a detective in search of facts, it was not sufficient to know that He would be called by a new name. I wanted to know what that name would be. Therefore, I examined the Scriptures with care to see if I might find it.

I made a very welcome discovery; I actually *did* find a new name by which the Promised One might very well be known. The more I tested it, the firmer it held, and this name was repeated time after time in connection with the prophecies of *the time of the end.*

It was given so often, that there seemed little doubt that this would be one of the titles by which He, the Messiah, would be known in that day. He would be recognized as the 'Glory of God' or the 'Glory of the Lord'.

Isaiah prophesied that the plain of Sharon and the holy mountain, Carmel, would both be centres for the light and presence of the 'Glory of the Lord' in the *last days.* He said:

'. . . the excellency of Carmel and Sharon; they shall see *the Glory of the Lord,* and the excellency of our God.'[1]

Once again in the chapter preceding the one in which he, Isaiah, promises that God will raise up a 'righteous man from the East,' he foretells:

'And *the Glory of the Lord* shall be revealed, and all flesh shall see it together: for the mouth of God hath spoken it.'[2]

In the next chapter but one Isaiah adds the warning:

'Hear, ye deaf; and look ye blind, that ye may see.'[3]

One group among the millennial scholars of the 1844 period was so certain that 'the Glory of God' would appear on the side of Mount Carmel, as foretold by Isaiah, that they sold all they owned and sailed for the Holy Land.

This group was originally under the leadership of Leonard H. Kelber. Their home was in Germany, where they were known as Templars. They were disillusioned when Christ did not appear, as expected, between 1843 and 1845, so they abandoned their former life and settled at the foot of Mount Carmel to await the great day of His coming.

They were positive that the 'Glory of God' would appear on the side of Mount Carmel. Their study of the Scriptures assured them that this promise would be kept. In the stone arches above their doorways, they chiselled the words which held their hopes:

DER HERR IST NAHE (The Lord is near).

Further search uncovered additional evidence that the title 'Glory of the Lord' or 'Glory of God' would be the *new name* by which the Messiah could be identified in the latter days.

The *Book of Revelation*, which, as we have already seen, gave the date of 1844 (1260) for the end of the 'times of the Gentiles', and which promised the *new name* and the *new city*, also confirms the name or title of Him Who will be the central Light of that new city of God.

St. John declares:

'And I John saw the holy city, *new* Jerusalem . . . and the city had no need of the sun . . . for *the Glory of God* did lighten it.'[4]

Christ Himself links the hour of His return with this same wondrous Figure 'the Glory of the Lord' or the 'Glory of God'. He promises that in the *last days* He will appear in this very likeness of God, and in His glory:

'For the Son of man shall come in *the Glory of his Father*.'[5]

This vision of the 'Glory of God' promised by Christ and

seen by St. John and Isaiah, is identical with the vision which came to Ezekiel. He saw the 'Glory of God' on more than one occasion, and associated it with a Promised One who would come into His House in a latter day. His coming, Ezekiel said, was:

> '. . . the appearance of . . . *the Glory of the Lord*. And when I saw it, I fell upon my face.'[6]

It was this same 'Glory of God' that appeared to Daniel as well. When Daniel had his vision of the *last days,* he spoke movingly of the Prince, Michael, who came to help him, Michael who would stand up for the children of God at *the time of the end.*

When Daniel had his vision, he was unable to bear the glory of it. In his own words:

> '. . . I set my face toward the ground, and I became dumb.'[7]

The meaning of the word MICHAEL when translated into English is: *One who looks like God*. Thus, it appeared, that Daniel, too, had seen the 'Glory of God'.

I uncovered another important clue which seemed to confirm the belief that this Figure seen by Daniel was identical with the one promised by Christ Himself for the time of His return.

Christ clearly explained the conditions of His *second* coming. He foretold that in that day everyone would see

> '. . . the Son of man coming in the clouds of heaven . . .'[8]

This exact same picture was given by Daniel as the vision he saw of the 'latter days'. In fact, in almost the exact same words Daniel said:

> '. . . one like the Son of man came with the clouds of heaven . . .'[9]

41

Furthermore, in that same chapter, for the second time, I found that Daniel foretold the hour when this would take place. This wondrous event, the coming of the Messiah, Daniel promised, will come to pass after

'. . . a time and times and the dividing of time.'[10]

There seemed to be no end to the references that brought me back to the year 1844. Here once again I had found that same prophecy of 1260 days, forty and two months, three and a half years, and now, 'a time and times and the dividing of time'. Students of Scripture agreed that all these phrases referred to one period of time, namely 1260 years.

This meant that I had found another reference to when the Messiah would come. According to Daniel, He would appear in the year 1260, and I knew already that in the calendar of the land in which Daniel saw his vision (Persia), the year 1260 coincided with the year 1844 of the West.

Daniel and Christ both had promised the coming of 'the Son of man.' Daniel had been overwhelmed and had fallen to the ground because of the glory of his vision.

In other places too numerous to detail, I found this same prophecy of the coming of the 'Glory of God.' Isaiah promised the faithful that

'. . . *the Glory of the Lord* shall be thy rereward.'[11]

And again:

'Arise, shine; for thy light is come, and *the Glory of the Lord* is risen upon thee . . . I the Lord am thy Saviour and thy Redeemer . . .'[12]

I was satisfied that I had uncovered sufficient evidence to indicate that the title by which the Messiah would be known when He appeared would be: 'The Glory of the Lord.' This would be the *new name*, just as Christ, 'the Anointed One', had been the *old name*.

In making the investigation into His name, I had also discovered additional information pointing to His coming with this *new name* in the year 1844.

I felt I was making progress.

12. For None Can Read

I was puzzled. If it were possible for me to discover these *clues* after careful search, why hadn't more people done the same before 1844? They had had nearly two thousand years to make the investigation.

The words of a verse ran through my memory:

'The sun, that God-like distant torch
  Sustains the life of all mankind.
  Alas, the pity! that it shines
  Upon these cities of the blind.'

Was this the answer? Was it possible that for nearly two thousand years students of Scripture had been blinded to the truth concerning the return of Christ? If so, the indifference of the people could certainly not be the fault of Christ. My research revealed that He had warned them repeatedly: 'Watch!'

He had said:

'Watch therefore: for ye know not what hour your Lord doth come.'[1]

'Take ye heed, watch and pray: for ye know not when the time is.'[2]

'Watch ye therefore ... Lest coming suddenly he find you sleeping.'[3]

'And this know, that if the goodman of the house had

known what hour the thief would come, he would have watched . . . Be ye therefore ready also: for the Son of man cometh at an hour when ye think not.'[4]

These were but a few of Christ's warnings that He would catch mankind unawares unless they looked for His coming with spiritual eyes. He had warned, not only His disciples, but through them, all humanity:

'And what I say unto you I say unto all. Watch.'[5]

I was curious to learn why the keen interest in the return of Christ had died out a few hundred years after His crucifixion, only to be taken up with such renewed zeal in the nineteenth century.

I searched carefully until I found a possible answer. Scripture itself explained why the interest in the *second coming* had died out, and why it had been revived. The explanation was given plainly in both the *Old* and the *New Testaments*. They both declared that until *the time of the end* no one would be able to read and grasp the meaning of these prophecies because the 'books were sealed.'

It was that simple. This same truth was explained by Isaiah, Daniel, and by both the Apostles Peter and Paul. The books were sealed until the latter days. After that time came, they would be unsealed.

I had already mentioned clearly that *the time of the end* came to pass in 1844; therefore, I could now reduce this to plain terms: until 1844 understanding of the holy Scriptures was hidden; after 1844 it would be revealed.

Daniel, as we have already seen, foretold in astonishingly accurate prophecies both the *first* and *second* comings of Christ. He foresaw that the Messiah would be cut off (crucified) in His thirties, and that this same spirit of the Son of man would return again in 1844. Yet no one understood the meaning of these prophecies until 1844. Not even Daniel himself. Why?

Daniel certainly asked for the explanation and meaning of his wondrous vision. He asked God to tell him the meaning, and he received a very blunt answer:

'O Daniel, shut up the Words and seal the Book, even to *the time of the end* . . .'[6]

It is in this same chapter that Daniel makes another of his references to 1844 (1260), giving this as the date when 'all these things shall be finished'.

Daniel was not satisfied when he was told to 'seal the Book.' He pressed God for an answer to the meaning of his remarkable vision. In his own words:

'. . . then said I, O my Lord, what shall be the end of these things?'[7]

There was no mistaking the answer he received this time:

'And he (the Lord) said, Go thy way, Daniel: for the words are closed up and sealed till *the time of the end*.'[8]

The meaning seemed self-evident: no one would be able to discover the meaning of the prophecies in the Book until *the time of the end* when the return of the Son of man (Christ) took place.

Isaiah reinforces this view:

'And the vision of all is become unto you as the words of a book that is sealed.'[9]

Isaiah goes a step further. He prophesies that not only the people, but even the educated and wise would be unable to grasp the meaning of the Book until the last days. According to Isaiah, the Bible would be a book,

'. . . which men deliver to one that is learned, saying, Read this, I pray thee: and he saith, I cannot; for it is sealed.'[10]

45

My study of the facts suggested that these seals mentioned by Isaiah and Daniel would not be opened by Christ in His *first* coming, but only in His *second*. It would happen only at *the time of the end*. Furthermore, I found that the New Testament upheld this reading of the case. In the words of St. Paul:

> '. . . judge nothing before *the time, until the Lord come,* who . . . will bring to light *the hidden things of* darkness.'[11]

Apparently when Christ returned, all would be clear. Until then it would remain hidden. The Apostle Peter left a similar warning to the followers of Christ not to interpret the prophecies according to their own deficient understanding before the day of His return:

> 'We have also a more sure word of prophecy . . . that no prophecy of the scripture is of any private interpretation.'[12]

Peter told them that there was only *one* way in which prophecy came to man, and only *one* way in which it could be interpreted:

> 'For the prophecy came not in old time by the will of man: but *holy men of God* spake as they were moved by the Holy Ghost.'[13]

Until this Holy Spirit appeared again in the Son of man at *the time of the end,* the meaning of the prophecies would remain hidden. There seemed to be little doubt that the truth was 'closed up' and the 'books sealed' and that none would be able to read them correctly until that time.

I found that Christ made no claim that *the time of the end* or the day of the *one fold and one Shepherd,* were fulfilled by Himself. On the contrary, He revealed a prayer which was both a prayer and a prophecy of the future. He said:

'. . . *Thy kingdom come,* thy will be done *on earth,* as it is in heaven.'

I found ample evidence that Christ never tried to 'unseal' the Books Himself. He left this for a future date. Rather, He spoke in parables and *hidden* meanings. He even prophesied that while He (Christ) spoke in parables, there would be a time in the future, when the Son would return in the Glory of the Father, and would speak plainly to them. Christ said:

'These things have I spoken unto you in proverbs: *but the time cometh,* when I shall no more speak unto you in proverbs, but *I shall shew you plainly* of the Father.'[14]

This promise to explain *the hidden meanings* is given by Jesus in the very same chapter in which He speaks of the coming of the *Spirit of Truth* who will guide His followers unto all truth. When this 'Comforter' comes, Christ promises:

'. . . *he shall teach you all things,* and bring all things to your remembrance, whatsoever I have said unto you.'[15]

Christ, in these words, seems to offer the clear promise that the new Messiah would, in the day of His coming, 'unseal the books' and bring to light the 'hidden things of darkness'.

If He had appeared in 1844, that would certainly account for all the renewed enthusiasm.

13. A Mysterious Springtime

I turned away from the Scriptures long enough to test my theory. I was intrigued to discover that certainly some creative power had 'brought to light' the 'hidden things' during that epoch of 1844. My search through secular history revealed the astonishing fact that beginning in that decade an entirely new spirit of invention and discovery had made itself apparent.

47

It proved without doubt the accuracy of Sir Lawrence Bragg's graph, to which we have already referred.

I also read the report given by an official of the United States Patent Office who, in 1844, stated that in his opinion everything worthwhile had already been invented, and that the Patent Office might as well close its doors. From that time on the Patent Office was overwhelmed with new inventions and discoveries. The most cursory survey vindicates Bragg's graph and shows that a whole new world seemed to be in the making following 1844.

Some of the great steps forward were these:

1. The First Congress of Women's Rights took place.
2. The First Congress for Universal Education.
3. Initial measures were taken to abolish child labour.
4. The Emancipation Proclamation, freeing the slaves in the United States, was signed.
5. Great new advances took place in the fields of medicine, literature, music and art.

The following are but a few of the vast downpouring of discoveries and inventions that lighted the age: 1844, Telegraph, Vulcanised rubber; 1845, Turret lathe; 1846, Rotary press; 1854, Elevator; 1855, Gas burner; 1858, Atlantic Cable; 1867, Typewriter, Dynamite; 1869, Air brakes; 1876, Telephone; 1877, Gas engine; 1878, Incandescent lamp; 1879, Arc lamp; 1880, Centrifugal creamer; 1844, Fountain pen, Trolley car, Cash register; 1885, Automobile, Linotype; 1888, Film, Transparent photo; 1891, Armourised plate; 1892, Diesel motor; 1893, Motion pictures, Coke oven; 1899, Wireless telegraphy; 1903, Airplane.

New and far-reaching developments took place in the fields of: Thermodynamics, Steam power, Electro-magnetism, Electric motor power, Gaslight, Electric light, High-speed press, Lithography, X-ray, Antiseptic surgery, Anaesthetics, Steamboats, Railways, Canal construction.

Great progress was made in bacteriology and medicine with such men as Lister, Koch, Pasteur in the lead. In the field of metallurgy, Sorby in Britain and Chernoff in Russia led the way. In music Chopin, Schubert, Tschaikowsky and a flood of creative genius appeared. Literature produced such names as Emerson, Tolstoi, Fitzgerald, Tennyson, Lowell, Whitman, James, Dickens, Thoreau, Dostoevski, to name but a few.

Man's life was enriched by an increasing number of inventions and benefits, a process which has continued from 1844 to the present day, taking even higher the graph of human accomplishment: Airlines, Jets (Planes, Ships, Submarines), Streamlined trains, Luxury liners, Air-conditioning, Radio, Television, Electronics, Antibiotics, Wonder drugs, Missiles, Rockets to the moon, All the magic of nuclear physics.

The endless stream of wonders still continues. The whole concept of life has altered. Newspapers, magazines, books, radio, television, telephone, telegraph, schools, education, travel—have all vastly increased man's knowledge and information.

Is there any doubt that these were the events foreseen by Daniel for *the time of the end*? In the very chapter in which he spoke of the (1) coming of Michael, Who looks like God, (2) in the year of 1844, (3) when the Book will be unsealed, Daniel prophesied:

'. . . many shall run to and fro, and knowledge shall be increased.'[1]

According to the sacred Writings there was a definite promise that when all these things took place the 'book' would be 'unsealed'. This unique event was foretold in

Isaiah, Daniel and *Revelation* in a remarkable series of prophecies.

In one chapter, Isaiah prophesies that (1) the Book is sealed, and (2) that in the *last days* the Book will be opened:

1. *Sealed*
'And the vision of all is become unto you as the words of a book that is sealed, which men deliver to one that is learned, saying, Read this, I pray thee: and he saith, I cannot; for it is sealed.'[2]

2. *Unsealed*
'And *in that day* shall the deaf hear the words of the book, and the eyes of the blind shall see ... They also that erred in spirit shall come to understanding, and they that murmured shall learn doctrine.'[3]

Daniel made the same two promises: (1) that the Books would be sealed until *the time of the end*, and (2) that they would be opened and explained in the last days:

1. *Sealed*
'Go thy way, Daniel: for the words are closed up and sealed till *the time of the end*.'[4]

2. *Unsealed*
'I beheld till the (other) thrones were cast down, and the Ancient of days did sit . . . and ten thousand times ten thousand stood before him: the judgment was set, and the books were opened.'[5]

This last promise is given by Daniel in the same chapter in which he says that 'one like the Son of man came with the clouds of heaven.'

The *Book of Revelation* seems to end all question on this subject. The basic theme of this entire book is the *second* coming of Christ. *Revelation* states plainly that those books which were sealed until *the time of the end* would then be unsealed and would be sealed no more:

'Seal not the sayings of the prophecy of this book; *for the time is at hand*.'[6]

Revelation, like *Daniel*, repeats the same vision of the coming of the Son of man (Christ) when the books were unsealed:

'And I looked, and behold a white cloud, and upon the cloud one sat like unto the Son of man . . .'[7]

In yet another place, *Revelation* describes this Messiah as one:

'. . . clothed with a vesture dipped in blood: and his name is called *The Word of God*.'[8]

Revelation says of this Lamb of God who will appear in the *last days:*

'Thou art worthy to take the book, and to open the seals thereof . . .'[9]

I felt that I had found at last a satisfactory answer to those puzzling questions:

Why had interest in Christ's return died out after His crucifixion?

Why had such an enthusiastic revival of this interest taken place in 1844?

Obviously something strange and special had taken place in the world following the 1844 period. My job was to find out what it was, and how it was related to *The Case of the Missing Millennium*.

Had the return of Christ actually taken place? If so, where was He? How had we missed Him? Had we made the same mistake all over again? Had we followed the same path as those scholars at the time of His *first* coming? Had we tried to read the 'books' that were 'sealed' and misunderstood their fulfilment?

Like Daniel, I too was dissatisfied. I wanted a lot more information. What I had uncovered so far was very fascinating, but it was not nearly enough. I wanted to actually close in on my quarry. In fact, like Daniel, I wanted to know the answer to the question: 'What shall be the end of these things?'

14. The Living and the Dead

An interesting question occurred to me: suppose this were the time of the *first* coming of Christ and I wanted an answer to my questions? Suppose I were asking the church-goers or religious leaders of that day, 'Who is the Messiah? Has He come? Where is He?'

The chances are that I wouldn't have received very much encouragement, and it was logical to expect that it would be the same now.

Therefore, I carefully studied the pattern of Christ's *first* coming, looking for a clue. I found, according to Scripture, that the generality of humanity in that day was spiritually 'dead' and did not recognize Him nor accept Him. A small minority was spiritually 'alive' and knew Him and believed in Him.

Christ Himself referred to those who believed in Him as 'alive' and those who didn't as 'dead'. One young man offered to follow Jesus and serve Him as soon as he had buried his father. Christ said:

'. . . let the dead bury their dead.'[1]

This could only mean : 'Let the spiritually dead man bury the physically dead one. This reminded me of the same literal-minded people referred to as spiritually dead by the prophet Jeremiah. He bluntly called them:

'O foolish people, and without understanding; which have eyes, and see not; which have ears and hear not.'[2]

My search disclosed that Christ had not appeared the *first* time in the magical, glamorous manner which the people had expected of their Messiah. On the contrary He was denied, called a false prophet, and slain; His little handful of followers was ridiculed by the masses for believing such obvious nonsense, as that Messiah could come 'from Nazareth' with no attendent fanfare of Nature.

After all, the people said, this Jesus of Nazareth was born of woman and walked abroad in the flesh of a normal human being. He ate and drank, grew tired and slept, knew grief and anger. Surely this was not the manner of a great Messiah!

The disciples of Christ, I found, were deeply troubled because religious leaders, influential people, business men and scholars neither believed, accepted, nor understood His message. They went to Christ for help.

'Why do the people not believe?' they asked him. Surely the signs were plain. Christ answered:

'Because it is given unto you to know the mysteries of the Kingdom of Heaven, but to them it is not given . . . their ears are dull of hearing, and their eyes they have closed . . . But blessed are your eyes, for they see: and your ears, for they hear.'[3]

Thus Christ comforted them, explaining that it took special 'eyes' and 'ears' to recognize the Messiah in the day of His appearance. The disciples were spiritually 'alive' while the others were 'dead'. The believers in the old Faith said: 'Reason should tell you that this Jesus cannot be the Messiah.

If He were the Messiah, then Elias would have already come. Does not our Holy Writ say that Elias must come first? If this man of Nazareth is the Messiah, then where is Elias? Who has seen him? Tell us this?'

The disciples found this question too difficult to answer. They, too, had been taught that Elias must appear before the coming of the Messiah. If Christ *was* the Messiah, then where was Elias? They went to Christ and put the question to Him directly.

Jesus told them that Elias *had* come. Elias had already appeared among the people, He said, but no one had recognized him, nor understood this truth. Elias, Christ said, had come in a manner in which the people did not expect, and for this reason they did not know him. Patiently Christ explained this symbolical truth to the disciples:

'If ye will receive it, this (John the Baptist) is Elias, which was for to come.'[4]

This was an astonishing explanation. John the Baptist was Elias? Christ prefaced His explanation with the words: '*If ye will receive it.*'

He meant apparently: If you can understand and accept this symbolical interpretation of the facts. Then Christ immediately added the words:

'He that hath ears to hear, let him hear.'[5]

This time there could be no doubt. He was warning His disciples that it would take spiritual ears to hear and believe in this truth. It was to be understood inwardly, not outwardly.

This *return*, which Christ said had happened, had taken place in the *spirit* and not in the *flesh*. This is confirmed by John the Baptist himself.

He was asked: 'Art thou Elias?' He answered: 'I am not.'
He was asked: 'Art thou that prophet?' He answered:
'No.'[6]

Certainly Christ was not a liar. He knew that John was not
Elias in the flesh. This is why it took spiritual 'eyes' to see and
accept John as Elias. Once understood symbolically, the truth
was simple: Elias had returned in the spirit in John the
Baptist.

If men were unable to understand the significance of this
inward truth and accept it, Christ explained, they would continue to believe Him, Jesus, to be false.

The *return* of Elias had come. John was the return of Elias
—not in the flesh, but in the spirit.

I found that this very event had been prophesied for John
the Baptist in the *Gospel of Luke:*

'. . . he (John) shall be filled with the Holy Ghost, even
from his mother's womb . . . And he shall go before him
in the spirit and power of Elias . . .'[7]

This was one of the most important clues I had yet found
in the teachings of Christ. It was still another confirmation of
why the Messiah, when He came again, would have a *new
name*.

Christ demonstrated in this example of John and Elias that
a Messenger of God does not return in the flesh. It is the Holy
Spirit that returns; but through another channel, in another
age, and with another outward name.

The disciples had much trouble grasping this truth. In
another place we read how they came to Christ concerning this
matter:

'. . . his disciples asked him, saying, Why then say the
scribes that Elias must first come?'[8]

Christ explained it with the utmost simplicity:

'Elias truly shall first come, and restore all things. . . .
But *I say unto you, that Elias is come already*, and they knew
him not, but have done unto him whatsoever they listed . . .
Then the disciples understood that he spake unto them of
John the Baptist.'[9]

Elias had come. No one believed it because it was the 'spirit'
of Elias which had returned in the flesh of John. Since this
return was not in the manner expected by the people, they did
not understand it or accept it. They had been taught that it
would be a literal return, and the real truth, the spiritual
return, was contrary to their teachings.

If this pattern had been repeated in 1844, it would easily
account for the fact that no Messiah had appeared, at least,
not as the people expected. Perhaps there might again be a
small minority who had 'eyes to see' and minds to understand a symbolical return. It would be worth checking.

In *The Coming World Teacher*, Pavri, a student of the last
day prophecies, recognizes this danger. He says: 'Perchance
some in the Christian Church will recognize Him by His
wisdom and supreme compassion. But if they insist on His
coming in the garb their thoughts have made for Him and
forget that "God fulfils Himself in many ways" and not
according to their measure of Him, He may pass unrecognized
because of His not fulfilling the expectations which they have
become accustomed to associate with Him. Last time when
He came, "He was not Jew enough for the Jew, not Roman
enough for the Roman, not Greek enough for the Greek. He
was too big for them all." So this time He will not be
Protestant enough for the Protestant, Catholic enough for the
Catholic, Broad Church enough for the Liberal. He will be
too big for them all. Coming again with a message for all

mankind, He will not be Hindu enough for the Hindu, Mohammedan enough for the Moslem, Buddhist enough for the Buddhist, nor Christian enough for the Christian. He will be too big for them all.'

Christ Himself gave still another indication that His return would require this spiritual insight to recognise it when He said:

'When ye therefore shall see the abomination of desolation, spoken of by Daniel the Prophet, stand in the holy place, (whoso readeth, let him understand.)'[10]

These last words show that His return would not be clear to the outward vision, but would have an inward significance.

Peter the Apostle in his *First Epistle* points out the same symbolical truth, that it is the *Spirit of Christ* which is in the Holy Messengers who appear. He says of these prophets:

'. . . the *Spirit of Christ* which was in them did signify (prophesy) . . .'[11]

That the Messiah will come among us in that day, living like other men, is shown in many places. In *The Testament of the Twelve*, regarded as authoritative by the early church, we read: 'The Most High will visit the earth, coming as a man, eating and drinking with men in quiet.'[12]

In the book of Justin Martyr, Trypho the Jew says: 'All of us (Jews) expect the Messiah to come as a man from among men.'[13]

Roderic Dunkerley in *Beyond the Gospels* quotes Christ as follows in a chapter on some of the sayings of Jesus:

'I stood in the midst of the world and in the flesh was I seen of them, and I found all men drunken, and none found I athirst among them, and my soul grieveth over the sons of men, because they are blind in their heart.'[14]

I now felt that the evidence fully justified my looking for the return of Christ in a new physical identity but with the same *Holy Spirit*. Christ Himself suggests this in His warning to His disciples, a warning which He gave them when speaking about the return of Elias in John. He said:

> 'Likewise shall also the Son of man suffer of them.'[15]

For my own benefit, I wrote on the margin of my typescript of this chapter: 'He who hath an ear to hear, let him hear.'

15. The Mouthpiece of God

Having decided to search along these lines, I combed the Scriptures for other clues which Christ might have given concerning the coming of One other than Himself. I found this symbolical interpretation of His return to be strongly fortified by His own words.

I discovered that Christ repeatedly made two clear distinctions regarding His *second* coming. On some occasions He would refer to His own appearance, at other times He would refer to the appearance of One other than Himself.

A few examples of this dual reference of Christ make the point evident:

1. *That He would return Himself:*

> 'I will not leave you comfortless: I will come to you.'[1]

> 'I go away, and come again unto you.'[2]

> 'A little while, and ye shall not see me: and again, a little while, and ye shall see me.'[3]

> 'And if I go and prepare a place for you, I will come again . . .'[4]

2. *That another other than Himself would come:*

'Nevertheless I tell you the truth; it is expedient for you that I go away: for if I go not away, the Comforter will not come unto you.'[5]

'. . . but if I depart, I will send him unto you. And when he is come, he will reprove the world of sin . . .'[6]

'I have yet many things to say unto you, but ye cannot bear them now.
Howbeit when he, the Spirit of truth, is come, he will guide you into all truth.'[7]

'But when the Comforter is come, whom I will send unto you from the Father, even the Spirit of truth, which proceedeth from the Father, he shall testify of me.'[8]

In the following words Christ made it clear that He, as well as the One Who would return in His name would be human channels for the same Holy Spirit. Of Himself Christ said:

'. . . the word which ye hear is not mine, but the Father's which sent me.'[9]

In yet another place, Christ repeats this:

'the words that I speak unto you I speak not of myself.'[10]

Christ makes this same statement about the One Whom He promises will return after He, Christ, departs:

'. . . he shall not speak of himself; but whatsoever he shall hear, that shall he speak.'[11]

That another Messenger would come in His (Christ's) name with the same power of the Holy Spirit is made unmistakably clear from still other words of Christ to His disciples:

'. . . the Comforter, which is the Holy Ghost, whom the Father will send in my name, he shall teach you all things, and bring all things to your remembrance, whatsoever I have said unto you.'[12]

Christ issued a stern warning to the people of Jerusalem, telling them that since they had denied Him in His day, they would have no opportunity to believe in Him again until the day of His return. In one single sentence He links Himself once more with the One to come after Him:

'For I say unto you, Ye shall not see me henceforth, till ye shall say, Blessed is he that cometh in the name of the Lord.'[13]

There seemed sufficient evidence to show that when Christ spoke of His *own return*, He was speaking of the Christ-spirit, the Holy Spirit, within Him, which would reappear; and when He spoke of the coming of another, He was speaking of a different human channel, a man with a *new name* other than Christ, but Who would be filled with this same Holy Spirit.

In yet another way Christ expressed the same truth, that it is not the name and the flesh that matter, but the Spirit which the Messenger brings:

'God is a Spirit: and they that worship him must worship him in spirit and in truth.'[14]

I found that this same principle of the return in spirit but not in flesh was found in other sacred scriptures. Sri Krishna, holy Messenger of Hinduism, had in ancient days stated this same basic truth. He said that the Holy Spirit returns in new channels in each age, according to the command of God. It is written in the Bhagavad Gita:

'Know thou, O Prince, that whenever the world declineth in virtue and righteousness; and vice and injustice mount the throne, then come I, the Lord, and revisit My world in visible form, and mingle as a man with men, and by my influence and teachings do I destroy the evil and injustice, and re-establish virtue and righteousness. Many times have I thus appeared; many times hereafter shall I come again.'

In this same Book, Krishna also foretold the coming of a Great World Teacher at *the time of the end*.

The same story of the 'return of the Spirit' is given by Gautama, the Buddha:

'I am not the first Buddha Who came upon earth, nor shall I be the last. In due time another Buddha will arise in the world, a Holy One, a supremely enlightened One . . . an incomparable Leader of men . . .

He will reveal to you the same eternal truths which I have taught you.'

At least all the doors were not now closed. There was a possibility that the *return* of Christ had taken place in the *Spirit* and not in the *flesh*. In fact, the evidence was indeed quite strong that this *had* taken place.

Therefore, I was prepared to search the history of the 1844 period for some holy, Christ-like Figure bearing a different name than Christ, but One who was filled with that same gentleness, kindness, and love shown by Jesus.

But there was one important thing which I still did not know. Where would the Messiah appear? In what part of the world?

My next task was to try and discover this very fact. I began checking the Scriptures for some concrete evidence which would help me narrow down the geographical area of my search.

As I sought for this clue, I received quite a setback. I found to my astonishment that a great many of my fellow-Christians didn't believe that Christ would *ever* return to this earth. I discovered that the Christian world held a great variety of views on the subject. In fact, the great majority of Christians, because of their disappointments down through the centuries, had long since given up any hope of a real return of Christ.

I decided that perhaps I'd better settle this point once and for all in my own mind before going on.

16. One Shepherd but Many Folds

WORLD COUNCIL OF CHURCHES SPLITS OVER CHRIST'S COMING AGAIN

Find it Impossible to Reach Vote

This was not an imaginary headline. It was taken from the bold-face type on the front page of the *Chicago Daily Tribune* of August 26th, 1954.

This news story was written following the opening session of the World Council of Churches in Evanston, Illinois, a gathering which brought together 163 Christian denominations from 48 countries.

Chesly Manly, who wrote the story, began by saying: 'Delegates to the second assembly of the World Council of Churches disagreed sharply and fundamentally yesterday as to whether the Christian hope for the establishment of God's kingdom can be fulfilled in this world or only after the second coming of Christ.'

One thousand nine hundred and fifty-four years after His birth, there was still a basic lack of agreement among Christ's followers as to whether He had ever really promised that He would come again.

George Goyder, delegate from the Church of England,

according to the newspaper story 'shamed the distinguished theologians and ecclesiastics who wrote the main theme report for being "lukewarm about the second coming of Christ".'

'The document speaks of "curiosity" about the date of His coming,' said the English delegate. 'What we need is a new Declaration of Independence on Christ. Never in history has there been such chaos, confusion, and despair in the world.'

There was even an apparent split in thinking between some of the Christian leaders of Europe and those of the United States. *Time* magazine in its April 19th issue wrote: 'The "Main Theme" of the Assembly, which all delegates will discuss together during the gathering's first week, sounds non-controversial enough: Christ—The Hope of the World. Yet it contains a question that—before it is answered—may draw a dramatic line between theologians of the Old World and the New. How much of the Christian Hope depends upon the Second Coming of Christ?'

The article quotes Norway's well-known Bishop Eivind Berggrav as saying that 'the outlook of American Christianity often looks . . . rather earthbound, expecting the fulfilment of God's Kingdom here on earth—one might even say expecting its realisation in the U.S.A.'

The article adds that to such European Protestants as Bishop Berggrav, 'the Christian hope rests more on the Biblical expectation that Christ will one day return to end the earthly enterprise.'

H. H. Rowley in *The Relevance of Apocalyptic* says: '. . . the hope of that Advent (of Christ) is integral to New Testament thought.'

O. Cullmann in *The Return of Christ According to the New Testament* writes: '. . . to reject this hope (of the Advent) is to mutilate the New Testament message of salvation.'

A. J. Gordon states: 'Any doctrine of the resurrection dissociated from the Advent must be false.'

Christabel Pankhurst, the British suffragette, wrote in her book *Behold He Cometh*, 'My practical political eye saw that the Divine Programme (the return of Christ) is absolutely the only one that can solve the international, social, political and other problems of the world.'

I learned that this debate had been going on for centuries, and that the World Council of Churches was merely another evidence of the disagreement. Many denominations did not participate in this World Council at all.

There was a widespread belief that when Christ spoke of His own return, or of the One who would come after Him, He was not speaking of an actual return, but of a symbolical one. This theory proposed that the *Comforter*, the *Spirit of Truth*, the One who would come in His name, all these in reality referred to the Holy Ghost Which had descended on the Church at the time of Pentecost; therefore, it was said, the *return* had been fulfilled at that time. It was over and done with.

In my search, I found that this particular doctrine that Christ had returned in the Holy Ghost at the time of Pentecost was more a doctrine of expediency than one of desire. It had developed long after the time of Jesus. When He did not return as expected, some explanation for this failure had to be discovered. Since Christ's words were true words, therefore His return *must* be figurative.

But belief in the *return* of Christ did not cease shortly after the crucifixion, never to be revived until 1844, not by any means. In fact, the Christian world suffered so many disappointments because of 'days of expectancy' down through the ages, that after the seventeenth century there was little sincere belief in the return until men's hearts were once again caught up by the vision, in the advent of the early nineteenth century. Rather, strong measures were taken to stamp out such 'vain hopes' and the Pentecostal theory gained great favour.

Those who adopted the Pentecostal theory of the return as the only possible answer to the enigma, sincerely believed that although Christ had used such terms as *the Comforter*, *the Spirit of Truth*, as well as the pronoun *he* upon several occasions, still He (Christ) was alluding to the symbolical coming of the Holy Ghost at that time.

This, of course, aroused a flood of opposition. It was pointed out that, according to this theory, when the Holy Ghost appeared in *the Spirit of Truth*, it was 'to lead men to all truth,' while in reality since that time the Church had become separated and divided into hundreds and hundreds of sects— each claiming the true path, and each going its own way.

Rev. William B. Riley in *Is Christ Coming Again* writes: 'To speak of the Lord's return as a mere figure of speech that is to know no literal fulfilment, is little less sacrilegious than the total denial of inspiration.' He adds, 'If the plain references to the return of the Lord do not involve a personal coming, language has lost its meaning.'

With such a raging controversy on the second coming of Christ being waged, even after all these years, among the Christians themselves, I decided to make my own investigation from the Scriptures.

I would settle the point in my own mind, and then either go on with my search or abandon it. It would depend on what I found. Until I knew the truth I would not be willing to admit that no answer could be found to the century-old mystery of *The Case of the Missing Millennium*.

I realised by now, of course, that even if Christ *had* returned in the 1844 period, there was no reason to expect that the knowledge of that return would be general, any more than it had been a hundred years after His *first* coming. If a World Council of Jews had been held a century after the crucifixion, it is obvious that the historical fact of the first Advent would have been unknown to it.

I was determined not to be influenced by any of the conflicting views until I had made my own personal search into the promises of Christ concerning His return. Either He promised to return or He didn't. I decided to find out which.

17. The Unmistakable Signs

My enthusiasm for *The Case of the Missing Millennium* returned with a rush.

I soon learned that there is no subject spoken of with more frequency and more power in all the New Testament than that of the *return of Christ*. It is mentioned on innumerable occasions. There is nothing vague or doubtful about the event whatever.

The disciples of Christ were very familar with His promise that He would return. They spoke of it often. They were eager for a clear understanding of the conditions under which He, Christ, would return. They asked Him plainly:

'What shall be the sign of thy coming?'

It was in answer to this direct question that Christ gave His three well-known promises that He would return when:

1. His gospel was preached in all the world for a witness.
2. The times of the Gentiles was fulfilled.
3. Ye see the abomination of desolation spoken of by Daniel the prophet.

None of these promises had been fulfilled by the time of

Pentecost, nor could they have been. In the very chapters (*Matt.* xxiv, *Luke* xxi) in which this question is asked concerning the time of His return, Christ gives plain answers. He refers repeatedly to His return, saying:

1. '. . . then shall the end come.'[1]
2. 'so shall also the coming of the Son of man be.'[2]
3. 'And then shall appear the sign of the Son of man.'[3]
4. '. . . they shall see the Son of man coming . . .'[4]
5. 'when ye shall see all these things, know that it is near, even at the doors.'[5]
6. 'so shall also the coming of the Son of man be.'[6]
7. 'so shall also the coming of the Son of man be.'[7]
8. 'Ye know not what hour your Lord doth come.'[8]
9. '. . . in such an hour as ye think not the Son of man cometh.'[9]
10. 'Blessed is that servant whom his Lord when he cometh shall find so doing.'[10]
11. 'The lord of that servant shall come in a day when he looketh not for him, and in an hour that he is not aware of.'[11]
12. 'And then shall they see the Son of man coming in a cloud, with power and great glory.'[12]
13. 'when these things begin to come to pass, then look up, and lift up your heads; for your redemption draweth nigh.'[13]
14. 'when ye see these things come to pass, know ye that the kingdom of God is nigh at hand.'[14]
15. 'And take heed . . . lest . . . that day come upon you unawares.'[15]
16. 'Watch ye therefore, and pray always, that ye may be accounted worthy . . . to stand before the Son of man.'[16]

When I had finished my study of the *New Testament*, I was more intrigued than ever with my search. I had discovered other clear promises of Christ's return:

1. 'I will not leave you comfortless: I will come to you.'[17]

2. 'I go away, and come again unto you.'[18]

3. 'And if I go and prepare a place for you, I will come again.'[19]

4. 'For the Son of man shall come in the glory of his Father . . .'[20]

It is not surprising that millennial zeal had seized the Christian world and held it in its grip for centuries, especially when we realize that the above references in the New Testament do not in any way exhaust the promises of Christ's return given in that Book.

The following are some of the additional references to His coming:

Matthew		Luke
	24 : 46	
	24 : 50	
6 : 10	25 : 6	9 : 26
7 : 22	25 : 10	12 : 36
10 : 23	25 : 13	12 : 37
16 : 27	25 : 31	12 : 38
16 : 28	26 : 29	12 : 40
23 : 39	26 : 64	12 : 43
24 : 3		12 : 46
24 : 14	Mark	13 : 35
24 : 15		17 : 24
24 : 27	8 : 38	17 : 26
24 : 30	9 : 1	17 : 30
24 : 33	12 : 9	18 : 8
24 : 37	13 : 26	21 : 27
24 : 39	13 : 33	21 : 28
24 : 42	13 : 35	21 : 31
24 : 44	14 : 62	21 : 34

Luke
21 : 36

John
5 : 28
14 : 16
14 : 18
14 : 26
14 : 28
15 : 26
16 : 7
16 : 8
16 : 13
16 : 22
21 : 22

Acts
2 : 20
3 : 19
3 : 20

I Corinthians
1 : 7
4 : 5
11 : 26
15 : 23
15 : 24

Philippians
1 : 6

3 : 20

I Thessalonians
1 : 10
2 : 19
3 : 13
4 : 15
4 : 16
4 : 17
5 : 2
5 : 3
5 : 4
5 : 23

II Thessalonians
1 : 7
1 : 10
2 : 2
2 : 3
2 : 8
3 : 5

I Timothy
6 : 14

II Timothy
4 : 1
4 : 8

Titus
2 : 13

Hebrews
9 : 28

James
5 : 7
5 : 8

I Peter
1 : 7
1 : 13
5 : 1
5 : 4

II Peter
1 : 19
3 : 3
3 : 4
3 : 9
3 : 10
3 : 12

I John
3 : 2

Revelation	3 : 3	14 : 15
1 : 7	3 : 11	14 : 16
1 : 8	3 : 20	22 : 7
1 : 13	4 : 8	22 : 10
2 : 5	6 : 17	22 : 12
2 : 16	14 : 1	22 : 20
2 : 25	14 : 14	

Even these do not exhaust the list of all the references to the return of Christ. Rev. R. A. Torrey, Dean of the Bible Institute of Los Angeles, California, in his book *The Return of the Lord Jesus*, listed over 250 separate passages on the certainty and consequences of the Second Coming of Christ.

However, these references were more than sufficient to convince me that Christ had indeed left a firm promise of His coming, including the words in the final book of Christian Scripture, where in the next to the last verse it says:

'He which testifieth these things saith, Surely I come quickly. . . . Even so, come, Lord Jesus.'[21]

Therefore, instead of deflecting me from my course, the widespread disbelief which I found, even among the Christians themselves concerning the return of Christ, only succeeded in arousing my enthusiasm.

Far from being discouraged, I realised from my own researches that this very lack of faith among Christ's own followers concerning His return was one of the certain signs that that return had taken place, and that He was already among men.

In the words of a later millennial scholar: 'The scepticism and unbelief so prevalent concerning the Second Advent of

Christ is in itself a "sign" of the last days. St. Peter tells us: ". . . there shall come in the last days scoffers, walking after their own lusts, and saying, Where is the promise of His coming? for since the fathers fell asleep, all things continue as they were from the beginning of the creation" (II *Peter* iii. 3–4). One hears these very words everywhere today. Even among the leaders of the Church this terribly momentous event (return of Christ) is regarded with incredibility, as "visionary".' (M. H. Goyer.)

The *Epistle of James* tells us:

'Be patient therefore, brethren, *unto the coming of the Lord.*'[22]

St. Paul wrote:

'Now we beseech you, brethren, by *the coming of our Lord Jesus Christ* . . . that ye be not soon shaken . . .

Let no man deceive you by any means: for that day shall not come, except there come a falling away first. . . .'[23]

St. Peter left the same warning about scepticism and doubt:

'. . . there shall be false teachers among you, who privily shall bring in damnable heresies, even denying the Lord that bought them . . .

And many shall follow their pernicious ways: by reason of whom the way of truth shall be evil spoken of.'[24]

The answer was clear. The evidence was overwhelming. Christ had indeed promised to return. These facts confirmed my growing theory that just as the people had not recognised the return of Elias in John, in spite of Christ's clear explanation, in like manner they might not have recognised the return of Christ in the new Messiah.

I hurried on with my search.

18. Lightning from the East

I now began an earnest search for clues which would tell me something about the place in which the Messiah would appear.

Two interesting things came to light. For the first coming, Daniel had given the *time* and Micah had given the *place*.

Daniel had prophesied exactly when the Messiah would appear the *first* time and when He would be slain. Micah had said of the place:

'But thou, *Bethlehem* . . . out of thee shall he come forth unto me that is to be ruler in Israel.'[1]

Daniel had also prophesied with even greater exactness the *time* of the second coming of the Messiah in 1844 (see p. 20). Therefore, I turned to Micah for a possible clue as to the *place* of His second appearance.

I was richly rewarded. In *Micah* vii. 7 and 12 I found:

'I will wait for the God of my salvation . . . *In that day* also he shall come even to thee from *Assyria*. . .'[2]

The Assyrian Empire at one time covered the entire area in which both Daniel and Micah lived out their lives. Therefore, I chose to study those parts of the Empire in which these two prophets traditionally lived and taught.

To my surprise, I found that there were many other clues to follow as well. Gradually one led to another, until a definite picture began to emerge, and I knew at least in which direction to turn my gaze.

The book of *Ezekiel* spoke of a great Figure who would come in those days. He said:

'And, behold, the glory of the God of Israel came *from the way of the east*.'[3]

This was clearly a reference to the *second* coming of Christ and not the *first*, for Jesus did not come from the way of the East, He came from north and west of Jerusalem.

Isaiah in like manner spoke of the wondrous Figure who would come from the East. Isaiah said that it was God Himself Who had

'. . . raised up the righteous man from the east, called him to his foot, gave the nations before him, and made him rule over kings.'[4]

Even Christ Himself pointed to the direction from which He would appear in the day of His *second* coming. Speaking of that day, He said:

'For as the lightning cometh out of the East . . . so shall also the coming of the Son of man be.'[5]

The Jewish Oracles, the Sibylline books, prophesied that the 'King Messiah' of *the time of the end* would come 'from the sunrise'.[6]

Daniel had written his words of millennial prophecy while in the East. In fact, he was in Elam, a part of ancient Persia, when he foretold with such startling accuracy the exact time of both the *first* and the *second* comings of Christ.

It was in the capital city of Persia, Shushan, that Daniel had the prophetic vision which revealed the year 1844 as the time for the return of the Messiah.

Daniel not only gave the *time*, 1844, but he also directed attention to the *place*, saying that 'Elam' (Persia) would be given as a place of 'vision' in the latter days.[7]

The Prophet Jeremiah speaks of things that 'shall come to pass in the latter days' and in the verse preceding this, he says:

'And I will set my throne in Elam (Persia) . . . saith the Lord.'[8]

I came across a prophecy well known among the Arabs. Speaking of *the time of the end*, it said:

> When the promised One appears, the 'upholders of His faith shall be of the people of Persia.'[9]

All these prophecies clearly showed that the Messiah would come from the East, and they put a strong emphasis on the territory of Persia. It was something definite to go on. The circle was narrowing.

19. The Vision of the Last Days

I uncovered another remarkable series of prophecies. They also pointed to Persia as the place where the Messiah would appear. Furthermore, they linked together in one unit the promises of Christ, Daniel, and *Revelation* regarding the time (1844) of His return.

These prophecies spoke of precisely such a troubled age as that in which we now find ourselves, devastated by two world wars, hovering on the brink of a third, faced with the ultimate in destruction—atomic warfare. In just such an age it was promised that Christ would already have come, unexpected, unknown, unaccepted, unwanted.

We are living in a day when, with the explosion of a hydrogen bomb, the elements do indeed melt with fervent heat. The Apostles of Christ warned mankind that when Christ returned He would catch them asleep. When would this happen?

> '*But the day of the Lord* will come as a *thief in the night*; in the which the heavens shall pass away with a great noise and the elements shall melt with fervent heat. . . .'[1]

All these awesome events, I learned, were foretold by Scripture. They must take place before the Messiah would be

74

recognised and accepted by the generality of mankind. Only then would He be able to usher in the day of the 'one fold and one shepherd'.

The Prophet Joel warned of these *last days*, saying:

'The sun shall be turned into darkness . . . before the great and the terrible day of the Lord come.'[2]

Christ echoes these same words, saying that after they have been fulfilled, He will return:

'. . . shall the sun be darkened . . . and they shall see the Son of man coming. . .'[3]

The Prophet Joel said of *the time of the end*:

'There hath not been ever the like, neither shall be any more after it.'[4]

Christ reaffirms that this time of trouble will be the time of His return. He repeats this very same statement of Joel, saying:

'For then shall be great tribulation, such as was not since the beginning of the world to this time, no, nor ever shall be . . . then shall appear the sign of the Son of man. . . .'[5]

Revelation gives the same two identical signs: (1) the darkening of the sun, and (2) the coming of the Lord's great and dreadful day. When the Lamb of God (the Messiah) appeared in the last days and 'unsealed' the holy Books, St. John the Divine records that he beheld the following:

'. . . there was a great earthquake; and the sun became black as sackcloth of hair . . .'[6]

This took place, *Revelation* said, in a day when all the people of the earth

'... hid themselves in the dens and in the rocks of the mountains ... for the great day of his wrath is come; and who shall be able to stand.'[7]

Daniel also foretells the suffering that will follow the coming of the Messiah in *the time of the end*. He prophesies that this suffering will last until His truth has been accepted. He uses the same words as Jesus, Joel and *Revelation*. He warns that in the day of the coming of the new Messiah,

'... there shall be a time of trouble, such as never was since there was a nation even to that same time ...'[8]

In these prophecies, Daniel links Christ inseparably with the One Who has the appearance of the 'Glory of God'. Speaking of this *time of the end*, Daniel promises that:

'... at that time shall *Michael* stand up ... and at that time thy people shall be delivered.'[9]

Enoch also mentions the same Michael, saying:

'And I will give thee ... the great Captain Michael, for thy writings and for the writings of thy fathers ... And I shall not require them *till the last age* ...'[10]

My next assignment was to identify this Michael who would deliver the children of God in the last days. The answer can be found in chapter ten of *Daniel*. There Daniel speaks of the overpowering vision which came to him in the land of Persia, and he says:

'But the prince of the kingdom of Persia withstood me one and twenty days: but, lo, *Michael*, one of the chief princes, came to help me. ...'[11]

In the next verse, Daniel is told that this vision concerns *the time of the end* and:

'. . . what shall befall thy people (Israel) *in the latter* days.'[12]

Then the Lord makes the following promise to Daniel:

'I will shew thee that which is noted in the scripture of truth . . .'[13]

In this very same verse, Daniel is told by the Lord that only Michael, the Chief Prince of Persia, understands the meaning of this latter day vision. The Lord says to Daniel:

'. . . and there is none that holdeth with me (God) in these things, but Michael your prince.'[14]

Michael is obviously a prince of Persia, but a spiritual prince, and unlike the prince of the kingdom of Persia who resisted Daniel. The Lord calls Michael 'your prince' in speaking to Daniel.

The name Michael, translated into English, means One who looks like God. This is yet another way of saying 'the Glory of God'.

It is interesting to note that Daniel, like Ezekiel, fell to the earth, overcome, when he beheld the glory of this Messenger. Daniel says:

'And when he had spoken such words unto me, I set my face toward the ground and I became dumb.'[15]

The same thing happened to Ezekiel when he beheld the 'Glory of God' who came from the East.

The final chapter of *Daniel* speaks of *the last days*, and says yet again:

'And at that time shall Michael stand up, the great prince which standeth for the children of thy people .. and at that time thy people shall be delivered . . .'[16]

There could no longer be any doubt but that Michael was

a spiritual prince, a representative of God. Could he be the Messiah? Would he come at the time foretold, which I had already ascertained from the Bible? The next question, therefore, was: When would this wonder take place? When would Michael, Prince of Persia, Who looked like God, appear and deliver the people?

Daniel was told when this would take place:

1. 'In the latter days . . .'[17]
2. 'At the time of the end shall be the vision.'[18]
3. 'The words are closed up and sealed till the time of the end.'[19]
4. 'Shut up the words, and seal the book, even to the time of the end.'[20]

Then in vision, Daniel sees the last days, and the coming of the 'Ancient of days', the Promised One Who will unseal the books. Daniel says:

'. . . ten thousand times ten thousand stood before him: the judgment was set, and the books were opened.'[21]

In this same chapter Daniel says that in this hour

'. . . one like the Son of man came with the clouds of heaven.'[22]

A few verses later Daniel repeats:

'. . . the Ancient of days came, and judgment was given to the saints of the Most High; and the time came that the saints (believers) possessed the kingdom.'[23]

In this same chapter, Daniel says that this will come to pass following:

'a time and times and the dividing of time.'[24]

78

This we know to be three and a half years, or 1260 days; or in the measure of biblical prophecy: 1260 years.

In the final chapter of *Daniel*, it is said again that Michael, Prince of Persia, the Ancient of days, will stand for the people of the Lord, and deliver them in the hour when the books are unsealed. This also will take place, Daniel prophesies, after:

'. . . a time, times, and a half.'[25]

Therefore, we again come to this same identical time of 1260 years.

In Persia, the land where Daniel wrote his prophecy, the land of Michael, Who looks like God, the year 1260 is identical with the year 1844 of the calendar of the West.

Thus, once again, I learned: (1) that the year 1844 would be the time for the appearance of the Messiah; (2) that He would be 'One Who looks like God' or 'the Glory of God'; (3) that He would appear in the land of Persia.

I now had two converging clues, of time and place, in *The Case of the Missing Millennium*.

20. The Avalanche

The next logical step was to search through the history of Persia in the first half of the nineteenth century for some *clue* as to the identity of the Messiah. Before doing this, I made a list of all the additional information and evidence which I had accumulated during my search through the Scriptures and secular history.

I shall leave the intriguing details until we take up the next section *The Solution*. Here I shall merely place on record the facts. Each one of these points I shall later, clearly and separately, substantiate from the sources.

In addition to those given in the preceding chapters, I uncovered the following statements concerning the Messiah of
the time of the end:

1. He shall come from Persia (additional evidence).
2. He shall go to the valley of the Tigris and Euphrates
   rivers in the land of Babylon.
3. He shall withdraw from the city into the barren places,
   as Christ had gone into the desert in the day of His *first*
   coming.
4. He shall openly proclaim His Mission in Babylon (or its
   modern equivalent), and there He shall 'redeem' Israel
   and the world.
5. He shall come from the Tigris and Euphrates valley to
   the Holy Land, Israel, as Abraham had come. He shall
   make the same journey from the land of the Chaldees to
   the promised land of Canaan.
6. He shall come from a fortified city to a fortified city on
   his journey to Israel.
7. He shall come out of the 'fortress' and journey to the
   freedom of the 'river.'
8. On His journey from the East to Israel, He shall come
   from 'mountain to mountain.'
9. The land of Israel shall be desolate when He comes, but
   it will later 'blossom as the rose.'
10. He shall dwell in the 'midst of Carmel' and from there
    He shall 'feed His flock' with His Teachings.
11. His ministry on earth shall last for exactly 'forty
    years'.
12. He shall come to the valley of Achor where He shall be
    found by those who 'have sought' Him in the last days.
13. The place where His feet have walked in the Holy Land,
    Israel, shall 'be made glorious'.

14. The place of His 'rest' or 'sanctuary' or tomb shall become beautified with trees, paths, and flowers.
15. He shall come from the 'seed' of Abraham.
16. He shall 'glorify' Christ in the day of His coming.
17. There shall be signs in the physical heavens in the day of His appearance.
18. He shall 'unseal the books' and explain their 'hidden meanings' so that all may understand (additional evidence).
19. He shall overthrow the power and thrones of wicked kings.
20. He shall set up a spiritual 'kingdom' in all parts of the world—the Kingdom foretold by Christ in His prayer: 'Thy Kingdom come, Thy Will be done, on earth as it is in heaven.'

I had never dreamed there would be such an avalanche of *clues* and *proofs* for the coming of Christ when I had started to unravel this mystery seven long years before.

I heartily affirmed Christabel Pankhurst's summation in *Behold He Cometh:* 'A few years ago there was excuse for the critical having doubts of Bible prophecies. But recent events are fitting into the mould of prophecy so marvellously as to remove all grounds for doubt.'[1]

Certainly no Messiah had ever come with such an astonishing array of proofs to fulfil. It should now be quite easy to prove the truth or the falsehood of anyone who claimed to be the Messiah. He need only be measured against these prophecies.

The hardest part of the detective's job was now over. The drudgery of assembling the facts, evidence and clues was ended. The rest was a matter of careful arrangement, then I could begin an all-out search for a Messiah Who would fulfil these promises. This should be the most interesting and exciting part. I certainly had more than enough to go on, including Christ's own words:

> '... when ye shall see all these things, know that it (His return) is near, even at the doors.'[2]

I knew exactly where to begin: Persia, 1844.

I took a second folder from my files. I labelled it: *The Solution*.

Would there be one?

PART TWO

THE SOLUTION

THE story told in the following chapter was gleaned from many sources, and was verified over a number of years. It is presented here in only the briefest form.

I hope it will give you the same stab-like thrill it gave me when I found the first 'clue' to this astonishing story.

In order to determine the truth of this account, I made several trips to the Middle East. In fact, the final two sections of this book were completed within sight of the famous Cave of Elijah (Elias) on Mount Carmel.

My search began in a radio studio in Wisconsin. It ended in the Holy Land, Israel, the land of promise.

W. S.

Haifa, Israel,
October 1959

1. The Mystery Begins to Unravel

A young man was being led captive through the crowded streets. His neck was encased in a huge iron collar. Long ropes were fastened to the collar by means of which he was pulled through the rows of people lining the streets.

When he faltered in his steps, the guards savagely jerked him on his way, or delivered a brutal well-aimed kick. Occasionally someone would dart out of the crowd, break through the guards, and strike the young man with a fist or a stick.

Cheers of delight from the crowd accompanied each successful attack. When a stone or a piece of refuse, hurled from the mob, struck the young captive in the face, the guards and the crowd would burst into laughter.

'Rescue yourself, O great hero!' one of the pursuers called mockingly. 'Break asunder your bonds! Produce for us a miracle!' Then he spat in derision at the silent figure.

The young man was led at last to his place of execution. It was twelve o'clock noon. In the barracks' square of a sun-baked city, the firing-squad was assembled. The blazing summer sun flashed from the barrels of the raised muskets, pointed at the young man's breast. The soldiers awaited the command to fire and to take his life. The crowd leaned forward expectantly, hoping to witness, even at this last moment, a miracle.

Late comers were still pouring into the public square. Thousands swarmed along the adjoining rooftops looking down upon the scene of death, all eager for one last look at this strange young man who, in six short years, had so troubled their country.

He was either good or evil, and they were not sure which it was. Yet he seemed so young to die, barely thirty. Now that the end had come, this victim of all their hatred and persecution did not seem dangerous at all. The crowd was disappointed. They had come, hungering for drama, and he was failing them.

The young man was a strange paradox: helpless yet confident. There was a look of contentment, even of eagerness, on his handsome face as he gazed into the menacing barrels of the seven hundred and fifty cocked rifles.

The guns were raised. The command was given.

'Fire!'

In turn, each of the three columns of two hundred and fifty men opened fire upon the young man, until the entire regiment had discharged its volley of bullets.

There were over ten thousand eye-witnesses to the spectacle that followed. Several historical accounts have been preserved. One of these states:

'The smoke of the firing of the seven hundred and fifty rifles was such as to turn the light of the noonday sun into darkness. . . . As soon as the cloud of smoke had cleared away, an astounded multitude (looked) upon a scene which their eyes could scarcely believe. . . . The cords with which (the young man had been) suspended had been rent in pieces by the bullets, yet (his) body had miraculously escaped the volleys.'[1]

M. C. Huart, a French author, and a Christian, also wrote an account of this episode: 'The soldiers in order to quiet the excitement of the crowd . . . showed the cords broken by the bullets, implying that no miracle had really taken place.'[2]

The soldiers picked up the fragments of rope. They held them up to the milling crowd. The mob was becoming dangerous, and the soldiers wished to pacify them.

'The musket-balls have shattered the ropes into pieces,' their actions explained. 'This is what freed him. It is nothing more than this. It is no miracle.'

M. C. Huart, in further describing that remarkable event, states: 'Amazing to believe, the bullets had not struck the condemned but, on the contrary, had broken the bonds and he was delivered. It was a real miracle.'[3]

A.-L.-M. Nicolas, the famous European scholar, also recorded this spectacle.

'An extraordinary thing happened,' he said, 'unique in the annals of the history of humanity . . . the bullets cut the cords that held (him) and he fell on his feet without a scratch.'[4]

I first read this story in an account written by the famous British Orientalist, Professor E. G. Browne of Cambridge University. (This was the same Professor Browne whom I mentioned earlier.) He likened this story to that of the coming of Christ, saying:

'I am very anxious to get as accurate an account of all the details . . . as possible, for in my eyes the whole (story) seems one of the most interesting and important events that has occurred since the rise of Christianity . . . I feel it my duty, as well as pleasure, to try as far as in me lies to bring the matter to the notice of my countrymen, that they may consider it . . . for suppose anyone could tell us more about the childhood and early life and appearance of Christ, for instance, how glad we should be to know it. Now it is impossible to find out much . . . but in the case of (this young man) it *is* possible . . . So let us earn the thanks of posterity, and provide against that day now.'[5]

If this great scholar, and others like him, after considerable study and search, felt that this event was akin to 'the appearance of Christ' and the recording of it would win 'the thanks of posterity', can you blame me for feeling a rising tide of excitement.

I had to know more.

2. The Remarkable Parallel

I began searching the libraries for all the available documents. You can imagine my feelings of awe and wonder when I uncovered the following facts.

The death of this young man occurred in July 1850. He was slain publicly because of his words and his teaching. Everything I learned about his life reminded me of Christ. In fact, after carefully searching into his background, I could find but one parallel in all recorded history to his brief, turbulent career; only the moving story of the passion of Jesus Christ himself.

As part of my record of 'findings', I here set down the remarkable similarity in the story of their lives:

1. They were both youthful.
2. They were both known for their meekness and loving kindness.
3. They both performed healing miracles.
4. The period of their ministry was very brief in each case, and moved with dramatic swiftness to its climax.
5. Both of them boldly challenged the time-honoured conventions, laws, and rites of the religions into which they had been born.
6. They courageously condemned the unbridled graft and corruption which they saw on every side, both religious and secular.
7. The purity of their own lives shamed the people among whom they taught.
8. Their chief enemies were among the religious leaders of the land. These officials were the instigators of the outrages they were made to suffer.
9. They both had indignities heaped upon them.

87

10. They were both forcibly brought before the government authorities and were subjected to public interrogation.

11. Both were scourged following this interrogation.

12. They both went, first in triumph then in suffering, through the streets of the city where they were to be slain.

13. They were both paraded publicly, and heaped with humiliation, on the way to their place of martyrdom.

14. They both spoke words of hope and promise to one who was to die with them; in fact, almost the exact same words: 'Thou shalt be with me in paradise.'

15. They were both martyred publicly before the hostile gaze of the onlookers who crowded the scene.

16. A darkness covered the land following their slaying, in each case beginning at noon.

17. Their bodies were both lacerated by soldiers at the time of their slaying.

18. They both remained in ignominious suspension before the eyes of an unfriendly multitude.

19. Their bodies came finally into the hands of their loving followers.

20. When their bodies, in each case, had vanished from the spot where they had been placed, the religious leaders explained away the fact.

21. Only a handful of their followers were with them at the times of their deaths.

22. In each case, one of their chief disciples denied knowing them. This same disciple, in each case, later became a hero.

23. Each of them had an outstanding woman follower who played a dramatic part in making the disciples turn their faces from the past, and look toward the future.

24. Confusion, bewilderment and despair seized their followers, in each case, following their martyrdom.
25. Through their disciples (the Peters and Pauls of each age) their Faiths were carried to all parts of the world.
26. They both replied with the same exact words to the question: Are you the promised One?
27. Each of them addressed their disciples, charging them to carry their messages to the ends of the earth.[1]

The words of Christ I already knew. With great interest I read the words of this young man:

'Verily I say, this is the Day spoken of by God in His Book . . . Ponder the words of Jesus addressed to His disciples, as He sent them forth . . . "Ye are even as the fire which in the darkness of the night has been kindled upon the mountain top. Let your light shine before the eyes of men. Such must be the purity of your character and the degree of your renunciation, that the people of the earth may through you recognize and be drawn closer to the heavenly Father who is the Source of purity and grace."[2]

'Verily I say, immensely exalted is this Day above the days of the Apostles of old. Nay, immeasurable is the difference! You are the witnesses of the Dawn of the promised Day of God . . . Scatter throughout the length and breadth of this land, and, with steadfast feet and sanctified hearts, prepare the way for His coming . . . Has He not established the ascendancy of Jesus, poor and lowly as He was in the eyes of men . . . Arise in His name, put your trust wholly in Him, and be assured of ultimate victory.'[3]

No wonder that the great Jowett of Oxford University said of this new Faith:
'It is too great and too near for this generation to comprehend. The future alone can reveal its import.'[4]

It was these comments of Jowett and of Browne which had originally directed me to this particular path of search. Now I understood their keen interest.

I felt the excitement of the chase! Was I on the trail at last? Had I found a possible solution to the century-old mystery of *The Case of the Missing Millennium*?

I decided to spend the next year assembling all the information I could gather about this young man and his Faith. I would then measure my findings against the required proofs in my file. If this *were* the Messiah, I was now in a position to test it thoroughly. I could settle the matter once and for all in my mind.

The blade of my enthusiasm, however, had been made razor-sharp by the answer to two questions:

When did his Faith begin?

In 1844!

Where?

In Persia!

3. The Twin Fires of Heaven

It took me three years instead of one before I could close my file of 'findings'. In the end, however, I knew that I had unearthed a truly remarkable story. The hard-boiled newspapermen had been right. If a man picked up his Sunday paper and read this story on the front page, he would indeed be rocked back on his heels. Nothing would ever be quite the same again.

Can you blame me for feeling excited? The search had been long, but the reward promised to be great. I might at last solve my mystery.

One of the first things I learned was this:

1. On May 24th, 1844, in the West, Samuel Morse sent his

famous telegraphic message, quoting from the Scriptures: 'What hath God wrought?'

2. On May 23rd, 1844, the preceding day, in the East, this young man arose to make a staggering claim.

He declared that this was the day foretold in all the Scriptures of the past. This day, he said, was the day when the promised One of all religions would appear. This was to be the day of the 'one fold and one shepherd'.

This took place in Persia in 1844. Naturally my attention was arrested immediately by the date and the place.

I learned that he was called the Báb. Just as the name Christ means 'the anointed', the name Báb means 'the gate' or 'the door'. This young man proclaimed that he was the 'gate' or the 'door' through which would come the One promised in all the Holy Books, the One Who would establish the one fold of God.

I remembered the promise given by Christ:

'But he that entereth in by *the door* is the shepherd of the sheep . . . And other sheep have I which are not of this fold: them also I must bring, and they shall hear my voice; and there shall be one fold and one shepherd.'[1]

The Báb said that he was the herald and forerunner of one greater than himself. His mission was to call men back to God and to prepare the way for the great world Saviour foretold by Christ and all the prophets of the past. Just as John the Baptist had been the forerunner of Christ, the Báb claimed to be the forerunner of this Promised Redeemer of all ages.

In the sacred writings of Persia, the land promised by Daniel as a 'place of vision' in the latter days, there are several prophecies of the twin heavenly Messengers who will appear. One foretells:

'One day, the disturbing *trumpet-blast* shall disturb it, which the *second blast* shall follow: men's hearts on that day shall quake.'

In yet another place:

'. . . on the resurrection day the whole Earth shall be but his handful. . . . And there shall be a *blast on the trumpet* . . . Then shall there be *another blast on it*, and lo! . . . the earth shall shine with the light of her Lord.'

In another instance, it speaks of the two who will come together at *the time of the end*:

'Verily I say, after the Qá'im (He who shall arise) the Qayyúm will be made manifest.'[2]

Pavri, in *The Coming World Teacher*, writes: 'When Sri Krishna was to come, the Sage Narada and others announced His coming several years beforehand . . . Such proclamation beforehand is necessary . . .'

I found this association of two Figures with a Divine Revelation to be common to several of the religions of the world.

Zoroastrian: Ushídar-Máh and the Sháh Bahrám.
Shí'ih Islám: The Qá'im and the Imám Husayn.
Sunní Islám: The Mihdí and Jesus the Christ.
Christianity: John the Baptist and Christ; Elijah and Christ.
Judaism: Messiah ben Joseph and Messiah ben David.
    Elijah (Elias) and the Messiah.

In the land in which the Báb appeared, there was still another prophecy of the coming of two holy Figures. The tradition related by Bokhari says:

'At the time of the end God shall manifest himself to all mankind with all the attributes of divinity and majesty, but very few shall advance towards him. . . . Then again he will appear *a second time* manifesting all the qualities of servitude and the people will flock around him and believe in him and praise and laud his uncreated virtues.'

Zechariah, speaking of the *last days*, prophesied of the twin holy souls who would appear, saying:

'Then said he, These are the *two* anointed ones, that stand by the Lord of the whole earth.'[3]

In addition to the two 'woes', *Revelation* speaks of the 'two olive trees' and the 'two candlesticks'.

Malachi, speaking of *the time of the end*, prophesied:

'Behold I will send you Elijah the prophet before the coming of *the great and dreadful day of the Lord*.'[4]

This was the very land, Persia, in which Daniel beheld:

'. . . one like the Son of man came with the clouds of heaven . . .'[5]

The Báb foretold that this great Redeemer would appear exactly *nine* years after His own coming. He would, therefore, as prophesied in the Old Testament, 'suddenly come to his temple'. He would thus come just as Christ had so often emphasised in the book of *Revelation*:

'Behold I come quickly.'

Malachi, who called it the great and dreadful day of the Lord, foretold the appearance of two at *the time of the end*, saying:

'Behold, I will send *my messenger*, and he shall prepare the way before me: and *the Lord*, whom ye seek, shall suddenly come to his temple . . .'[6]

The Báb repeatedly said that He was the *Dawn*, but that the

Promise of all Ages Who was soon to come after him would be the *Sun*. He foretold that this great world Saviour would usher in an age of unprecedented progress and peace.

Naturally, I now wanted to learn everything that I could about the Báb as well as about the One who was to follow. After all, three of my most basic *proofs* had been fulfilled:

1. This faith had begun at a time when 'the Gospel of Christ had been preached in all the world for a witness' (1844).
2. This faith brought its message to the world at the exact year 'when the times of the Gentiles' had been fulfilled (1844).
3. This faith had appeared in the year foretold by Daniel, and at the time when, according to Christ, mankind should 'stand in the holy place' (1844).

All three of these vital initial *clues* had been fulfilled by the coming of this faith in 1844; therefore I knew I had to go on.

4. The Witnesses

Margaret Fuller, friend of Emerson, said of the world-wide zeal around 1844: 'One very marked trait of the period was that the agitation reached all circles.'[1]

I was anxious to learn exactly what had happened to the Báb in that hour. What were the very beginnings of this faith? The millennial zeal was at its fever pitch when Morse sent his famous message on May 24th, 1844. The evening of May 22nd, 1844, two hours and eleven minutes after sunset in far off Shíráz, Persia, the Báb spoke to a humble Persian student, much as Christ had first spoken to simple fishermen. He said:

'This night, this very hour will, in the days to come, be

94

celebrated as one of the greatest and most significant of all festivals.'[2]

The young student to whom the Báb first revealed his message, has left a vivid impression of that unforgettable occasion and these first words of the Báb:

'Verily, the dawn of a new Day has broken. The promised One is enthroned in the hearts of men.'[3]

'I sat spellbound by His words,' this student recalled. 'I forgot all sense of time. This Truth, so suddenly thrust upon me, came as a thunderbolt. It numbed my senses. Then excitement, joy, awe, and wonder stirred the depths of my soul. Most of all I felt a sense of gladness and strength. I was changed into a new person.'[4]

I studied a 700-page document on the early history of the Báb and his followers. I read of their sufferings and martyrdom, a story like that of Christ and His apostles. I read the words of the French historian Ernest Renan, author of a life of Christ, who called those martyrdoms of the followers of the Báb, 'A day without parallel perhaps in the history of the world.'[5] I re-read several times the recollections of the young man to whom the Báb spoke first. He has left to posterity the following memory of that first announcement:

'Sleep departed from me that night. I sat enthralled by the music of that sweet voice. Predominant among all my emotions was a sense of gladness and strength which seemed to have transfigured me. How feeble and impotent I had felt previously. Now, I felt possessed of such courage and power that were the world, all its peoples and rulers, to rise against me, I would alone and undaunted withstand their onslaught. I seemed to be the voice of Gabriel calling unto all mankind: "Awake, for lo! ... His Cause is made manifest. The portal of

His grace is open wide; enter therein, O peoples of the world! For He who is your promised One is come!" "[6]

The story of the life of the Báb touched me deeply. I felt certain that such an epic drama as this could not have passed without some record in contemporary history. It might be misunderstood, but it could hardly be overlooked. I was correct. I found that I was not alone in my impression. I was able to find many accounts of this event in European history. The French historian, A.-L.-M. Nicolas wrote of the Báb, saying: '(His life) is one of the most magnificent examples of courage which it has been the privilege of mankind to behold . . .'[7]

Nicolas also likened this age to that of Christ, in these words: 'He sacrificed himself for humanity' . . . Like Jesus, He (the Báb) paid with his life for the proclamation of a reign of concord, equity and brotherly love.[8]

Edward Granville Browne, who first put me on the trail of this story, wrote of the Báb: 'Who can fail to be attracted by the gentle spirit of (the Báb)? His sorrowful and persecuted life; his purity of conduct, and youth; his courage and uncomplaining patience under misfortune . . . but most of all his tragic death, all serve to enlist our sympathies on behalf of the young Prophet of Shíráz.'[9]

The Case of the Missing Millennium had suddenly taken on great stature. I was very much impressed by the new developments. I realised that this was no little thing which I had uncovered. It did not concern some obscure hidden little group. Neglected, yes; but only by the twentieth century, certainly not by the nineteenth.

A noted French publicist testified: 'All Europe was stirred to pity and indignation. . . . Among the *littérateurs* of my generation in the Paris of 1890, the martyrdom of the Báb was still as fresh a topic as had been the first news of His death. We wrote poems about Him. Sarah Bernhardt entreated Catulle Mendès for a play on the theme of this historic tragedy.'[10]

The great scholar Arminius Vambéry spoke of the Báb in the French Academy, saying that 'he has expressed doctrines worthy of the greatest thinkers'.

A drama was published in 1903 entitled *The Báb*. It was played in one of the leading theatres of St. Petersburg. The drama was publicised in London and was translated into French and into German (by the poet Fiedler).

Sir Francis Younghusband, in his history of the times, writes: 'The story of the Báb . . . was the story of spiritual heroism unsurpassed . . . his life must be one of those events in the last hundred years which is really worth study.'[11]

Yet who had made an effort to study this story since that day?

The famous Oxford scholar, the Reverend Dr. T. K. Cheyne, called the Báb: '. . . that Jesus of the age . . . "a prophet and more than a prophet." His combination of mildness and power is so rare that we have to place him in a line with super-normal men.'[12]

Now, I was more eager than ever to investigate the great One foretold by the Báb; for, if the Báb had so affected the people, what of the Redeemer yet to come? According to the Báb, His power would far transcend his own. It would be as the candle to the sun.

The Forerunner, John the Baptist, said of Christ:

'He that cometh after me is mightier than I, whose shoes I am not worthy to bear.'[13]

The Báb said of the One yet to come:

'Of all the tributes I have paid to Him Who is to come after me, the greatest is this, My written confession, that no words of Mine can adequately describe Him, nor

97

can any reference to Him in My Book . . . do justice to His Cause.'[14]

The Báb considered himself only a 'ring upon the hand' of Him Who was yet to come. He said that he would be the first to bow down before Him. He told his own followers:

'I, verily, am a believer in Him, and in His Faith, and in His Book, and in His Testimonies . . . and pride Myself on My belief in Him.'[15]

The Báb said of the Christian who would believe in the Messiah yet to come:

'. . . the same will I regard as the apple of Mine eye.'[16]

In the days preceding his death, the Báb wrote:

'I have educated all men, that they may recognize this Revelation (of the Messiah to come) . . . that belongeth neither to the East nor to the West. . . . How, then, can anyone be veiled from Him?'[17]

I had never felt so hopeful of finding a solution to my century-old mystery. What I had started to do in the beginning for fun, I was now doing in earnest.

My next assignment was self-evident. Who was the one foretold by the Báb? What was his name? Where did he come from? Did he fulfil the proofs which I had assembled?

Until I knew the answer to these questions I couldn't close *The Case of the Missing Millennium.*

5. The Hidden is Revealed

I carefully studied all of the writings of the Báb which had been translated into English. I was seeking every possible clue which would lead me to the place and person of the

98

great World Redeemer, Who, he had promised, would soon appear.

The Báb clearly stated the exact year in which this promised One would arise:

'Ere *nine* (*years*) will have elapsed from the inception of this Cause, the realities of the created things will not be made manifest. . . . Be patient, until thou beholdest a new creation.'[1]

That was plain enough. The year nine (1269) of Persia was the year 1853 of the West. Not before 1853 would He come. In another place the Báb wrote:

'In the year nine ye will attain unto all good.'[2]

And still again:

'In the year nine ye will attain unto the presence of God.'[3]

Nine years from his own announcement would bring us from 1844 to 1853. I also found in his writings other *clues* which gave the place of the Messiah's appearance; in fact, the very city.

When he bade farewell to the young student who was the first to believe in him, the Báb said:

'Follow the course of your journey towards the north, and visit . . . Teheran. Beseech almighty Providence that He may graciously enable you to attain, in that capital, the seat of true sovereignty, and to enter the mansion of the Beloved. A secret lies hidden in that city. When made manifest, it shall turn the earth into paradise.'[4]

On another occasion, the Báb said:

Direct your steps to Teheran 'which enshrines a Mystery of such transcendent holiness as . . . Shíráz (his own birth-place) (cannot) hope to rival.'[5]

Was this to be the *mystery* I had spent so many years search-

99

ing for? Was this the key that would unlock the door to the missing millennium for which Christians, Jews, Muslims, Buddhists, Hindus and Zoroastrians had longed for in vain?

I found a documented account of the Báb's visit to a sacred spot near the city of Teheran. He addressed the following words to the saint buried there:

'Well is it with you to have found your resting-place ... under the shadow of My Beloved.'[6]

There seemed little doubt as to the place and the date: Teheran, 1853. My curiosity was doubly increased when I encountered still another prophecy in the sacred writings of Persia which spoke of the coming of twin Messengers of God in the *last days*. It promised:

'In the year Ghars (1844) the earth shall be illumined by His light. ... If thou livest until the year Gharasí (1853) thou shalt witness how the nations, the rulers, the peoples, and the Faith of God shall all have been renewed.'[7]

My investigation of Persian history, and further study of the writings of the Báb, soon brought to my attention information concerning the birth of a remarkable person. He was born in *Teheran*, the capital. He was, as Daniel had prophesied, of noble lineage. He was descended from the ancient kings of Persia.

I was able to find the following account of his early years: 'From childhood He was extremely kind and generous. He was a great lover of outdoor life, most of His time being spent in the garden or the fields. He had an extraordinary power of attraction, which was felt by all. People always crowded round Him, Ministers and people of the Court would surround Him, and the children also were devoted to Him.'[8]

I also found a record of some of His activities as a youth. It was much like the story about Jesus as a boy: 'When He was only thirteen or fourteen years old, He became renowned for His learning. He would converse on any subject and solve any problem presented to Him. In large gatherings He would discuss matters with the (leading priests) and would explain intricate religious questions. All of them used to listen to Him with the greatest interest.'[9]

Obviously the effect he had on people was remarkable. Even the Prime Minister of Persia recognized his greatness and was disturbed by it. When his name was suggested for a post in the government, the Prime Minister said: 'Leave him to himself. Such a position is unworthy of him. He has some higher aim in view. I cannot understand him, but I am convinced that he is destined for some lofty career. His thoughts are not like ours. Let him alone.'[10]

In an historical record of His life, I found yet another similarity to Christ: 'As Jesus washed His disciples' feet, so (He) used sometimes to cook food and perform other lowly offices for His followers, He was a servant of the servants, and gloried only in servitude, content to sleep on a bare floor if need be, to live on bread and water, or even at times on what He called "the divine nourishment, . . . hunger!" His perfect humility was seen in His profound reverence for nature, for human nature, and especially for the saints, prophets and martyrs. To Him, all things spoke of God, from the meanest to the greatest.'[11]

His mission began in the East as foretold by Ezekiel and by Christ. It began in Persia as promised by Daniel. It began in Teheran as prophesied by the Báb. And it started exactly nine years later.

The Báb wrote:

'Look ye upon the Sun of Truth. . . . This, verily, is the thing We promised thee. . . . Wait thou until nine (years) will have elapsed. . . . I am the first servant to believe in Him and in His signs.'[12]

Lest anyone should misunderstand, the Báb wrote the following words:

'Glorified art Thou, O my God! Bear Thou witness that, through this Book, I have covenanted with all created things concerning the Mission of Him Whom Thou shalt make manifest (the Messiah) . . .'[13]

And finally:

'After (1853) a Cause shall be given unto you which ye shall come to know.'[14]

On many occasions, I found, the Báb referred to the great Messiah Who would appear in nine years, in the year 1853. He said that Persia would be blessed with what he called 'the footsteps of His (God's) Most Great Name and Mighty Announcement'.

This was not circumstantial evidence. It was concrete. It could be tested.

6. The Glory of God

I studied the story of the young Persian student to whom the Báb had made his first announcement. He, too, had sought the One promised by the Báb. He went to Teheran, and inquired among the people.

'Is there any person who is distinguished above all others in this city? Someone who is renowned for his character?'

He was told that there was only one such person.

'What is his occupation?'

'He cheers the disconsolate and feeds the hungry.'

'What of his rank and position?'

'He has none apart from befriending the poor and the stranger.'

'What is his name?'

'It is Husayn 'Alí, Bahá'u'lláh.'

'His age?'

'Eight and twenty.'[1]

In this way, too I learned that his name was Husayn Alí, just as the name of Christ was Jesus. Jesus was known by the title of Christ (in English, 'the Anointed'). Husayn Alí was known by the title of Bahá'u'lláh (in English, 'the Glory of God').

Bahá'u'lláh was born in Persia, the land in which Daniel had seen his vision of the Prince Michael whose name means 'One who looks like God'.

When Daniel was told to 'seal the books' until *the time of the end*, he also was promised:

'At that time shall Michael stand up, the great prince which standeth for the children of thy people . . .'[2]

Bahá'u'lláh was born in the province of Mazandaran in Persia. This part of Persia had long been known as a land of future promise. It has been written of Mazandaran: 'There are many legends regarding the province. It was said that there would grow a celestial tree, with branches reaching to heaven. The fruit of this tree would be for the life of the nations. Many people travelled to this region hoping to find the wonderful tree. Another legend was that the king of war and hatred had been imprisoned in one of these high mountains.'[3]

The author of this account goes on to explain that these were symbolic parables of the coming of a Great Figure from that province, one who would bring peace to mankind.

Similar legends were noted in *Revelation* and in *Daniel*.

Daniel in the very chapter in which he prophesies that Michael, who looks like God, will deliver the people in the last days, also prophesies that it will be the great *resurrection day* as well. A similar *resurrection day* is promised by Christ at the time of His return.

F. Hudgings, scholar of Jewish prophecy, writes of these present days in his *Zionism in Prophecy:* 'Yes, it seems that we are actually in the "time of the end", exactly as the Prophet (Daniel) saw it in vision.'

Husayn 'Alí, Bahá'u'lláh. It was a strange name to me. It took me some time to get used to it. Gradually the story of his life melted away my original coolness. The name was oriental, from the Middle East. I realised of course that I had reacted exactly as the Roman historian who had praised the Emperor for 'stamping out the cult of the Nazarene'. He, too, as a westerner, had objected to the strange oriental name. Yet in reality all the Messengers of God had come from the East with names that were strange at first.

About this time I came across a most remarkable statement. Or so it seemed to me. It had been written, not by a follower of the Báb or Bahá'u'lláh, but by a Bible scholar of Oxford University and a well-known Christian clergyman. He wrote: 'If there is any prophet in recent times, it is to Bahá'u'lláh that we must go. (He) was a man of the highest class—that of prophets.'[4]

I read the account of Dr. J. Estlin Carpenter in his book *Comparative Religions* in which he asked the pointed question: 'Has Persia, in the midst of her miseries, given birth to a religion that will go around the world?'

Nothing could have induced me to give up my search at this point. I was now on the threshold of a possible solution to *The Case of the Missing Millennium*. Would I be disappointed, as so many had been down through the centuries?

At least I was in a far more favourable position. I had a long list of definite proofs which *any* claimant to the throne of the *Messiah* would have to fulfil before He could hope to be accepted.

It was difficult to restrain my growing enthusiasm. The thrill so far had been far more exciting than that of unearthing a mine of precious gems. Could it possibly sustain itself?

I knew that I was now at the crucial point. I took down my list of *proofs* and slowly, one at a time, I began to check them against the life of Bahá'u'lláh. I planned to measure him by each *proof* separately.

I learned much about Bahá'u'lláh, and that like Christ he had suffered great indignities and humiliation at the hands of the leaders of his day.

He was brutally scourged in the prayer-house at Amul. Two years after the martyrdom of the Báb, he was arrested by soldiers and marched many miles on foot to an underground prison in Teheran. He was stripped of his garments, *en route*, and was overwhelmed with abuse and ridicule.

An historical account of that time records: 'On foot and exposed to the fierce rays of the midsummer sun, He was compelled to cover, barefooted and bareheaded, the whole distance from Shimiran to the dungeon. All along the route, He was pelted and vilified by the crowds. . . . As He was approaching the dungeon, an old woman tried to stone Him. She pleaded with the soldiers. "Give me a chance to fling my stone in his face!"

'Bahá'u'lláh saw her hastening behind him. He said to his guards: "Suffer not this woman to be disappointed. Deny her not what she regards as meritorious in the sight of God." '[5]

In order to silence the magic power of his tongue, Bahá'u'lláh was separated from his followers. He was exiled from his native land.

Under armed escort, he was taken over the borders of Persia into Iraq. Perhaps you, too, will feel the same tingling sensation that I experienced when I learned of his destination.

The valley of the Tigris and Euphrates rivers!

The very spot where Ezekiel had had *his* vision of the 'Glory of the Lord'.

Babylon! Bahá'u'lláh means 'The Glory of the Lord'!

I put away my file of papers marked *Solution*. On the front of the manila folder I wrote a big? Then I turned my full attention to my list of *proofs*. The outcome of *The Case of the Missing Millennium* would depend on what happened from now on.

PART THREE

THE PROOF

1. The King from the Sunrise

The deeper I dug, the more evidence I unearthed that Bahá'u'lláh had fulfilled the requirement that the Messiah should come from the East. He came, I found, from a family of noble lineage in Persia, which is to the *East* of Israel.

The Christian clergyman, Reverend John Cumming, in his book about the last days, *The Great Tribulation*, quotes a prophecy of Zoroaster concerning the Messiah which states that this Messenger of God will come from the land of Núr in Persia.

Núr is in the province of Mazandaran. It is the homeland of Bahá'u'lláh. His father, Mírzá Buzurg of Núr, was an honoured Minister to the King of Persia (known as the Sháh).

In the book *Religious Debates* by Nategh, are found the following prophecies of Zoroaster concerning the One who will come from the *East:*

1. 'God will give you (Persia) a good ending.'
2. 'If there is but one minute remaining in the whole world, I will send someone from this nation (Persia) Who will renew religion.'
2. 'When Persia and the other countries are overtaken by the Arabs, I will choose one from the generation of the Kings of Persia, so that He will call the people of the world from East to West to worship one God.'

In my search, I also found the following record: 'A manuscript has been found, giving his (Bahá'u'lláh's) genealogy which goes back more than 1300 years to the kings of ancient Persia.'[1]

There is a prophecy of the Great Messiah to come which is known to the Buddhists. The prophecy is attributed to Buddha Gautama Himself, and states that in the fulness of time, there would arise:

'A Buddha named Maitreye, the Buddha of universal fellowship.'[2]

This great Messiah, the Buddhists believe, will come: *not from the East*, but *from the West*.

Mr. Edward Irving, a Christian clergyman of Britain, who was keenly anticipating the return of Christ during the millennial zeal of the 1800's, said: '. . .What is very remarkable, a friend of mine, who . . . stood on the Himalaya mountains in India, by the holy pool, where never Christian had dwelt before, found there also an expectation of a religion *from the west* which in the space of forty years was to possess the earth . . .'[3]

Bahá'u'lláh came from Persia which is to the *East* of Israel, but to the *West* of India. His ministry from the time of its beginning until his last days on earth was *forty years*.

The prophets of Syria and Palestine foretold the coming of the promised Messiah from the *East*. The prophets and seers from India and the Far East, said that He would appear in the *West*. Persia, the birthplace of Bahá'u'lláh lies in between these two, and fulfils the requirements of each.

In the book of *Enoch*, it is prophesied that the Messiah of the last days shall come from the East of Israel, and that He shall come from the land now known as Persia. Enoch foretells:

'And *in those days* the angels will assemble, and turn their heads *towards the East,* toward the people of *Parthia and Medea,* in order to excite the kings, and that a spirit of disturbance came over them, and disturbed them from off their thrones.'[4]

Parthia and Medea make up what is now the land of Persia, the birthplace of Bahá'u'lláh.

The Jewish oracles, the Sibylline books, also mention the coming of the Messiah from the *East,* saying:

'And then *from the sunrise* God shall send a king who shall give every land relief from the bane of war . . . nor shall he do these things by his own counsel, but in obedience to the good ordinances of the Mighty God.'[5]

Joseph Klausner, in *The Messianic Idea in Israel,* writes: 'The "king from the sunrise" is, without any doubt, the King-Messiah.'

The prophet Ezekiel also foretold that the Messiah would come to the Holy Land, Israel, from the *East.* He even gave the title by which He would be known in that day: *The Glory of God.* Ezekiel recorded his vision of the *last days,* saying:

'And, behold, *the Glory of the God* of Israel came from the way of *the east . . .*'[6]

In another place, Ezekiel says:

'And *the Glory of the Lord* came into the house *by way of the gate* whose prospect is toward *the east.*'[7]

I had already learned that the name Bahá'u'lláh was Persian, and when translated into English means, *The Glory of God* or *the Glory of the Lord.*

His herald was called the Báb. This is also Persian, and translated into English means, *The Gate.*

The Báb was the *Gate* by which Bahá'u'lláh, *the Glory of God,* entered into the hearts of men. Bahá'u'lláh had come to Israel in exile from Persia which is to the *East.*

I was more than satisfied with my findings. I learned that Bahá'u'lláh had completed the prophecies of Isaiah, Jeremiah, Ezekiel, Daniel, Micah, Zoroaster, Buddha, Muhammad, and many secular prophecies as well—all of which pointed to the time and the place from which this Shepherd of the day of the 'one fold' would come.

I marked the first proof: *Fulfilled.*

2. Ancient Land of Mystery

The *second proof* I sought concerned Babylon, ancient land of mystery. From the *clues* I had uncovered, there seemed little doubt that the Redeemer of the last days should come from the valley of the Tigris and Euphrates, from the land once called Babylon.

When the people lamented their lack of a Redeemer to save them, Micah rebuked them severely. He also promised them that their redemption would come from Babylon. He denounced their faithlessness and said:

'Now why dost thou cry out aloud? is there no king in thee?'[1]

Then Micah prophesied of the future, saying:

'Be in pain, and labour to bring forth, O daughter of Zion, like a woman in travail: for now shalt thou go forth out of the city, and thou shalt dwell in the field, and *thou shalt go even to Babylon; ... there the Lord shall redeem thee ...*'[2]

Micah was speaking of *the time of the end,* for he begins this very chapter saying:

'But in the *last days* it shall come to pass ...'[3]

This would be the day when Israel would be 'gathered', and the nations would 'beat their swords into plough-shares'.

My task as a detective was to measure Bahá'u'lláh against this prophecy of Micah, to see if he had:

1. Given birth in Babylon;
2. Gone forth out of the city;
3. Dwelt in the field;
4. Come to Babylon, and there redeemed the people.

I had already learned that Bahá'u'lláh's faith had begun in 1844, and that on January 12th, 1853, he had been exiled from Persia to Iraq. He was taken under armed guard to the valley of the Tigris and Euphrates. His dwelling-place was in old Baghdad, the section called Karkh.

There could be no doubt that this was the land of ancient Babylon. Thomas Newton, Bishop of Bristol, in his *Dissertations on the Prophecies* (1754), writes: Tavernier, who is a very celebrated traveller, relates that 'at the parting of the Tigris, which is but a little way from Bagdat, there is the foundation of a city, which may seem to have been a large league in compass. There are some of the walls yet standing, upon which six coaches may go abreast: They are made of burnt brick, ten foot square, and three thick. The chronicles of the country say here stood the ancient Babylon.'

In *Hanway's Travels*, the author, Hanway, writes of the famous city of Baghdad, saying that in its neighbourhood once 'stood the metropolis of one of the most ancient and most potent monarchies in the world. The place is generally called Bagdat or Bagdad, though some writers preserve the ancient name of Babylon.'

Will Durant, in *The Age of Faith*, writes of the site of Baghdad, saying: 'It was an old Babylonian city, and not far from ancient Babylon; bricks bearing Nebuchadrezzar's name were found . . . under the Tigris there.'

I discovered that Bahá'u'lláh came to the city of Baghdad on the banks of the Tigris. I also learned the following:

1. There, in the valley of the Tigris and Euphrates, in ancient Babylon, Bahá'u'lláh, in the midst of much pain and suffering brought forth his faith.

2. As foretold by Micah, Bahá'u'lláh went 'out of the city' into the mountains of Kurdistan on April 10th, 1854, as Christ had gone into the desert in the days of His *first* coming.

3. He did indeed 'dwell in the field' as promised by Micah. A record of that time states that Bahá'u'lláh was 'entirely alone in His wanderings through the wastes of Kurdistan' as he prepared himself for the fateful days ahead.

4. From these desolate wastes, Bahá'u'lláh did 'go even unto Babylon'. He came to Baghdad, and there announced publicly that He was the Redeemer foretold for the *last days*.

When Ezekiel had his vision of the *Glory of God* Who came from the *East*, he was a prisoner in the land of Babylon. He says:

'I was among the captives by the river Chebar . . . the heavens were opened, and I saw visions of God.'[4]

In that same chapter, Ezekiel mentions that he saw the rainbow in the sky, the sign of the Covenant of God promised to Noah. This, too, was by the river Chebar. In the midst of Ezekiel's vision was the figure of a man:

'This was the appearance of the likeness of *the Glory of the Lord*. And when I saw it, I fell upon my face . . .'[5]

I looked up the history of the river Chebar. It was known to ancient geographers as the river Khabar, as well as by other names. The Chebar had its source west of Baghdad and emptied into the Euphrates in ancient Babylon. It was in this very region that Bahá'u'lláh announced his Mission.

Ezekiel says further of his vision:

'Then the spirit took me up, and I heard behind me a voice of a great rushing, saying, Blessed be *the glory of the Lord* from his place... Then I arose, and went forth into the plain: and, behold, *the glory of the Lord* stood there, as the glory which I saw by the river of Chebar: and I fell on my face.'[6]

Bahá'u'lláh appeared in the land of the Chebar, the land of ancient Babylon. His name means: *the Glory of the Lord* or *the Glory of God*.

I uncovered another prophecy. It came from India. It also referred to the appearance of the promised One in Babylon in the *last days*. It was called the *Red Robe Tradition*, as follows: 'It is related that an account is given of an Indian Muslim, a holy man of the eighth century A.D., who, speaking of the "Great Day of God" to come, uttered these words: "In that day the Holy One will be found abiding in a land called Karkh. He will walk beside the river, wearing the dervish turban, and wrapped in a *red robe*. He will be teaching His followers on the banks of the river. Would that I might be privileged to enter His Presence, and to shed my life-blood in His Path." '[7]

I learned that Bahá'u'lláh wore such a red robe. It had been prepared for him by his wife and daughter while he was away in the wilderness of Kurdistan. They had made it from the pieces of tirmih (red cloth) which they had preserved from the few possessions which had not been stolen during Bahá'u'lláh's imprisonment in Persia.

Bahá'u'lláh taught along the banks of the river Tigris.

The name of the section of Baghdad in which he lived was called Karkh. It was in the land of ancient Babylon.

What a fascinating story!

3. Begotten in Babylon

I was able to discover several additional *clues* concerning my second *proof* and Babylon.

The prophecies of Islám, among which were references to the return of the Spirit of Jesus the Christ, made mention of Baghdad (ancient Babylon). The Qur'án alluded to that city as the 'Abode of Peace' to which God Himself 'calleth'.[1] To that city, in that same Book, further allusion had been made in the verse:

> 'For them is a Dwelling of Peace with their Lord . . . on the Day whereon God shall gather them all together.'[2]

Isaiah also spoke of Babylon and the *last days* when the people would be 'gathered' together. In successive chapters leading up to his promise for Babylon, Isaiah declares:

1. 'Look unto me, and be ye saved, all the ends of the earth; for I am God, and there is none else.'[3]
2. 'Hearken unto me, O house of Jacob, and all the remnant of the house of Israel . . . even I will carry, and will deliver you.'[4]
3. 'As for our Redeemer, the Lord of hosts is his name, the Holy One of Israel.'[5]

Then Isaiah calls upon them all to hear the words of the one he (God) hath chosen among them in Babylon:

4. 'All ye, assemble yourselves, and hear; which among them hath declared these things? *The Lord hath loved him:*

he will do his pleasure on *Babylon,* and his arm shall be on the Chaldeans.'[6]

5. 'I, even I, have spoken; *yea, I have called him: I have brought him, and he shall make his way prosperous.*'[7]

6. 'Come ye near unto me . . . *the Lord God, and his Spirit, hath sent me.*'[8]

7. 'Thus saith the Lord, thy Redeemer . . . which leadeth thee by the way that thou shouldst go.'[9]

Isaiah concludes with the words:

8. 'Go ye forth of Babylon, flee ye from the Chaldeans, with a voice of singing declare ye, tell this, utter it even to the end of the earth; say ye, *The Lord hath* redeemed his servant Jacob.'[10]

Thus Isaiah, like Micah, prophesied that Israel would be redeemed in Babylon.

Bahá'u'lláh came to Baghdad (Babylon) and there proclaimed his mission to the world. Unwanted, and unwelcome, he did 'go forth of Babylon' and did 'flee from the Chaldeans' until he reached the Holy Land which became the world centre of his faith. This, too, had been foretold by Isaiah in these same chapters.

'I have spoken it, I will also bring it to pass; I have purposed it, I will also do it . . . and my salvation shall not tarry: and I will place my salvation in Zion for Israel my glory.'[11]

However, it was in the *Book of Zechariah* that I found the most striking evidence of all that the great Redeemer of the *last days* would come from Babylon.

When Zechariah saw the vision of the one who would say: '*I am returned to Jerusalem*', he also beheld two olive trees. He asked God to tell him the meaning of the appearance of these two olive trees which appeared in his vision.

'Knowest thou not what these be?' the Lord asked.

'No, my Lord,' Zechariah answered.

Then God explained the meaning. Zechariah records it thus:

'Then he answered me and spake unto me saying, This is the word of the Lord unto Zerubbabel . . .'[12]

In addition to being the name of a ruler, this title 'Zerubbabel' has a special symbolical significance when we examine its true meaning as given in these verses of Zechariah.

The word Zerubbabel, according to the Oxford University Press red-letter edition of the King James version of the Bible, means 'Begotten in Babylon'. Other references say that it means 'Scattered in Babylon'. Cruden, in his *Unabridged Concordance*, declares it to mean 'Banished in Babylon' or 'Stranger in Babylon'. ('Born' in other editions.)

All these descriptions fit Bahá'u'lláh. He was 'banished' to Babylon from Persia. He was a 'stranger' in that land. There in Babylon, his faith was 'begotten'. He was in the end 'scattered' with his followers, until he, himself, reached the ancient land of Canaan promised by God to Abraham as an inheritance in the *last days*.

The faith of Abraham and the faith of Bahá'u'lláh were both 'begotten' in Babylon. The Holy Spirit descended upon each of them in Babylon, and they poured forth the light from their houses of truth in that ancient land. This, too, was foreseen and foretold by Zechariah in his vision:

'Moreover the word of the Lord came unto me, saying, The hands of Zerubbabel (Begotten in Babylon) have laid the foundation of this house; his hands shall also finish it; and thou shalt know that *the Lord of hosts* hath sent me unto you.'[13]

The *Word of God*, Abraham, laid the foundation of the house of Israel in Babylon. The *Word of God*, Bahá'u'lláh finished it, and brought it to fulfilment. Both were 'begotten in Babylon'. Thus, it was to them, *Zerubbabel*, that Zechariah directed the message of God:

> 'This is the word of the Lord unto Zerubbabel (Begotten in Babylon), saying, Not by might, nor by power, but *by my Spirit*, saith the Lord of hosts.'[14]

Lest there be any mistake, Zechariah asked God once more concerning the meaning of the two olive trees. The Lord answered him, saying:

> 'These are the *two anointed ones,* that stand by the Lord of the whole earth.'[15]

These *two olive trees* were *Abraham* who began the concept of the oneness of God in Babylon, and *Bahá'u'lláh* who brought the concept of the oneness of God and religion to its fulfilment in Babylon. In yet another way, these *two olive trees* were the *Báb* and *Bahá'u'lláh*, who in the *last days* 'stand by the Lord of the whole earth'.

I also discovered that the meaning of the word Baghdad, the city in which Bahá'u'lláh declared his Mission, is: '*The Gift of God*'.

Once again Bahá'u'lláh had fulfilled the promises of the sacred Scripture. He had kept the prophecies of Micah, Isaiah, Zechariah, and those of Islám and India, which foretold that the Messiah would come to the land of Babylon, withdraw into the wilderness, then, from that land of ancient mystery, proclaim His mission to the whole world.

I marked the second proof: *Fulfilled.*

4. The Amazing Micah

In one small Book of the *Old Testament*, I found a series of successive *clues*. They traced the history of the Messiah from beginning to end. All by themselves they would have been sufficient to prove the mission of the Messiah of the *last days*. This is why I was tempted to call the prophet who gave them, 'The Amazing Micah'.

In almost the first words of his first chapter, Micah says:

'For, behold, the Lord cometh forth out of his place, and will come down, and tread upon the high places of the earth.'[1]

I found that Bahá'u'lláh fulfilled this verse, both symbolically and actually, concerning these 'high' places.

Symbolically: He walked in the land made holy by the feet of Abraham. He was exiled to Israel, a land considered holy by the Jews, Christians and Muslims. He walked where the feet of Christ and the prophets of old had walked.

Actually: He spent many months in prayer and meditation in the *mountains* of Kurdistan in Iraq, prior to his public declaration of his mission. In the last years of his life, he walked on the side of *Mount Carmel*, called the 'mountain of God', the 'nest of the prophets', the 'snow white place'.

There, on that sacred mountain, above the Cave of Elijah, Bahá'u'lláh wrote the words:

'Call out to Zion, O Carmel, and announce the joyful tidings: He that was hidden from mortal eyes is come!'[2]

In his next chapter, Micah prophesies as follows:

'I will surely assemble, O Jacob, all of thee; I will surely gather the remnant of Israel; I will put them together ... as the flock in the midst of their fold ...'[3]

I had already learned that this prophecy began its fulfilment in 1844, the exact year of the beginning of Bahá'u'lláh's faith. In 1844 the Edict of Toleration was signed, permitting the descendants of Jacob to return to Israel with freedom and security after twelve centuries of separation.

Following the appearance of Bahá'u'lláh himself in the land of Israel, the Jews began to return in greater numbers to the Holy Land, until, in the year 1948, the State of Israel itself was formed.

Bahá'u'lláh himself prophesied that this great event would take place in the not too distant future. Carl Alpert, a prolific writer on Zionism, spoke of this prophecy of Bahá'u'lláh. In his article in *The Reconstructionist*, I found the following: 'While still in his Turkish jail in Acre, more than 75 years ago, Bahá'u'lláh wrote: "The outcasts of Israel shall gather and create a state that will become the envy and admiration of both their friends and their enemies, and outwardly and spiritually they will attain to such glory that their 2,000 years of abasement will be forgotten." '[4]

To return to Micah, there can be no doubt that he is speaking of the *second* coming of Christ, and not the first. For he continues his prophecy, saying that it will take place in *the last days:*

> 'But *in the last days* it shall come to pass, that the mountain of the house of the Lord shall be established in the top of the mountains, and it shall be exalted above the hills; and people shall flow unto it.'[5]

I visited the shrine where the herald of Bahá'u'lláh's faith is entombed on the side of Mount Carmel in Israel. I also visited the world administrative centre of his faith which is established on the side of this same mountain. I was an eye-witness to the crowds that 'flow unto it' every day. While investigating the history of this area, in order to complete this book, I witnessed a throng of nearly two thousand people flow in and out of these sacred places in less than three hours.

I learned that it goes on day after day. People come from all parts of the world; in fact, from 'the ends of earth'.

In this same chapter, Micah promises that in these *last days* from this 'house of the Lord' both the 'law shall go forth' as well as the 'word of the Lord'. When the truth of the Messiah is known, men shall 'beat their swords into ploughshares'.

While in Israel, I learned that the 'law' of Bahá'u'lláh now 'goes forth' to over 250 countries of the earth where his followers reside; and that in over 8,000 centres of the world these followers consider Bahá'u'lláh's teachings to be the 'word of the Lord'. [1975—330 countries and 72,000 centres.]

I walked on the site of the future Universal House of Justice of Bahá'u'lláh's faith, from which the 'law' will go 'forth' to the National and Local Houses of Justice in all parts of the planet. (The Universal House was elected in 1963.)

In these chapters, Micah foretells both the *first* and *second* coming of Christ, prophesying that He will come *first* from Bethlehem and *second* from Assyria. That following the first coming, great suffering and tribulation will fall upon the children of Israel:

> 'Therefore shall Zion for your sake be plowed as a field, and Jerusalem shall become heaps . . .'[6]

In 70 A.D. Jerusalem was destroyed by the Roman Titus. In 132 A.D. the Roman Emperor Hadrian crushed the soldiers of Bar Kochba and ploughed under the site of the city.

Then, says Micah, of the Messiah from Bethlehem:

> 'Therefore will he give them up, until the time that she which travaileth hath brought forth: then the remnant of his brethren shall return unto the children of Israel.'[7]

Micah has just pointed out that 'she which travaileth' is the *daughter of Zion*. Where did she bring forth? Micah foretold this, too, saying:

120

'. . . thou shalt go *even to Babylon:* there shalt thou be delivered . . . '8

In that day, Micah says of the Messiah:

'. . . shall he be great unto the ends of the earth.'9

And Micah foretells that when the Messiah comes the *second* time, this time from Assyria, it shall bring about the day of the one fold and one shepherd when:

'. . . nation shall not lift up a sword against nation, neither shall they learn war any more.'10

Millennial Bible scholars were well aware of this special promise for Assyria and Elam and Persia, but they could not understand it. Reverend H. Bonar, speaking as one of fourteen Christian clergymen at a special conference on the Second Coming of Christ called *Our God Shall Come,* declared: 'There is another nation reserved for blessing and restoration. Elam. I take these as the overlooked specimens of a certain class of God's doings in the latter days, when the whole earth is given to Christ for His inheritance.' Bonar accepts these prophecies concerning Assyria, Elam and Persia, although, as he says, 'I cannot venture on giving any reason why Elam, or Assyria, should be so especially blessed in the latter days . . .'11

Both Christ and Micah gave the same identical signs for this day of His *return.* Christ said He would come from the *East* in a day when men were eating, drinking, marrying, living in material pleasures as in the days of Noah. Micah said He would come from the *East* (Assyria) in a day when:

'The good man is perished out of the earth: and there is none upright among men; . . . they hunt every man his brother with a net.

That they may do evil with both hands earnestly, the

prince asketh, and the judge asketh for a reward; and the great man, he uttereth his mischievous desire . . . the best of them is as a brier: the most upright is sharper than a thorn hedge . . .'¹²

Christ said that this was the day to 'Watch!' for the Lord would come as a 'thief' and 'break up' the house of the faithless. Micah said that this hour was:

'. . . the day of thy *watchmen* and thy visitation cometh . . .'¹³

Micah then let loose an astonishing downpour of prophecy. He foretold the exact steps by which the Lord would come to Israel, and the things that would befall Him. No detective had a clearer set of *clues*. Micah promised that:

1. He would come from Assyria.
2. He would come from the fortified cities.
3. He would come from a fortress to a river.
4. He would come from sea to sea.
5. He would come from mountain to mountain.
6. The land to which he came would be desolate.
7. He would feed his flock in the midst of Mount Carmel.
8. He would work his wonders for a period equal to the days which the Jews spent coming out of Egypt.

Frankly, I felt that a fulfilment of these prophecies would be sufficient by itself to establish the authenticity of the Messiah, for in addition to these eight prophecies, Bahá'u'lláh had also fulfilled Micah's prophecies that the Messiah must:

1. Come as a Messenger of God and tread upon the high places of the earth.
2. Appear in the day when the children of Israel would be gathered into their own land.
3. Establish His house in the mountain.
4. Draw the people of the world to it in a flow of love.

5. Send forth His love from that mountain.
6. Go to Babylon.
7. Withdraw from the city.
8. Dwell in the wilderness and the field.
9. Give birth in Babylon that would redeem the children of Israel.

No wonder I called him 'the Amazing Micah'. I now felt that if Bahá'u'lláh also fulfilled these eight additional prophecies, I might indeed be coming to the end of my search. I had to admit that I had already assembled a powerful array of evidence pointing to a solution of *The Case of the Missing Millennium*.

5. The Eight Astonishing Steps

When the faithless people and the enemies of Micah ridiculed him, and taunted him, saying:

> 'Where is the Lord thy God?'[1]

Micah answered them with an undeviating confidence:

> 'I will look unto the Lord: I will wait for the God of my salvation: my God will hear me.'[2]

It was then that Micah gave the remarkable sequence of prophecies which would proclaim the appearance of the Messiah so that every 'eye' that could 'see' might know that He dwelt amongst them.

1. '. . . he shall come . . . from *the fortified* cities.'[3]

Bahá'u'lláh, I discovered, was exiled from Baghdad (Babylon) in the valley of the Tigris and Euphrates rivers to *the fortified city* of Constantinople.

In a last desperate effort to destroy him and his teachings, the religious and civil authorities of Persia and Turkey combined to send him to *the fortified city of* 'Akká (Acre).

2. '. . . he shall come . . . *from the fortress even to the river.*'[4]

Bahá'u'lláh was imprisoned for two years in a cell of *the fortress* of 'Akká. So impregnable were its defences that Napoleon could not capture it; he left his cannon balls buried in the stone walls as a memory of his attempt. When Bahá'u'lláh was released from the *fortress* and the prison-city of 'Akká, he journeyed to an island in *the river* called Na'mayn.

3. '. . . he shall come . . . *from mountain to mountain.*'[5]

Bahá'u'lláh, I learned, withdrew to the *mountain called Sar-Galú* in the Kurdistani mountains where he prepared for his life of suffering. From that mountain, he returned to Baghdad and thence to the exile that carried him to the side of the *mountain called Carmel* which had been blessed by the footsteps of Christ during His *first* coming.

4. '. . . he shall come . . . *from sea to sea.*'[6]

I traced the exile of Bahá'u'lláh from Iraq to Israel. *En route* to the fortified city of Constantinople, he made the last part of this journey *by way of the Black Sea*. When banished to the fortress city of 'Akká, he made the last part of this journey *by way of the Mediterranean Sea*.

5. '. . . the land shall be desolate . . .'[7]

Bahá'u'lláh was exiled to the prison-city of 'Akká in a *land so desolate* that it was believed that he would perish and be heard of no more. So foul, insanitary, and filled with disease was the land that a proverb written about that land said: 'If a bird flies over 'Akká, it dies!'[8] It was a land filled with

typhoid, malaria, diphtheria, and dysentery. It was called 'the
metropolis of the owl',[9] a land that was, in the words of an
historian of the time, 'desolate and barren'.

'In that day,' Micah promised, the Messiah would:

6. 'Feed thy people with thy rod, the flock of thine heritage,
   which dwell solitarily in the wood, in the midst of
   Carmel.'[10]

My records showed that when Bahá'u'lláh was released
from captivity in the final years of his life, he pitched his tent
in a small *wood in the midst of Carmel*. Seated in that tiny clump
of cypress trees on the side of that stony, barren mountain,
Bahá'u'lláh pointed out the spot where the shrine of the Báb,
his herald, should be erected. From there he poured out his
teachings to his followers. He *fed his people* and *his flock* with
his words of love and kindness:

'The world is but one country, and mankind its citizens
. . . Let not a man glory in this that he loves his country;
let him rather glory in this, that he loves his kind.'[11]

There *in the midst of Carmel*, Bahá'u'lláh linked his own
mission with that of Jesus. He addressed the following words
to that holy mountain where the feet of Christ had walked:

'Render thanks unto Thy Lord, O Carmel. The fire of
thy separation from Me was fast consuming thee, when the
ocean of My presence surged before thy face, cheering thine
eyes and those of all creation. . . . He, verily, loveth the spot
which hath been made the seat of His throne, which His
footsteps have trodden, which hath been honoured by His
presence, from which He raised His call, and upon which He
shed His tears.'[12]

The final prophecy of Micah was, perhaps, the most remarkable of all. He foretold the exact length of time during which

God would shower His truth upon the Messiah 'in those days'. He prophesied that it would be:

7. '*According to the days of thy* (Israel) *coming out of the land of Egypt will I shew unto him marvellous things.*'[13]

The time of the coming out of Egypt was *forty years*. For *forty years*, under the holy guidance of Moses, the Jews wandered in the desert until finally they reached the promised land. For an equal period of time, *forty years*, Almighty God would fill the mouth of His Messenger with 'wonders' in *the last days*.

Joseph Klausner, in his *The Messianic Idea in Israel*, quotes R. Eliezer (ben Hyrcanus) as saying: 'The Days of the Messiah will last *forty years* . . .'

It is also written in the *Psalms*:

'*Forty years* long was I grieved with this generation . . .'[14]

The millennial Bible scholar, Edward Irving, a Christian clergyman, called attention to the Indian prophecy of the religion 'which in the space of *forty* (*years*) was to possess the earth'.[15]

Hooper Harris, in his book of *Lessons*, writes: 'This mention of forty is indissolubly connected with a time which was to be a time of exile, siege, banishment, imprisonment and persecution of some Great One, on whom tribulation and burdens were to be laid, during which time the teachings of God, nevertheless, were to flood the earth.'

Bahá'u'lláh, like unto Moses, wandered in exile with his family and followers for *forty years*. He was sent as a prisoner, still in exile, to the prison *fortress* of 'Akká. This once lay in the ancient land of Canaan which God had promised would be inherited in the last days by one from the seed of Abraham. These *forty years* of wandering, banishment, and imprisonment mark the exact period of time of Bahá'u'lláh's ministry on earth.

He was thrown into the dungeon called 'The Black Pit' in Teheran in August 1852. In that prison, but a few weeks later, Bahá'u'lláh, in his own words, experienced the following:

'. . . lo, the breezes of the All-glorious (God) were wafted over Me, and taught Me the knowledge of all that hath been. This thing is not from Me, but from One Who is Almighty and All-knowing. And He (God) bade Me lift up My voice between earth and heaven. . . This is but a leaf which the winds of the Will of thy Lord . . . have stirred. Can it be still when the tempestuous winds are blowing?'[16]

Bahá'u'lláh was released from that prison, and his years of enforced exile and imprisonment began. They ended only with his death in the Holy Land in May 1892.

Thus from the beginning of his mission to the last days of his life, there were *forty years*, exactly 'according to the days of thy coming out of the land of Egypt'.

It was with a feeling of awe that I marked all seventeen of the prophecies of 'the amazing Micah', *Fulfilled*!

Was there ever such a remarkable story to be told? What a pity, I thought, that the world had not yet read such 'headlines' as these.

6. No Need of the Sun

Many Bible scholars in the millennial days were seeking the Messiah by the title 'the Glory of God'. I had already discovered that Bahá'u'lláh's name meant 'the Glory of God'. However, I found additional *clues* regarding this name.

Isaiah foretold that for those of the House of Israel who were faithful to the end:

'... *the glory of the Lord* shall be thy rereward. ... And they that shall be of thee shall build the old waste places ...'[1]

Wherever the feet of Bahá'u'lláh have walked in Israel, *the old waste places have been built up* and beautified. His name means '*the Glory of God*'.

Isaiah prophesied:

'And the Redeemer shall come to Zion ...'[2]

In the next verse he declared:

'... this is my covenant with them, saith the Lord ...'[3]

In the very next verse, Isaiah proclaims:

'Arise, shine; for thy light is come, and *the glory of the Lord* is risen upon thee.'[4]

Bahá'u'lláh came to Zion (Israel) from the *East*. He wrote a special book called the *Book of the Covenant*, in which he outlined the future of his faith through all time. His faith has its world-centre on the side of the 'mountain of God'. His name means 'The Glory of God'.

In yet another place, Isaiah says:

'... behold your God will come ... he will come and save you ... the excellency of *Carmel* and *Sharon*; they shall see *the glory of the Lord* ...'[5]

Bahá'u'lláh pitched his tent on *Mount Carmel* which faces the silver city of 'Akká and is backed by the plain of *Sharon*. His name means '*the Glory of God*'.

In yet another chapter, Isaiah speaks of the day of the One Shepherd and His fold. He says:

'Behold, the Lord God will come with a strong hand . . .
He shall feed his flock like a shepherd: he shall gather the
lambs with his arm . . .'[6]

He also foretells of that time:

'And *the glory of the Lord* shall be revealed, and all flesh
shall see it together; for the mouth of the Lord hath spoken
it.'[7]

Bahá'u'lláh came to Israel, where he declared that all men
were the sheep of one sacred fold, that his mission was to
gather the scattered 'lambs' of God into one family, one mankind. His name means '*the Glory of God*'.
Ezekiel said:

'And, behold, *the glory of the God of Israel* came from the
way of the *east* . . . and the earth shined with his glory.'[8]

And again:

'And *the glory of the Lord* came into the house *by way of the
gate* whose prospect is toward the *east*.'[9]

Christ also spoke of the great Shepherd of the one fold,
saying:

'But he that entereth in *by the door* is the shepherd of
the sheep.'[10]

Christ also said:

'. . . the Son of man shall come in *the Glory of his
Father*.'[11]

This was yet another way of saying: '*the Glory of God*'.
Bahá'u'lláh came from the *East*. He came by way of the door,
the Báb. His name means '*the Glory of God*' or '*the Glory of the
Lord*'.

The *Book of Revelation*, like *Isaiah*, mentions both the *first* and *second* coming of Christ; and in the *second* appearance foresees 'the *Glory of God*'. St. John recounts his vision, saying:

'And I saw a *new* heaven and a *new* earth: for the *first* heaven and the *first* earth were passed away . . .

And I John saw *the holy city, new Jerusalem*, coming down from God out of heaven . . .

And the *city* had no need of the sun, neither of the moon, to shine in it: for *the glory of God* did lighten it . . .'[12]

Christ Himself foretold this day of *the new Jerusalem*, when He would come in the Glory of the Father. A Samaritan woman objected strongly to the fact that Christ was changing the place of worship which had been sacred to her people from ancient times. She rebuked Christ, saying:

'Our fathers worshipped in this mountain; and ye say, that in Jerusalem is the place where men ought to worship.'[13]

Christ answered her, saying:

'Woman, believe me, *the hour cometh*, when ye shall *neither in this mountain, nor yet at Jerusalem*, worship the Father.'[14]

I found through my research that *the new Jerusalem* is the Law of God which comes down from heaven with the Messenger or Messiah. Wherever He dwells is *the new Mount Zion*. Jerusalem means 'possession of peace'. Zion means 'monument raised up'.

Revelation states that God

'. . . showed me *that great city, the holy Jerusalem*, descending out of heaven from God.

Having *the Glory of God:* and her light was like unto a stone most precious . . .'[15]

The *Book of Enoch* also speaks of this *new name* in the *last days*:

'They blessed, glorified, and exalted because the *name* of the Son of man was revealed to them.'[16]

Enoch also said:

'He (God) spoke to holy Michael to discover to them the sacred name, that they might understand that secret name.'[17]

This *new name* was established, Enoch says, through 'the instrumentality of the holy Michael.'[18]

This is the same *Michael* whom *Daniel* said was like unto God, a Prince of Persia, who would stand up for the children of God in the last days. He gave the date for this event, 1844.

Bahá'u'lláh, I found, in his *Tablet of Carmel*, declared that *the new Jerusalem* had appeared upon *the new Mount Zion*. He said:

'Haste thee, O Carmel, for lo the light of the Countenance of God . . . hath been lifted upon thee. . . . Rejoice, for God hath in this day, established upon thee His throne.'[19]

In that same Tablet, I found the following words written by Bahá'u'lláh:

'Call out to Zion, O Carmel . . . *the City of God* . . . hath descended from heaven.'[20]

He adds:

'Beware lest thou hesitate or halt.'

The *Book of Habakkuk* declared:

'The earth shall be filled with the knowledge of *the glory of the Lord* as the waters cover the sea.'[21]

To my surprise, I found that although the world at large was still quite unaware of the coming of Bahá'u'lláh, there were believers in his faith in over 8,000 centres of the world, scattered in more than 250 countries, and in most of the islands. I carefully studied a map of the world which was dotted with places to which his faith had spread. [See p. 120.]

Habbakkuk foretold that this vision he had of *the Glory of the Lord* would take place at *the time of the end*. He said:

'Write the vision, and make it plain upon tables, that he may run that readeth it.

For the vision is yet for an appointed time, *but at the end* it shall speak, and not lie: though it tarry, wait for it.'[22]

Habakkuk also warned that men would see this wondrous truth and would not believe the testimony of their own eyes and ears. At the *time of the end* when the *'Glory of God'* was *'in His Holy Temple'*, Habakkuk prophesied that men would

'. . . regard, and wonder marvellously: for I will work a work in your days, which ye will not believe, though it be told you.'[23]

Had I found the 'work' which God had 'worked?' Of one thing I felt confident. Beside the *proof*, He shall be known as *'the Glory of God'*, I could write: *Fulfilled.*

7. The Families of the Earth Shall Be Blessed

The next *proof* by which Bahá'u'lláh was to be tested concerned the 'seed of Abraham'. The millennial scholars were agreed that when the Messiah came, He would be of this sacred 'seed'. I checked the antecedents of Bahá'u'lláh to see if he fulfilled this important requirement.

I had already discovered *one* remarkable way in which Abraham and Bahá'u'lláh were linked together, as set out in Section 3. I now found another statement which linked them together and demonstrated that Bahá'u'lláh was descended from the Father of the Faithful. This said: '*He derived His descent*, on the one hand, *from Abraham* through his wife Katurah, and on the other from Zoroaster, as well as from Yazdigird, the last king of the Sásáníyán dynasty. *He (Bahá'u'lláh) was moreover a descendant of Jesse*, and belonged, through His father, Mírzá 'Abbás, better known as Mírzá Buzurg—a nobleman closely associated with the ministerial circles of the Court . . . to one of the most ancient and renowned families of Mázindarán.'[1]

Thus Bahá'u'lláh was of the 'seed' of Abraham, being descended through Abraham's third wife, Katurah. This in itself I found to be a most interesting *clue*, for among the writings of the British Israelites, as well as among those of some millennial scholars, reference is made to the fact that the *latter-day Messiah* would be descended from Katurah, the third wife of Abraham.

In *the latter days* of His life, Abraham took Katurah to wife. In *the latter days* in the life of His House, Israel, it is promised that the sons of Katurah, with all the young lions of her family shall stand for the Lord God in the land of Israel.

This belief was based upon the prophecies in *Ezekiel* which speak of the battle of Armageddon. When the great princes of evil come down from the north from the land of Gog and Magog against 'my people of Israel', the Lord promises that:

'*Sheba, and Dedan*, and the merchants of Tarshish, with all the young lions thereof, shall say unto thee (Gog), Art thou come to take a spoil? hast thou gathered thy company to take a prey?'[2]

133

Then, promises the Lord, He will destroy Gog, with the help of these faithful ones:

> 'I will rain upon him (Gog), and upon his bands, and upon the many people that are with him, an overflowing rain, and great hailstones, fire, and brimstone.'[3]

This is the same description given for *the last days* by *Revelation*, and the *Second Epistle of Peter*, when the 'Lord will come as a thief in the night'. These young lions of *Sheba and Dedan* who will be in Israel at the side of the Lord, are the promised descendants from the line of Katurah, Abraham's third wife. This descent is given in the book of Genesis:

> 'Then again Abraham took a wife, and her name was *Keturah*. And she bare him . . . Jokshan . . . and Jokshan begat *Sheba and Dedan*.'[4]

Ezekiel says that all this will take place in '*the latter years*'.[5] In the chapter preceding the account of the descendants of *Sheba and Dedan*, Ezekiel foretells that the two Houses of Israel will be united in that day. This, Ezekiel declares, will be part of the ancient Covenant which God made with Abraham. This prophecy foreshadows the reunion *in the last days*, not only the physical unity of Judah and Israel, but also the symbolical reunion of the two *spiritual* Houses of Judaism and Christianity.

The Lord tells Ezekiel:

> 'I will take the children of Israel from among the heathen, whither they be gone, and will gather them on every side, *and bring them into their own land:*
>
> And *I will make them one nation* in the land upon the mountains of Israel; and one king shall be king to them all: and *they shall be no more two nations, neither shall they be divided into two kingdoms any more at all . . .*'[6]

In the very year in which Bahá'u'lláh's faith began (1844), the Edict was signed which permitted this *gathering* of the children of Israel. Since the day of Bahá'u'lláh's arrival as a prisoner in Israel, the Holy Land has become an independent State, and *one nation*. Bahá'u'lláh's teachings declare that one of the fundamental principles of his faith is the union of the Jews and Christians.

Ezekiel concludes this prophecy with God's promise that the Shrine of the Messiah shall be eternally placed in Israel:

'I will make a covenant of peace with them ... and will set my sanctuary in the midst of them for evermore.'[7]

The 'sanctuary' of Bahá'u'lláh is a place of great beauty in the midst of Israel.

Isaiah speaks of this same great 'gathering'. He prophesies:

'Lift up thine eyes round about, and see: all they gather themselves together, they come to thee: thy sons shall come from afar, and thy daughters shall be nursed at thy side.'[8]

Three verses before, Isaiah foretells that when this 'gathering' takes place, the Lord will say to the holy mountain:

'Arise, shine: for thy light is come, and *the glory of the Lord* is risen upon you.'[9]

In yet another place, Isaiah speaks of this great 'gathering'. He says:

'And *the ransomed of the Lord shall return*, and come to Zion ...'[10]

Eight verses before in this same chapter, he prophesies that when this 'gathering' takes place

'... Carmel and Sharon; they shall see *the glory of the Lord*.'[11]

135

In yet another place, Isaiah prophesies the great 'gathering'. He says:

'He (the Messiah) shall feed his flock like a shepherd: *he shall gather the lambs* . . .'[12]

Six verses before in that same chapter, Isaiah foretells that when this 'gathering' takes place

'. . . *the glory of the Lord* shall be revealed, and all flesh shall see it together . . .'[13]

Almost invariably, the time of the '*gathering*' of the children of Israel was associated with the appearance of '*the Glory of the Lord*'.

This *gathering* or *return* began in 1844. It reached its climax in 1948 with the formation of the State of Israel. Bahá'u'lláh, after reaching Israel as a prisoner, himself prophesied that this would come to pass. His name, we know, means: '*The Glory of the Lord*.'

Ezekiel prophesied:

'My tabernacle also shall be with them . . . my sanctuary shall be in the midst of them for evermore.'[14]

No one knows where His Holiness Moses lies buried. There is much doubt and dispute about the resting-place and tomb of His Holiness Christ. Yet, the exact spot of the Shrine, 'tabernacle' or 'sanctuary' of Bahá'u'lláh *is* known. It has been placed in the 'midst' of Israel 'for evermore'. Each year thousands upon thousands of people visit this sacred spot. The Christian writer, Arthur Moore, says it is a 'place of international pilgrimage. On Sundays and holidays the citizens of Haifa of all faiths come for rest and recreation . . .'[15]

I was about to close my evidence on the relationship of Abraham and Bahá'u'lláh when I came upon another series of highly interesting and provoking prophecies which added considerable spice to *The Case of the Missing Millennium*.

8. The Lord of the New Era

Isaiah made three specific predictions in one single chapter concerning the 'seed' of Abraham. He foretold:

1. God shall assemble the outcasts of Israel, and gather to-together the dispersed of Judah from the four corners of the earth.[1]

2. God would set up an ensign, for the nations of the world to see.[2]

3. It would take place in the day when a Branch grew out of the roots of Jesse.[3]

Zechariah also foretold the coming of this *branch* from the line of Abraham.[4]

In those same chapters concerning *the last days,* he prophesied:

'Therefore thus saith the Lord; *I am returned* to Jerusalem with mercies . . .'[5]

And in another place:

'Thus saith the Lord; *I am returned* unto Zion . . .'[6]

The mountain of the Messiah in that day, Zechariah says shall be called 'the holy mountain'.

This was the day promised from the beginning to Abraham when God told him that his 'seed' would inherit this land. He said to Abraham:

'. . . he that shall come forth out of thine own bowels shall be thine heir . . . I am the Lord that brought thee out of Ur

of the Chaldees, to give thee this land (Canaan) to inherit
it.

'Unto thy seed have I given this land.'[7]

Abraham asked God:

'How shall I know that I shall inherit it?'

God answered him, this time with a symbol:

'Take me an heifer of three years old, and a she-goat of
three years old, and a ram of three years old, and a turtle-
dove, and a young pigeon.'[8]

What a strange answer to Abraham's question as to how and
when he, Abraham, would inherit Canaan. F. Hudgings, in
his *Zionism in Prophecy*, offers the following interesting explanation of this prophecy of the animals and the birds. He suggests
that we look at the inward truth behind this outward symbol.
Then, he tells us: 'A strange and remarkable story unfolds. It
is not the animals and birds that are of significance, but their
ages. The three animals are each three years old. The birds
are taken to be one year old as the term a "young" pigeon is
used. Thus we have three, three, three, one, one—or a total
of eleven. The meaning is that Abraham will inherit Canaan
and His seed inherit the earth when this prophecy came to
pass after eleven years: eleven symbolical years of "each day
for a year".'

Eleven multiplied by 360 equals 3960 years. After 3960
years the prophecy would be fulfilled.

The exact time when this prophecy was revealed to Abraham is not known. However, we do know that it must have
been immediately before the birth of Isaac.

Authorities differ on the date of Isaac's birth. However,
one of the later dates given is 2007 B.C.; 2007 years from 3960
years, brings us to the year A.D. 1953.

My task was to discover whether or not this year 1953 had any particular significance in the faith of Bahá'u'lláh. The results of my search were rewarding.

The year 1953 was the hundredth anniversary of the beginning of Bahá'u'lláh's Mission. It was the very year in which a great wave of pioneer teachers of his faith went out into all parts of the world so that the children of God might be *gathered together* in these *last days*, and their eyes and hearts be turned toward Israel, the world-centre of the Faith of Bahá'u'lláh.

In 1953 the Faith of Bahá'u'lláh launched a great spiritual world-crusade, which was destined to culminate in the raising up of a universal *House of Justice* so that as prophesied by Isaiah, the spiritual 'Law of God' would go forth from Zion.

Bahá'u'lláh began his exile one hundred years before, in 1853. He went to the valley of the Tigris and Euphrates, and from there, like Abraham before him, was banished to the ancient land of Canaan.

Even more significant are the prophetic words in the Bahá'í teachings concerning this date of 1953, words which say that this date

'Marks the inception of the Kingdom of God on earth.'[9]

This same unique date of 1953 is also one of the important dates given in the prophecies of the Great Pyramid. Worth Smith, in his *Miracle of the Ages*, says of this date 1953: 'That will be a period during which the whole earth is to be "cleansed of its pollutions," and which will prepare the people of earth for the actual beginning of Christ's "Millennial Rule" . . .'

In one year, from 1953 to 1954, the Faith of Bahá'u'lláh, I learned, was spread to 100 new countries. This, too, I found to be foretold in prophecy.

Professor Roerich, in his *Altai-Himalaya*, a five-year record of his expedition, points out that all through the East, in India, Mongolia, even in Siberia, there are prophetic records of this great new age of teaching which would come with the Messiah. He says: 'It is told in the prophecies how the new era shall manifest itself.'

I have recorded some of those prophecies here. This was the first:

1. 'First will begin an unprecedented war of all nations.'

This had certainly come to pass with the Second World War. The next prophecy said:

2. 'Then shall the *Teachers* appear and in all corners of the world shall be heard the true teaching.'

From the records of the Faith of Bahá'u'lláh, I learned that following the Second World War, the Bahá'ís (his followers) carried out a second Seven-year Plan of teaching which spread his Faith through the western hemisphere and Europe. Then in 1953 there began a Ten-year Crusade which carried the message of Bahá'u'lláh to all corners of the globe.

The next prophecy from the East foretold:

3. 'To this word of truth shall the people be drawn but those who are filled with darkness and ignorance shall set obstacles . . . even those who by accident help the *Teachings* of (this spiritual king of the world) will receive in return a hundred fold.'

It is also promised in the writings of Bahá'u'lláh's faith that whatever effort is made for the sake of God, the doer will receive in return a hundred fold.

Still another of these Eastern prophecies declares:

4. 'Only a few years shall elapse before everyone shall hear the mighty steps of *the Lord of the New Era.*'

At the time of the martyrdom of the Báb, only two countries were included among the followers of his Faith. At the time of the passing of Bahá'u'lláh, only fifteen countries. Following the outpouring of *teachers* in 1953, Bahá'u'lláh's Faith had reached over 3,000 centres in 235 countries.

Professor Dr. V. Lesny called Bahá'u'lláh the 'Saviour of the twentieth century.'[10]

Bahá'u'lláh has also been designated as *the Lord of the New Era.* The most widely distributed book concerning his teachings, a book translated into all the widely spoken languages, is called *Bahá'u'lláh and The New Era.*

The prophecies of the East continued as follows:

5. 'And one can already perceive unusual people. Already they (the teachers) open the gates of knowledge, and ripened fruits are falling from the trees.'

I found numerous references to these 'unusual' Bahá'ís, including the reference already given by Justice of the United States Supreme Court William O. Douglas who paid tribute to their high sense of integrity. Marcus Bach, member of the faculty of the State University of Iowa School of Religion, wrote in his article for the *Christian Century, Bahá'í; A Second Look:* ' "If these Bahá'ís ever get going, they may take the country by storm." So said a discerning Protestant minister as we talked one evening about America's most "ecumenical" faith. . . . Let all who are interested in the gospel of the abundant life take heed! It may be that the Bahá'ís are coming. . . . They ask no salaries, want no honour, and are literally more interested in giving than receiving . . . a second look shows that by way of its devotion and the opening door, it (the Faith of Bahá'u'lláh) may loose itself from captivity. It may also be that the minister was quite right when he said, "If these Bahá'ís ever get going, they may take the country by storm." '[11]

And the final prophecy from the East:

6. 'Those who accept Him (the Messiah) shall rejoice. And those who deny Him shall tremble. . . . And the warriors (teachers) shall march under the banner of Maitreya.'

Ballou and Spiegelberg in *The Bible of the World*, point out that according to the sacred scripture of the East, *Maitreya* is 'the compassionate Buddha who is to come in the distant future. Foretold by Gautama, as Christ foretold *his* second coming.'

Maitreya, the Buddha of 'universal fellowship' was expected to appear to the West of India and to the East of Israel. Persia, the home of Bahá'u'lláh, lies between them. His message is one of "universal fellowship" and the union of religions, nations, and races.

Isaiah also foretold the day when all the earth would hear the Messiah's teaching:

'All ye inhabitants of the world, and dwellers on the earth, see ye, when he lifteth up an ensign on the mountains . . .'[12]

Isaiah also prophesies:

'. . . blessed are all they that wait for him . . . he will be very gracious unto thee . . . *thine eyes shall see thy teachers.*'[13]

F. Hudgings worked out the prophecy concerning Abraham and Canaan to the date 1914. He attributed its fulfilment to the increased interest in Zionism at that time. However, I found that whatever date was taken for the fulfilment of the 3960 years foretold to Abraham by God for 'Canaan', it would still fall within the years of the rise of Bahá'u'lláh's Faith. In fact, the very year given by Hudgings, 1914, was significant for the Faith of Bahá'u'lláh. In that year, Bahá'u'lláh's son stood on the side of Mount Carmel and prophesied that the tiny city of Haifa would soon become an important port, and that it would grow in greatness until a wide highway would link the towns of Haifa and 'Akká, the twin holy cities of the Faith of Bahá'u'lláh. This prophecy has already come true.

He foretold that electric lights would illumine the sacred mountain Carmel, and the lights of the Holy places of Bahá'u'lláh's Faith would be seen far out to sea. This, too, has come to pass.

The Lord has indeed, as prophesied, 'built up Zion'. The Psalms of David had promised:

'When the Lord shall build up Zion, he (the Messiah) shall appear in his glory.'[14]

Isaiah foretold:

'And the sons of strangers shall build up thy walls . . .'[15]

This would be in the day when the *branch*, the root of Jesse, the 'seed' of Abraham had appeared on earth. In that same chapter, Isaiah declares of that sacred mountain:

'*The Glory of the Lord* is risen upon thee.'[16]

Bahá'u'lláh had come to Israel. He was known as '*the Glory of the Lord*'. He was a descendant of Katurah, the third wife of Abraham. His sanctuary was placed eternally in the Holy Land. His *teachers* had covered the earth as the waters cover the sea in the short space of a few years.

To all these prophecies I could write without equivocation: *Fulfilled.*

143

9. The Door of Hope

My next assignment was to search out the wonderful things which were supposed to take place in Haifa and 'Akká in the day when the Messiah appeared. I found there were promises not only for Mount Carmel itself, but for the plain of Sharon on one side, and the valley of 'Akká on the other.

In the *Book of Hosea* it was promised that:

> 'I will give her her vineyards from thence, and the valley of Achor for a door of hope: and she shall sing there as in the days of her youth . . .'[1]

When will this come to pass? It seemed clear to me that it would be *in the last days* when Israel would be forgiven for having turned away from the Messiah in His *first* coming, and would have embraced His truth in the time of His *second* coming. In that day, Hosea says:

> 'I will have mercy upon her that had not obtained mercy: and I will say to *them which were not my people, Thou art my people*; and they shall say, *Thou art my God.*'[2]

Hosea foretells that this will take place at *the time of the end*. First the valley of Achor will become a place of hope and refuge. Then Israel will return from disbelief, and seek their Beloved (David) from the stem of Jesse (seed of Abraham). Hosea says:

> '*Afterward* shall the children of Israel *return*, and seek the Lord their God, and David their king; and shall fear the Lord and his goodness *in the latter* days.'[3]

I had already learned that the '*latter days*' and '*the time of the end*' were synonymous. I had also learned that they began in 1844, the year of the birth of Bahá'u'lláh's Faith, and the year of the beginning of the *return* of the Jews to the Holy Land.

Isaiah made an identical prophecy to that of Hosea, saying:

'And I will bring forth a *seed* out of Jacob . . . an inheritor of my mountains; and mine elect shall inherit it, and my servants shall dwell there.

'And Sharon shall be a fold of flocks, and the valley of Achor a place for the herds to lie down in, for my people that have sought me.'[4]

Five verses later, Isaiah tells us that this will take place in the day when God shall

'. . . call his servants by another name.'[5]

In yet another place Isaiah prophesies

'. . . thou shalt be called by a *new name*, which the mouth of the Lord shall name.'[6]

And the city of the Messiah and the redeemed of the Lord would be called

'*Sought out*, A city not forsaken.'[7]

Ezekiel spoke of this city, the city of the great Shepherd of the 'one fold' and the 'flock of God'. He said that the name of this city, *the new Jerusalem* is:

'. . . the Lord is there!'[8]

I found in my research, that no one knows for certain where the valley of Achor is. The *Westminster Historical Atlas to the Bible* suggests that it might lie between Hyrcania and Gilgal in the wilderness of Judah west of the Dead Sea. George Adam Smith's *Historical Atlas of the Holy Land* for the University of Aberdeen makes the guess that it lies along what is now the river W. el Qelt near to Jericho and Gilgal on its way to the Jordan above the Dead Sea. However, both mark the spot with a '?'.

Ever since the day that Achan and his family had been

stoned and buried in the valley of Achor, it had been a place unwanted and forsaken. Their sin of disobedience to the laws of God had brought this punishment upon them.

Since Achor means *trouble*, and the valley of Achor *the valley of trouble*, there seemed little doubt that this was another symbol showing that when the Jews turned to the Messiah in the *last days*, their suffering and troubles would be ended. Such a day is foreshadowed by Joshua concerning the valley of Achor, when he said:

'The Lord turned from the fierceness of his anger.'[9]

In the *last days*, Bahá'u'lláh was sent, a prisoner and an exile, to the fortress of 'Akká, the old city of Accho, the ancient Ptolemais, the St. Jean d'Acre of the Crusaders. It has been described as 'the most detestable in climate' and 'the foulest in water'. Here, in what was once *the land of Canaan*, Bahá'u'lláh suffered cruel imprisonment and persecution at the hands of Turkish authorities. It was indeed *a valley of trouble*. I saw the words which Bahá'u'lláh himself wrote about this valley:

'Know thou, that upon Our arrival at this Spot, We chose to designate it as the "Most Great Prison". Though previously subjected in another land (Persia) to chains and fetters, We yet refused to call it by that name ... Ponder thereon, O ye endued with understanding!'[10]

On another occasion Bahá'u'lláh wrote of the prison of 'Akká:

'None knoweth what befell Us, except God, the Almighty, the All-Knowing.'[11]

In this valley of trouble (Achor), Bahá'u'lláh declared in his writings that his 'sufferings have now reached their culmination'. (That 'Akká was intended by Hosea is attested by Shoghi Effendi in *God Passes By*, p. 184.)

An account of Bahá'u'lláh's arrival at 'Akká and his later visits to Mount Carmel states: 'It is difficult to understand how Bahá'u'lláh could have been obliged to leave Persia, and to pitch His tent in this Holy Land, but for the persecution of His enemies, His banishment and exile.'[12]

Bahá'u'lláh first touched upon the soil of Israel at Haifa, directly below the cave of Elijah. There was great rejoicing among his followers when they learned that Bahá (Glory) had arrived in the Holy Land, for none had known what his destination would be when he was banished from Turkey.

His exile had ended at last. The *Glory of God* had come to the land of Israel. His exile, like that of the Jews from Egypt, ended with the arrival in the Holy Land.

There is a very curious prophecy mentioned by Samuel ben Judah Valerio. He was a Biblical commentator who wrote a commentary on the *Book of Daniel* which was printed in Venice in the second half of the sixteenth century. Valerio calculated that the end of the present exile (of the Jews) would be in the year 5628 of the Jewish calendar, which is the year 1868 of the Christian era.

Strangely enough, 1868 is the exact date on which Bahá'u'lláh arrived in Israel, the Holy Land. Thus 1868 marked the end of his long wanderings from Persia. He had come at last to the 'nest of the prophets'. He had also symbolically brought to an end the spiritual exile of the children of Israel.

This arrival had been foretold, it was said, by David in his Psalms:

'Lift up your heads, O ye gates; even lift them up, ye everlasting doors; and the King of glory shall come in. Who is this King of glory? The Lord of Hosts, he is the King of glory.'[13]

Bahá'u'lláh had touched upon what was once the soil of

Galilee, made holy by the feet of Christ and the prophets of old. He had come *by way of the sea* beyond Jordan.

Isaiah had prophesied both the *first* and the *second* coming of the Messiah on yet another occasion when he promised that the everlasting Father would come *by way of the sea*

'Nevertheless the dimness shall not be such as was in her vexation, when at the *first* he lightly afflicted the land of Zebulun and the land of Naphthali, and *afterward (the second time)* did more grievously afflict her *by way of the sea,* beyond Jordan, in Galilee of the nations.'[14]

That Isaiah was speaking of the *second* coming *by way of the sea,* and not of the *first* in the land of Naphthali and Zebulun where Christ spent so much of His time, is clear from the prophecies which Isaiah gives a few verses later:

'For unto us a child is born, unto us a son is given: and the government shall be upon his shoulder: and his name shall be called Wonderful, Counsellor, The mighty God, the everlasting Father, the Prince of Peace.
'Of the increase of his government and *peace* there shall be no end, upon the throne of David, and upon his kingdom, to order it, and to establish it with judgment and with *justice* from henceforth even for ever. *The zeal of the Lord of hosts will perform this.*'[15]

This prophecy has been attributed to Christ by Christian scholars, although it was frankly admitted by them that some of the prophecies had not been fulfilled, and could only come to pass in *the time of the end* with His second coming. Some of the prophecies appeared to fit His Holiness Christ, but most of them did not. For example:

1. The government was not upon his shoulders. Christ Himself said:

148

'Render therefore unto Caesar the things which are Caesar's; and unto God the things that are God's.'[16]

'My kingdom is not of this world.'[17]

2. The name of Christ was not *the mighty God*. Christ obviously considered Himself different from God:

'Why callest thou me good? there is none good but one, that is, God.'[18]

3. Christ was not *the everlasting Father*. He often said that the Father was one different than Himself. Although Christ said that He and the Father were 'one' in Their purpose, still, He said:

'My Father, which gave them (the sheep) me, is greater than all . . .'[19]

'The Son can do nothing of himself, but what he seeth the Father do . . .'[20]

4. Christ did not claim to be *the Prince of Peace*. Although He has been called this. He Himself said:

'Think not that I am come to send peace on earth; I came not to send peace, but a sword.'[21]

He also said:

'Suppose ye that I am come to give peace on earth? I tell you, Nay: but rather division.'[22]

5. Christ did not anticipate that there would be *an increase of His government and peace* after His death.
He said:

'For from henceforth there shall be five in one house divided, three against two, and two against three.'[23]

In these very prophecies, in the very chapter quoted above, Christ speaks of *the last days* when He will come like 'a thief' in the night.

I learned the following:

1. The *government was upon the shoulder* of Bahá'u'lláh. His Writings established local, national, and international institutions to preserve his faith, and to protect the human rights of mankind.

2. His name *could* be called *the Counsellor*, for his laws established the principle of 'consultation' for each of these governing institutions.

3. As Christ was called the Son, in like manner, I found that Bahá'u'lláh was called *the Father*. His mission was that of a Father: to gather together the human family into one household, the planet. To unite the nations, races, and religions was the purpose of his coming, Bahá'u'lláh declared. He was the Father of all religions, races and peoples, with complete equality.

4. Unlike Christ, Bahá'u'lláh's mission *was* to bring peace. His whole purpose was to establish universal peace. He was a *Prince of Peace*, as I found in the words which he spoke to Professor E. G. Browne in the Holy Land. I read Browne's own account of that memorable visit: 'A mild dignified voice bade me be seated. . . . "Thou hast come to see a prisoner and an exile. . . . We desire but the good of the world and the happiness of the nations. . . . That all nations should become one in faith and all men as brothers. . . . Yet so it shall be; these fruitless strifes, these ruinous wars shall pass away, and the '*Most Great Peace*' shall come." Such, so far as I can recall them,' says Professor Browne, 'were the words which, besides many others, I heard from Bahá. Let those who read them consider well with themselves whether such doctrines merit death and bonds, and whether the world is more likely to gain or lose by their diffusion.'[24]

5. There was indeed *an increase in the kingdom* of Bahá'u'lláh. It has spread from the day of its birth a little over one hundred years ago to all parts of the world. It continues to grow each year. The astonishing progress is almost entirely due, in this day, to the leadership of the great-grandson of Bahá'u'lláh, Shoghi Effendi Rabbani, who for thirty-six years was the World Head of Bahá'u'lláh's Faith.

Be honest. Aren't you saying to yourself, as I did, at this time: 'What a truly remarkable story?' My enthusiasm as the detective of *The Case of the Missing Millennium* was never greater.

All these things took place in Israel, the Holy Land, the promised 'valley of Achor'. They unfolded within sight of the 'plain of Sharon' on the side of 'Mount Carmel'.

Bahá'u'lláh, I learned, wrote over one hundred volumes, addressing many letters to the leaders of the world's governments and religions. Was this not the promise in the Psalms:

'Out of Zion, the perfection of beauty, God hath shined. *Our God shall come,* and shall not keep silence.'[25]

The world administrative centre of Bahá'u'lláh's Faith is on the north side of Mount Carmel, one of the most beautiful situations and views in all of Israel. Thus the *new* Zion fulfilled the prophecy of the *Psalms* for *the last days:*

'Great is the Lord, and greatly to be praised in the city of our God, in the mountain of his holiness.

'Beautiful for situation, the joy of the whole earth, is mount Zion, *on the sides of the north, the city of the great King.*'[26]

I decided to learn more about Mount Carmel, and Haifa, the city of Bahá'u'lláh, and about 'Akká, the place of his imprisonment.

10. Where the Poor are the Kings of Paradise

Almost immediately I found the following statement about this famous mountain: 'Carmel is renowned in Jewish history, and occurs frequently in the imagery of the prophets.'[1]

It is mentioned in: *Joshua, I Kings, II Kings, Songs of Solomon, Isaiah, Jeremiah, Amos, Micah* and *Nahum*, etc.

I also learned the following:

1. Mount Carmel is famous as the place where Elijah brought Israel to its allegiance to YHWH (God), and where he slew the priests of Baal.[2]

2. It was on Mount Carmel that Elisha restored to life the son of the Shunammite woman.[3]

3. The *Jewish Encyclopedia* says, 'It is reasonable to suppose that from very early times Carmel was considered a sacred spot.'[4]

4. An altar to YHWH (God) existed on *Mount Carmel* before the introduction of the worship of Baal into the kingdom.[5]

5. Elisha visited *Mount Carmel* from Jericho, and made it his abiding place.[6]

6. Pythagorus was attracted to *Mount Carmel* because of its sacred reputation.[7]

7. According to the Roman historian Tacitus, Vespasian went to *Mount Carmel* to consult the oracle of God which was believed to dwell on the side of the mountain.[8]

8. Elijah chose *Mount Carmel* as the place for the assembly of the people.[9]

9. Fire descended from heaven onto *Mount Carmel* in a contest of truth, and 'proved the God of Israel to be the true God'.[10]

10. The Cave of Elijah can still be seen on the side of *Mount Carmel*. This is the cave of the prophet Elijah who was to appear *in the last days* as the Forerunner and Herald of the expected Messiah.

There is still another very interesting prophecy concerning *Mount Carmel* and *the time of the end*. I found it in the *Book of Elijah*, one of the Midrashic apocalypses of the Jews.

Silver, in his *Messianic Speculation in Israel*, comments on this *Book of Elijah*, saying: 'The angel Michael, after showing Elijah the regions of heaven, reveals to him on *Mount Carmel*, *the time of the end*.'[11]

The following promises were also given for *Mount Carmel*:

1. The Messiah would dwell in the midst of *Carmel*.
2. The Messiah would feed His flock from *Carmel* with the rod of His teachings.
3. The Messiah, *the Glory of the Lord*, would be seen by *Carmel*.

In addition to the many prophecies concerning Mount Carmel and the city of 'Akká which have already been mentioned, I found some very interesting accounts in other Scriptures. I learned that the city of 'Akká (Accho, Acre, St. Jean d'Acre, Ptolemais), had been greatly lauded as a place of hope and promise.

For example, the Arabian Prophet also referred to 'Akká many times, calling it:

1. A city . . . to which God has shown His special mercy.'[12]
2. A city 'by the shore of the sea . . . whose whiteness is pleasing to God.'[13]

In the prophecies of Islám, it is written of 'Akká:

1. 'Blessed the man that hath visited 'Akká, and blessed be he that hath visited the visitor of 'Akka.'[14]
2. 'He that raiseth therein the call to prayer, his voice will be lifted up unto Paradise.'[15]
3. 'The poor of 'Akká are the kings of paradise and the princes thereof.'[16]

4. 'A month at 'Akká is better than a thousand years else-where.'[17]

And finally, one of the most remarkable prophecies of all, when one follows the history of the martyrdom of the Báb and of the exile of Bahá'u'lláh to the prison city of 'Akká. In the sacred Writings of the land of Bahá'u'lláh's birth, it states:

'All of them (*the companions of the Herald of the Messiah*) shall be slain *except One*, Who shall reach the plain of 'Akká, the Banquet-Hall of God.'[18]

Professor E. G. Browne of Cambridge University visited Bahá'u'lláh on the plain of 'Akká in 1890. He wrote of his experiences in that valley: '. . . here did I spend five most memorable days, during which I enjoyed unparalleled and unhoped-for opportunities of holding intercourse with those who are the very fountain-heads of that mighty and wondrous spirit, which works with invisible but ever-increasing force, for the transformation and quickening of a people who slumber in a sleep like unto death. It was in truth a strange and moving experience, but one whereof I despair of con-veying any save the feeblest impression . . . The spirit which pervades the (followers of Bahá'u'lláh) is such that it can hardly fail to affect most powerfully all subjected to its influence . . . it cannot be ignored or disregarded. Let those who have not seen, disbelieve me if they will; but, should that spirit once reveal itself to them, they will experience an emotion which they are not likely to forget.'[19]

When Professor Browne came face to face with Bahá'u'lláh, he said that he felt 'a throb of wonder and awe'. He added: 'The face of Him on whom I gazed I can never forget, though I cannot describe it. Those piercing eyes seemed to read one's very soul; power and authority sat on that ample brow . . . No need to ask in whose presence I stood, as I bowed myself before one who is the object of a devotion and love which kings might envy and emperors sigh for in vain!'[20]

The mansion in which Professor Browne visited Bahá'u'lláh, was in process of construction when Bahá'u'lláh was still a prisoner in 'Akká.

Just as Jesus the Christ had ridden, lowly, upon a donkey in the land of Israel, so did Bahá'u'lláh ride in the same manner. One day while passing this mansion which was being constructed by a wealthy Muslim, Udi Khammar, Bahá'u'lláh turned to his son 'Abdu'l-Bahá, and said with a twinkle in his eye: 'I wonder for whom they are building that mansion?'

No sooner was the mansion completed, than an epidemic of cholera broke out. The mansion was abandoned, and 'Abdu'l-Bahá was able to secure its use for Bahá'u'lláh at a very nominal rental.

When Bahá'u'lláh was released from the prison, he moved into the mansion. Above the stairway leading to the rooms which Bahá'u'lláh was to occupy, Udi Khammar had been inspired to have carved the following message in stone. It still remains to this day:

'Greetings and Peace be upon this Mansion! Its beauty will increase down through the ages. Within its walls wondrous and strange things will take place; things which all the pens of the earth shall be powerless to describe.'

In this mansion Bahá'u'lláh lived the last years of his earthly life. Within these walls he passed away on May 29th, 1892. To this sacred spot pilgrims now journey from all parts of the world.

There in the valley of 'Akká, in sight of holy 'Carmel', the entire prophecy of the fifty-third chapter of *Isaiah* was brought to its fulfilment.

Isaiah had foretold:

1. 'He is despised and rejected of men: a man of sorrows, and acquainted with grief . . .'[21]

Bahá'u'lláh was rejected by his own countrymen, and was sent into exile. His life was filled with grief and sorrow.

2. '. . . we hid as it were our faces from him; he was despised, and we esteemed him not.'[22]

The Emperor Franz Joseph passed within but a short distance of the prison in which Bahá'u'lláh was captive. Louis Napoleon cast behind his back the letter which Bahá'u'lláh sent to him, saying: 'If this man is of God, then I am two Gods!' The people of the world have followed in their footsteps.

3. 'Surely he hath borne our griefs, and carried our sorrows . . .'[23]

I read the following words of Bahá'u'lláh concerning his persecution and imprisonment: 'Though weariness lay Me low, and hunger consume Me, and the bare rock be My bed, and My fellows the beasts of the field, I will not complain, but will endure patiently . . . and will render thanks unto God under all conditions. . . . We pray that, out of His bounty— exalted be He—He may release, through this imprisonment, the necks of men from chains and fetters . . .'[24]

The prophecy of Isaiah continues:

4. 'But he was wounded for our transgressions, he was bruised for our iniquities; the chastisement of our peace was upon him; and with his stripes we are healed.'[25]

Bahá'u'lláh was twice stoned, once scourged, thrice poisoned, scarred with hundred-pound chains which cut through his flesh and rested upon the bones of his shoulders. He lived a prisoner and exile for nearly half a century.

5. 'He was taken from prison and from judgment . . .'[26]

Bahá'u'lláh was taken from the black-pit prison in Teheran for judgment before the authorities. His death was expected hourly, but he was banished to Iraq and finally to Israel. In the prison-city of 'Akká, on another occasion, '. . . the Governor, at the head of his troops, with drawn swords, surrounded (Bahá'u'lláh's) house. The entire populace, as well as the military authorities, were in a state of great agitation. The shouts and clamour of the people could be heard on all sides. Bahá'u'lláh was peremptorily summoned to the Governorate, interrogated, kept in custody the first night. . . . The Governor, soon after, sent word that He was at liberty to return to His home, and apologized for what had occurred.'[27]

6. 'And he made his grave with the wicked, and with the rich in his death . . .'[28]

Bahá'u'lláh was buried in the precincts of the Mansion of Bahji, owned by a wealthy Muslim. He was surrounded by enemies, members of his own family who betrayed his trust after his death and dwelt in homes adjacent to his burial-place.

7. '. . . he shall see his seed . . .'[29]

Bahá'u'lláh *did* see his 'seed'. He wrote a special document called the *Book of the Covenant*, in which he appointed his eldest son to be the Centre of his faith after his own passing. This very event was also foretold in the prophecies of the Psalms which proclaim:

'Also I will make him my first-born higher than the kings of the earth . . . and my covenant shall stand fast with him.'[30]

This 'first-born' son of Bahá'u'lláh, was named 'Abdu'l-Bahá, which means 'the servant of Bahá ('u'lláh). Bahá'u'lláh appointed him as his own successor in his *Will and Testament.* He called 'Abdu'l-Bahá *the Centre of his Covenant.*

Professor E. G. Browne said of 'Abdu'l-Bahá: 'Seldom have I seen one whose appearance impressed me more. . . . One more eloquent of speech, more ready of argument, more apt of illustration, more intimately acquainted with the sacred books of the Jews, the Christians and Mohammedans, could, I should think, scarcely be found. . . . These qualities, combined with a bearing at once majestic and genial, made me cease to wonder at the influence and esteem which he enjoyed even beyond the circle of his father's followers. About the greatness of this man and his power, no one who had seen him could entertain a doubt.'[31]

The well-known Bible scholar of Oxford University, the Reverend Dr. T. K. Cheyne, arranged a meeting for 'Abdu'l-Bahá at Manchester College, Oxford. Dr. Cheyne himself invited the public in an advertisement in the Oxford newspaper. In the Preface of his book *The Reconciliation of Races and Religions,* Cheyne mentions the fact that the Hungarian sage Vambéry was a believer in Bahá'u'lláh. Of his own belief, Cheyne says, 'I should express my own adhesion to the Bahá'í leader in more glowing terms.'

Cheyne is mentioned on the title page of his book as a member of 'the Bahá'í Community'.

This is the same Christian clergyman and Bible scholar who wrote: 'If there has been any prophet in recent times, it is to Bahá'u'lláh that we must go. Character is the final judge. Bahá'u'lláh was a man of the highest class—that of prophets.'[32]

8. Isaiah's prophecy continues:
'He (God) shall prolong his days, . . .'[33]

Bahá'u'lláh's days *were* prolonged. He was born in 1817 and passed away in the Holy Land in 1892. In the last years of his life, Bahá'u'lláh was released from his prison cell. He came out of the prison city of 'Akká and walked on the sides of Mount Carmel. His followers came from afar to be with him, and to surround him with their love, fulfilling the words of the prayer of David spoken within a cave:

'Bring my soul out of prison, that I may praise thy name: the righteous shall compass me about; for thou shalt deal bountifully with me.'[34]

These events in the valley of 'Akká with its strong fortress prison had been foreshadowed in *Ecclesiastes* (4 : 14):

'For out of prison he cometh to reign . . .'

Bahá'u'lláh, I found, had written that 'whatsoever hath been announced in the Books hath been revealed and made clear.' He declared that the Ancient Beauty 'ruleth upon the throne of David' and that the 'Most Great Law is come'.[35]

Alongside my record of the prophecies which the Messiah would have to fulfil concerning the 'plain of Sharon', 'the valley of 'Achor', and the sacred mountain 'Carmel', I wrote: *Fulfilled.*

11. The Blossoming Desert

I had still another *proof* to check. It had been prophesied that when the Messiah came, the 'desert would blossom as the rose'.

Isaiah had foretold clearly:

'The wilderness and the solitary place shall be glad for them; and the desert shall rejoice, and blossom as the rose.'[1]

It is in the next verse of this prophecy that Isaiah says that when this happens, *Carmel* and *Sharon* shall see *the Glory of the Lord*.

Carmel and Sharon had seen the appearance of Bahá'u'lláh, the Glory of the Lord, but had the desert blossomed as the rose?

My study revealed that the followers of Bahá'u'lláh came from as far away as his native land even while he was yet in prison. They knew that Bahá'u'lláh loved children, green fields, trees and flowers. They were heavy-hearted because of the nine years he had to spend in the prison-city surrounded by the sandy plain and the unfragrant atmosphere of that 'foul city'.

Bahá'u'lláh's followers brought flowers and plants from Persia, and his son, 'Abdu'l-Bahá planted a lovely garden nearby. An eye-witness to the events of those days has written: 'These wonderful pilgrims! How they came on that long, toilsome journey on foot, braving numberless dangers, malignant human enemies and bad weather, and through all the fatigue, carrying, as the greatest treasure, some plant for their adored one's garden. Often the only water, which the devoted pilgrims so urgently needed for themselves, was given to the plant.'[2]

I made a personal visit to that garden on the island of Na'mayn outside the city of 'Akká. The land is arid, thirsting for water; yet, in the midst of this desert grows a magnificent garden. Laurence Oliphant refers to it in his book on Israel. He says: 'This island (garden), which is about two hundred yards long by scarcely a hundred wide, is all laid out in flower-beds and planted with ornamental shrubs and with fruit-trees. Coming upon it suddenly it is like a scene in fairy land.'[3]

In another place, Oliphant says of this garden: 'The stream

is fringed with weeping willows, and the spot, with its wealth of water, its thick shade, and air fragrant with jasmine and orange blossoms, forms an ideal retreat from the heats of summer. The sights and sounds are all suggestive of languor ... the senses are lulled by the sounds of murmuring water, the odours of fragrant plants, the flickering shadows of foliage, or the gorgeous tints of flowers ...'[4]

From the sandy plain of 'Akká, I drove to the rocky side of Mount Carmel. There on the side of this sacred mountain, were lovely gardens, walks and paths of magnificent beauty virtually carved out of the rock.

Even while I was flying from Rome *en route* to the Holy Land, the beauty of this spot was called to my attention. I was given a folder from the *British European Airways*. On the cover was a picture of the entrance to the gardens of the Bahá'í Faith on Mount Carmel. The folder described it as: 'The most beautiful spot in the Middle East.'

Between the two great Bahá'í gardens that go halfway up the mountainside, runs a broad highway. Through the gates leading from this highway stream pilgrims and visitors from all parts of the world. They come with hearts full of joy and gladness, and the sound of their beautiful chanting can be heard on that mountainside. This, too, was foreseen by Isaiah:

'And an highway shall be there, and a way, and it shall be called The way of holiness ... the redeemed shall walk there.
And the ransomed of the Lord shall return, and come to Zion with songs and everlasting joy upon their heads: they shall obtain joy and gladness, and sorrow and sighing shall flee away.'[5]

Surrounding these beautiful Shrines and gardens are orange, lemon, and pomegranate trees. Beautiful coloured paths of red and white stone wind through multi-coloured flowers, graceful lawns, and dark green hedges. Wherever the feet of Bahá'u'lláh walked can be found these lovely gardens.

The Shrine of Bahá'u'lláh, the *sanctuary* where he is buried, is a place of great beauty and peace. It lies in the centre of a giant circle with many walks leading to it. This land was once an arid desert, but it now blossoms out in splendour. It is perfumed by rose, hyacinth, jasmine and geranium. Smooth white stones from the Sea of Galilee make a pathway directly to the door of his Shrine. Three hills carpeted in crimson shelter his sanctuary from wind and storm. These sacred Shrines are surrounded by cedars of Lebanon, fir trees, pine trees, cypress, box, and olive trees.

Isaiah had foretold:

'. . . his rest shall be glorious.'[6]

In still another chapter, Isaiah prophesies:

'. . . *the glory of the Lord* is risen upon thee.'

and a few verses later he foresees the following:

'The glory of Lebanon shall come unto thee, the fir tree, the pine tree, and the box together, to beautify the place of my sanctuary; and I will make the place of my feet glorious.'[7]

Bahá'u'lláh's name means '*the Glory of the Lord*'. The place of his 'rest' had been made glorious, as well as the place where his feet had walked.

Isaiah also prophesies:

'I will make the wilderness a pool of water, and the dry lands springs of water.

I will plant in the wilderness the cedar, the shittah tree and the myrtle, and the oil tree; I will set in the desert the fir tree, and the pine, and the box tree together:

That they may see, and know, and consider, and understand together, that the hand of the Lord hath done this, and the Holy One of Israel hath created it.'[8]

I also uncovered the prophecies which foretold that when *the Glory of God*' that 'Holy One' of Israel returned to Zion, there would be changes of climate, and that the arid would become green. In that day when His 'rest' and 'sanctuary' would be 'beautified', the water would flow where the desert once held sway.

A survey of the early development of modern Israel disclosed the following report: 'Even the climatic conditions of Palestine (Israel) are now showing marked improvement. In 1927 the Pools of Solomon, dry for centuries, began to overflow. At that time the High Commissioner of Palestine was asked to declare a day of public thanksgiving to God for this seeming miracle. The pools were measured and found to contain approximately sixty million gallons. In Bible times there were two copious rainy seasons in Palestine, the "early and the later rain". But for the past many centuries the "early rains" have been scant; while the "later rains" and the dews had disappeared completely. But now these have returned to gladden the land, with the result that some parts of Palestine now yield two or three crops a year.'[9]

Thus the prophecy of Joel was fulfilled:

'. . . he will cause to come down for you the rain, the former rain, and the latter rain in the first month.'[10]

Also the prophecy of Zechariah:

'Thus saith the Lord, *I am returned* unto Zion . . . I will not be unto the residue of this people as in the *former days* . . . the heavens shall give their dew; and I will cause the remnant of this people to possess all these things.'[11]

There in the sandy desert of the plain of 'Akká, as long ago as 1878, a fountain splashed and gurgled in the midst of Bahá'u'lláh's garden.

Fresh water flowed in abundance to the arid land that now nourishes the beautiful green lawns, trees and flowers in both 'Akká and on the side of Mount Carmel in Haifa, even as Isaiah had prophesied:

> '. . . in the wilderness shall waters break out and streams in the desert.
>
> And the parched ground shall become a pool, and the thirsty land springs of water.'[12]

In this same chapter, once again, Isaiah prophesies that these wonders shall take place in Israel when *Carmel* and *Sharon* shall see '*the Glory of the Lord*'.

Nearly twenty years before the turn of this century a Christian traveller described these waters of Bahá'u'lláh's garden in the midst of the desert wilderness, 'In the centre is a plashing fountain from which the water is conveyed to all parts of the garden. The flower-beds are all bordered with neat edges of stone-work, and are sunk below the irrigating channels. Over a marble bed the waters from the fountain come rippling down in a broad stream to a bower of bliss, where two immense and venerable mulberry-trees cast an impenetrable shade over a platform with seats along the entire length of one side, protected by a balustrade projecting over the waters of the Belus, which here runs in a clear stream, fourteen or fifteen feet wide and . . . three deep, over a pebbly bottom, where fish of considerable size, and evidently preserved, are darting fearlessly about, or coming up to the steps to be fed.'[13]

Bahá'u'lláh had successfully demonstrated every requirement for this specific *proof*. Since the day of his coming to Israel, the land had grown in beauty. The places where he dwelled and where he walked had become gardens of superb loveliness. The desert had indeed 'blossomed as the rose'. In fact, I saw with my own eyes, one huge plot where once only barren rock had pushed its head above the soil. Now there bloomed roses of every variety and hue, perfuming the air with a delicate fragrance.

The *proof* had demanded: In the day of the Messiah, the desert shall blossom as the rose. I marked it: *Fulfilled*.

12. Fire in the Sky!

I had one last point of *proof*. Christ Himself had foretold that when the Messiah came, the Spirit of Truth, He would glorify His, Christ's, name. Had Baha'u'lláh done this?

In order to come to this final evidence, I had set aside two important *proofs*:

1. '*He shall unseal the Books.*'
2. '*He shall topple the unjust kings from their thrones.*'

The fulfilment of these two *proofs* made such a thrilling and dramatic story, that I was not only able to write *Fulfilled* beside them, but I have felt impelled to write a separate book about each, so that you too, might enjoy the same delight which I felt when discovering these astonishing stories.

The first of these two books I have called *The Wine of Astonishment*. On the eve of the declaration of his Mission, Bahá'u'lláh wrote his *Book of Certitude*. This book, he himself said, offered to mankind the 'Choice Sealed Wine' whose seal is of 'musk'. It broke the 'seals' of the 'Book' referred to by Daniel, and disclosed the meaning of the 'words' destined to remain 'closed up' till the 'time of the end'.[1]

Bahá'u'lláh wrote over a hundred volumes. This *Book of Certitude* was completed in the space of two days and two nights, a continuous outpouring. His words have been described as 'a rushing torrent'.

An historian who was living at the time of Bahá'u'lláh in Baghdad, has testified that the words which 'streamed from his lips . . . in a single day and night' were the equivalent of a large volume. Moreover, 'As to those verses which He either dictated or wrote Himself, their number was no less remarkable than either the wealth of material they contained, or the diversity of subjects to which they referred.'[2]

I found the following eye-witness account of a business man of Shíráz, Persia, who knew both the Báb and Bahá'u'lláh. He says: 'I bear witness that the verses revealed by Bahá'u'lláh were superior, in the rapidity with which they were penned, in the ease with which they flowed, in their lucidity, their profundity and sweetness to those which I, myself, saw pour from the pen of the Báb when in His presence. Had Bahá'u'lláh no other claim to greatness, this were sufficient, in the eyes of the world and its people, that He produced such verses as have streamed this day from His pen.'[3]

In his writings, Bahá'u'lláh 'unseals' the truth and the 'hidden meanings' of those subjects which have long troubled and confused mankind, such as:

> The Day of Judgement
> Resurrection
> Baptism
> The Eucharist
> The Trinity
> Reincarnation
> The Creation of the World
> Proofs of the Existence of God
> Life After Death
> The Immortality of the Soul

The Story of Adam and Eve
Good and Evil
The Son of God
The Father
Heaven and Hell
The Stars Falling from Heaven
The Darkening of the Sun and the Moon
The Day of God
The City of God
The Seal of the Prophets
The Return

These and many other subjects are revealed in their true meaning by Bahá'u'lláh, whose fresh and clear explanations harmonize with science and education and broaden the outlook of humanity. These have been explored in detail in the book *The Wine of Astonishment*.

Enoch, in speaking of the Messiah of *the time of the end*, promised:

'This is the Son of man . . . who will reveal all the treasure of that which is concealed.'[4]

The second of these two books I have called *Fire in the Sky*. It tells the story of Bahá'u'lláh's letters to the kings and rulers of the world. (Published as *The Prisoner and the Kings*.)

Bahá'u'lláh addressed them saying:

'O Kings of the earth! We see you increasing every year your expenditures and laying the burden thereof on your subjects. This, verily, is wholly and grossly unjust . . . lay not excessive burdens on your peoples. Do not rob them to rear palaces for yourselves; nay rather, choose for them that which ye choose for yourselves. . . . Your people are your treasures. Beware lest your rule violate the commandments of God, and ye deliver your wards to the hands of the robber. By them ye rule, by their means ye subsist, by their aid ye conquer. Yet, how disdainfully ye look upon them! How strange, how very strange!'[5]

In another place Bahá'u'lláh wrote to the kings and rulers:

'O kings of the earth . . . Compose your differences, and reduce your armaments, that the burden of your expenditures may be lightened, and that your minds and hearts may be tranquillised. Heal the dissensions that divide you . . . and be ye the emblems of justice amongst them (mankind).'[6]

And again:

'If ye stay not the hand of the oppressor, if ye fail to safeguard the rights of the downtrodden, what right have ye then to vaunt yourselves among men?'[7]

Bahá'u'lláh informed the monarchs of the world by whose authority he spoke, saying:

'I am the One Whom the tongue of Isaiah hath extolled, the One with Whose name both the Torah (of Moses) and the Evangel (of Christ) were adorned . . .'[8]

Bahá'u'lláh addressed letters to:

Emperor Franz Joseph of Austria
Napoleon III of France
Kaiser William I of Germany
Czar Nicolaevitch Alexander II of Russia
The Sultán 'Abdu'l-'Azíz of Turkey
Násiri'd-Dín Sháh of Persia
Queen Victoria of Britain
The Presidents and Rulers of the Republics of the West
The Religious Leaders of the Christians, Jews, Muslims and Zoroastrians

The followers of Christ, Moses, and Muhammad
The peoples of the world

Napoleon III cast Bahá'u'lláh's letter aside scornfully, saying, 'If this man is of God, I am *two* Gods!'

Shortly after, Napoleon fell from power as prophesied by Bahá'u'lláh, and ended his days in exile, after suffering a humiliating imprisonment.

Only one of these Sovereigns responded, even in the slightest measure. It was Queen Victoria in Great Britain. This dynasty is the only one which still remains today of those once-mighty monarchies.

Bahá'u'lláh foretold that Queen Victoria would have a long and successful reign, although at the time her health was precarious and she was not in favour because of her German consort. Of far more arresting interest is the fact that still another Sovereign, a grand-daughter of Queen Victoria, became a follower of Bahá'u'lláh. I found these words of Queen Marie of Rumania concerning Bahá'u'lláh and his Faith, quoted in the *Toronto Daily Star*, May 4th, 1926: 'It (Bahá'u'lláh's Faith) is Christ's message taken up anew. . . . No man could fail to be better because of this Book. I commend it to you all.'

She was quoted in the *Philadelphia Evening Bulletin*, September 27th, 1926 as follows: 'Those who read their Bible with "peeled eyes" will find in almost every line some revelation.'

She also wrote in a personal letter: 'These Books (the writings of Bahá'u'lláh's Faith), have strengthened me beyond belief. . . . The Bahá'í teaching brings peace and understanding.'[9]

Bahá'u'lláh declared that he saw 'abasement hastening after' those unjust rulers who neglected the rights and welfare of the poor and humble among their subjects. They would, he said, be made an 'object lesson' for the world.

Three were assassinated and two went into exile, the royal thrones of all but one were overthrown!

These events, I found, were all foretold for the day of the coming of the Messiah, and were part of the *proof* expected by the millennial scholars. It had been written in Scripture of the Messiah:

1. *Psalms:* 'He shall cut off the spirit of princes: he is terrible to the kings of the earth.'[10]

2. *Job:* 'He shall break in pieces mighty men without number . . .'[11]

3. *Isaiah:* 'The Lord hath broken the staff of the wicked, and the sceptre of the rulers.'[12]

'And it shall come to pass *in that day* that the Lord shall punish the host of the high ones that are on high, and the kings of the earth upon the earth.'[13]

In the very chapter of *Daniel*, in which he speaks of *the time of the end*, saying:

'. . . behold, one like the Son of man came with the clouds of heaven . . .'[14]

Daniel also says:

'I beheld till the thrones were cast down, and the Ancient of days did sit (upon His throne) . . .'[15]

I found over twenty specific prophecies in sacred Scripture which referred to the overthrow of the kings of the earth in the day of the coming of the Messiah.

Enoch refers to the same '*Son of man*' mentioned by Daniel for the *last days*, saying:

'This is the Son of man whom thou hast seen shall . . . break the teeth of the sinners, and he shall put down the kings from their thrones and kingdoms . . .'[16]

Enoch even tells from what part of the world this '*Son of man*' will come in the *last days:*

> 'And *in those days* the angels will assemble, and turn their heads *toward the east*, towards the people of Parthia and Medea (modern Persia), in order to excite the kings, and that a spirit of disturbance came over them, and disturbed them from off their thrones.'[17]

The welfare and happiness of the under-privileged, the down-trodden, the common man was a favourite theme of Bahá'u'lláh. He had great love for those who suffered from hunger and persecution. He warned the rulers of earth:

> 'Know ye that the poor are the trust of God in your midst. Watch that ye betray not His trust, that ye deal not unjustly with them and that ye walk not in the ways of the treacherous.'[18]

Bahá'u'lláh's own words set the seal to those winds of adversity which have swept across the face of the earth since 1844, dethroning monarchs, extinguishing dynasties, and uprooting age old kingdoms:

> 'God hath not blinked, nor will He ever blink His eyes at the tyranny of the oppressor. More particularly in this Revelation hath He visited each and every tyrant with His vengeance.'[19]

This astonishing story concerning the downfall of kings and the fulfilment of prophecy is told with all of its dramatic detail in the book *Fire in the Sky*.

Beneath the two *proofs:* (1) the Messiah shall unseal the Books, and (2) He shall topple the unjust kings from their thrones, I wrote: *Fulfilled.*

13. He Shall Glorify Christ

This brought me to the final *proof* of all: *He, the Messiah, shall glorify Christ*.

Jesus Himself had promised that when the Messiah came:

1. 'He shall glorify me.'
2. 'He will reprove the world of sin . . . because they believe not on me.'
3. 'He shall take of mine, and show it unto you.'
4. 'He shall . . . bring all things to your remembrance, whatsoever I have said unto you.'

Had Bahá'u'lláh done this?

My final *clue* in *The Case of the Missing Millennium* was answered with the most resounding proof of all. I found the following words which Bahá'u'lláh had written about Jesus, the Christ. He had indeed glorified Jesus:

'. . . Whatsoever hath proceeded out of His (Christ's) blameless, His truth-speaking, trustworthy mouth, can never be altered.'[1]

Bahá'u'lláh penned the following tribute upon the crucifixion of Christ:

'Know thou that when the *Son of Man* yielded up His breath to God, the whole creation wept with a great weeping. By sacrificing Himself, however, a fresh capacity was infused into all created things. Its evidences, as witnessed in all the peoples of the earth, are now manifest before thee.'[2]

In his letters to the kings of the earth, Bahá'u'lláh 'reproved' the world for not believing in Christ. He pointed out the similarity of his own reception to that of Christ in the day of His *first* coming:

'And . . . when I came unto them in My glory, they turned aside. They, indeed are of the fallen. This is, truly, that which the Spirit of God (Christ) hath announced, when He came with (the) truth . . . (and) they perpetrated what hath made the Holy Spirit to lament, and the tears of them that have near access to God to flow.'[3]

Bahá'u'lláh throughout his writings called to 'remembrance' the words of Christ. He *did*, as Christ foretold, 'take of mine, and show it unto you'. Bahá'u'lláh called upon the people of the world to:

'Consort with the people of religions with joy and fragrance; to show forth that which is declared by the Speaker of the Mount (Jesus Christ); and to render justice in (all) affairs.'[4]

As prophesied by Jesus, Bahá'u'lláh frequently brought to mind the words of Christ: 'whatsoever I have said unto you'. In the teachings of Bahá'u'lláh's Faith, I read:

'Unity is the very spirit of the body of the world. . . . His Holiness Jesus Christ—may my life be a sacrifice to Him!—promulgated this unity among mankind. Every soul who believed in Jesus Christ became revivified and resuscitated through this spirit, attained to the zenith of eternal glory, realised the life everlasting, experienced the second birth and rose to the acme of good fortune.'[5]

I was convinced that no honest and sincere Christian would ever consider Bahá'u'lláh or the Bahá'í Faith an enemy of Christ or Christianity, once they had read such words as these in Bahá'í teaching:

'Jesus was a Manifestation (Messenger) of God. Everything of Him pertained to God. To know Him (Christ) was to know God. . . . To obey Him was to obey God. He was the source of all divine virtues. He was a vision of all divine qualities . . . through this mirror (of Jesus) the energy of God was transmitted to the world. The whole disc of the Sun of Reality (God) was reflected in Him (Christ).'[6]

Bahá'u'lláh linked his own life with that of Christ throughout his mission. After having suffered stoning, scourging and imprisonment, Bahá'u'lláh lifted up his voice to cry out:

'If ye be intent on crucifying once again Jesus, the Spirit of God, put Me to death, for He hath once more, in My person been made manifest unto you. Deal with me as ye wish, for I have vowed to lay down My life in the path of God.'[7]

Bahá'u'lláh, expressing the oneness of the Holy Spirit which appears in all the Messengers of God, associates Himself with Christ, and offers Himself as a target for the indignities which the world hurled against Jesus:

'Lay hands on Me and persecute Me, for I am His Well-Beloved, the revelation of His own Self, though My name be not His name. I have come in the shadows of the clouds of glory.'[8]

As Christ had foretold, Bahá'u'lláh 'reproved' the world 'because the Prince of the world (Christ) is judged' by the people. Wishing to share this same suffering at their hands, Bahá'u'lláh wrote:

'If ye have resolved to shed the blood of Him Whose coming . . . Jesus Christ Himself hath announced, behold Me standing, ready and defenceless before you. Deal with Me after your own desires.'[9]

Bahá'u'lláh *'glorified'* the name of Christ for all time in his writings. The greatness of Jesus Christ was a much-loved theme of Bahá'u'lláh, who said:

'We testify that when He (Jesus Christ) came into the world, He shed the splendour of His glory upon all created things. Through Him the leper recovered from the leprosy of perversity and ignorance. Through Him, the unchaste and wayward were healed. Through His power, born of Almighty God, the eyes of the blind were opened, and the soul of the sinner sanctified.'[10]

Of the *glory* of Christ, Bahá'u'lláh proclaimed:

'He (Christ) it is Who purified the world. Blessed is the man who, with a face beaming with light, hath turned towards Him.'[11]

In one volume alone in the teachings of Bahá'u'lláh's Faith, I found nearly *one hundred references* to the beauty, the majesty, the greatness, and the glory of His Holiness Jesus the Christ.[12]

Thus Bahá'u'lláh had fulfilled the final, and one of the most important *proofs*. Christ had prophesied that when the *Spirit of Truth* came: '*He shall glorify me.*'

To this *proof* I wrote the words: *Fulfilled*.

14. The End of the Avalanche

At this stage in my search, there seemed no doubt whatsoever to my mind that Bahá'u'lláh had brought a definite solution to the century-old mystery of *The Case of the Missing Millennium*.

With the exactness of the stars, and with an over-flowing abundance of *proof*, he had fulfilled each of the requirements concerning the *Messiah of the last days*.

He had fulfilled all of the following *proofs* from the Scriptures:

1. His faith had appeared in the year 1844.
2. He had appeared in the East.
3. He had come from Persia.

4. He was known as '*the Glory of God*'.

5. He went to the valley of the Tigris and Euphrates rivers.

6. He made his public announcement to the world in that land of ancient Babylon.

7. He was exiled from Babylon to Syria, as Abraham had been before him.

8. He came to the ancient land of 'Canaan' which God had promised to the seed of Abraham.

9. He came to Israel, the Holy Land, *by way of the sea*.

10. He came from *fortified city* to *fortified city*.

11. He came from *the fortress to the river*.

12. He came from *mountain to mountain*.

13. He came from *sea to sea*.

14. *Carmel* and *Sharon* had seen him, '*the Glory of God*'.

15. He had come from the *East by way of the Gate* (the Báb).

16. He had come to the valley of 'Akká, to the prison-city.

17. He had *dwelt* in the *midst of Carmel*.

18. His *Law* had *gone down* from the mountain.

19. The children of Israel had been *gathered* in the Holy Land in his day.

20. A '*house of prayer*' for *all nations* was being raised up on the mountain of God.

21. The *desert had blossomed* as the rose.

22. His ministry on earth had lasted for exactly *forty years*.

23. The place of his *sanctuary* and *rest* had been beautified.

24. The place where his *feet* had walked had been made *glorious*.

25. He had come from the *seed* of Abraham.

26. He had established a spiritual kingdom even to the ends of the earth.

27. He had *unsealed* the Books.

28. He had *toppled the kings* from their thrones.

29. He had *glorified Christ*.

The fulfilment of these prophecies did not by any means exhaust the story. However, these were the major *proofs* by which I had planned to test the truth of Bahá'u'lláh's Faith and his person.

Beside each one I could confidently place the word: *Fulfilled*. If my curiosity and interest had not been further aroused by additional information that came into my hands concerning his Faith, information which added greatly to the stature and to the proof of its truth, I would have closed the file on *The Case of the Missing Millennium* and marked it: *Solved*.

But there was still *more* to come, incredible though it seemed. Would the 'wonders' never cease?

I bitterly regretted the long years of obscurity which had kept this story from reaching the masses of humanity who hungered and longed for such a hope, for the hand of God to lift their sorrow and disillusionment.

PART FOUR

SIGNS IN THE HEAVENS

1. The Signs in the Heavens

In my study of the books and records of the 1844 period, as well as several relating to the preceding century I discovered another remarkable thread which excited the people of that time, and led to their zealous expectancy of the Messiah.

These prophecies did not speak of the date of the Messiah's appearance, but of the dramatic events which would gradually lead up to that wondrous day.

The story was both intriguing and entertaining. I felt that I had to record it. I began to understand much more clearly the zeal that aroused the populace as 1844 approached.

In the *Book of Revelation,* it promised that one from the seed of Abraham would unseal the Books in the last days. This *Lamb of God* was pictured in the visions as having *seven eyes.* These seven eyes were said to be the seven spirits (religions) of God which He had sent forth into the world up to that time. It was to be the Books of these seven great religions that the Messiah would unseal. Strangely enough, I had learned that up to the time of the coming of the Bahá'í Faith, there *had* been *exactly seven* great revealed religions. This story is told elsewhere in this volume.

When this *Lamb of God*, according to the sixth chapter of *Revelation,* opened the Books and unsealed their meaning, one of the seals which He broke open concerned the signs which would be written in the heavens. These signs would appear prior to the days or years of His coming. These signs, given in *Revelation* were the signs which the millennial scholars searched through history to find during their 1844 enthusiasm.

The *Book of Revelation* prophesied:

1. '. . . and, lo, there was a great earthquake.'[1]

This was the *first* sign which was to appear.

2. '. . . and the sun became black as sack-cloth of hair, and the moon became as blood;[2]

This was to be the *second* sign.

3. 'And the stars of heaven fell unto the earth, even as a fig tree casteth her untimely figs, when she is shaken of a mighty wind.'[3]

This was the *third* sign which was to appear. This was the final promise, and would be seen just before the coming of the Messiah in the *last days*.

Bahá'u'lláh wrote of these signs in the heavens in his *Book of Certitude*, saying that the meanings hidden in such words as those of *Revelation* were symbolical, although in some cases they had an outward physical fulfilment as well. Bahá'u'lláh's explanation of their true inner meaning is given in *the Wine of Astonishment* in the chapter *When the Stars Fall from Heaven*.

I discovered many interesting events unearthed by the millennial scholars and leading up to the year 1844. Some of them were quite astonishing. Others were certainly dramatic. These happenings caused a great stir among the people of those days.

The three signs of *Revelation* which would appear in succession, leading up to the day of the *return of Christ* were, in order:

1. The great earthquake.
2. The darkening of the sun and the moon.
3. The falling of the stars from the heavens.

The Books of *Isaiah, Joel, Daniel, Zechariah,* and the *New Testament* of Christ Himself, had all foretold that these things would take place. Following these events, the 'great and dreadful' day of the Lord would appear, and then the Messiah would come, bringing the end of the world.

Some Bible scholars felt that all of these events mentioned in *Revelation* would take place in one great upheaval, and that the world as we know it would pass away forever. Most of them, however, felt that these three events would take place successively, each one in turn heralding a closer approach of the footsteps of the Messiah, until, shortly after the last of the three, the star-fall, He would appear.

My own study indicated clearly that the 'end of the world' mentioned in Scripture was obviously symbolical. It was referred to in some writings as the 'end of the whirl' or the 'end of the cycle' or the 'end of the age'.

I found that there were two Greek words used for *world*. One was *kosmos,* the other was *aion. Kosmos* meant the material world and *aion* meant an age or era. This phrase 'end of the world' occurs seven times in the New Testament. *Aion* is used each time, never *kosmos.* When the disciples of Christ asked Him about the 'end of the world' and His return, it is *aion* that is used. When Christ refers to the 'harvest at the end of the world', it is *aion.* When Christ says, 'so shall it be at the end of the world', once again it is *aion.* Clearly Christ's return marks the end of an age or the end of an era.

Bizarre as it seemed to me at first, I did find a record of three just such events as are mentioned in *Revelation,* happening in exactly the order foretold. Incredible? Perhaps, but nevertheless true. Do you wonder that I was thrilled with *The Case of the Missing Millennium.*

I came across the account of one millennial scholar who made a study of the historical events leading up to the 1840 period. When he had completed his search, he made the following statement:

'As we look, we find the events recorded (in *Revelation*), following on in the order predicted.'[4]

These events which he listed were as follows:

1. The Lisbon earthquake, 1755.
2. The Dark Day, 1780.
3. The Falling Stars, 1833.

Was I on to something?

I decided to take up the three events one at a time and see for myself.

2. The Shaking Earth

My first *clue* was plain enough.

'. . . and, lo, there was a great earthquake.'

I found the earthquake in many historical records. It was called:

THE LISBON EARTHQUAKE OF 1755

Concerning the first of these three signs, this great earthquake, I read in the account of Professor W. H. Hobbs, geologist, the following words, taken from his book *Earthquakes:* 'Among the earth movements which in historic times have affected the kingdom of Portugal, that of November 1, 1755, takes first rank, as it does also, in some respects, among all recorded earthquakes. . . . In six minutes 60,000 people perished.'

As I continued my investigation, I found that millennial scholars took into account the gathering momentum of the shaking of the earth. The Reverend John Cumming in *The Seventh Vial* writes of this period, saying: '. . . in the 65 years that elapsed between A.D. 1800 and A.D. 1865, there occurred (within the limits of the old Roman Empire alone) no less than 35 great and disastrous earthquakes, arresting the attention of the historian. . . . In the Scandinavian Peninsula and in Iceland, from A.D. 1700 to 1850, (there have been) 224; in Spain and Portugal 178; in France, Belgium and Holland 600. . . . On the Italian Peninsula and the Eastern Mediterranean, upwards of 800 earthquakes have occurred within the period of fifty years between 1800 and 1850.'

It was the unique proximity and the succession of the three events (earthquake, dark day, falling stars), beginning with the destructive earthquake in Portugal which arrested the attention of these scholars, but (according to James Parton in his *Life of Voltaire*) it was the blinding speed of the destruction in Portugal which set that earthquake apart from all others. He says: 'The Lisbon earthquake of November 1, 1755, appears to have put both theologians and philosophers on the defensive. . . . At twenty minutes to ten that morning, Lisbon was firm and magnificent. . . . In six minutes the city was in ruins.'

Robert Sears, in his *Wonders of the World*, writes: 'The great earthquake of 1755 extended over a tract of at least four million square miles.'

Voltaire was profoundly moved by the destruction caused by the Portuguese earthquake. It is said that he described it as follows: 'It was the last judgement for that region; nothing was wanting to it except the trumpet.'[1]

The opening of Voltaire's new play was delayed by the disaster. His biographer, Tallentyre, said: 'The earthquake had made all men thoughtful. They mistrusted their love of the drama, and filled the churches instead.'[2]

In that very same year, 1755, another earthquake struck in the land of Persia killing 40,000 persons. Christ said:

'. . . there shall be . . . earthquakes in divers places . . .
these are the beginning . . . And then . . . they shall see
the Son of man coming . . .'[3]

Many students of the Bible felt that the great earthquake of
Revelation had come at last. It had arrived on the crest of a
period of unprecedented increase in the number of earthquakes.

Many were confident that the *first* of the three signs in the
sixth chapter of *Revelation* had taken place. They would now
carefully watch the heavens for the *second* sign which was to
follow: *The darkening of the sun.*

3. The Blast of the Trumpet

I was now on the trail of my second *clue*. The prophecy
said:

'. . . and the sun became black as sackcloth of hair, and the
moon became as blood.'

I discovered such an event in various documents. It was
called:

THE DARK DAY OF 1780

This event attracted so much attention that it made newspaper headlines in all parts of the United States, and in other
countries as well.

The following account was given by Dr. Samuel Stearns in
the *Boston Independent Chronicle* of June 22nd, 1780: 'That the
darkness was not caused by an eclipse is manifest by the various
positions of the planets of our system at that time; for the
moon was more than one hundred and fifty degrees from the
sun all that day.'

The event was so unique that it was placed in the 1883 edition of *Websters Unabridged Dictionary*, as follows:

'The Dark Day, May 19th, 1780—so called on account of a remarkable darkness on that day extending all over New England.... The true cause of this remarkable phenomenon is not known.'

In his *Collections for the Massachusetts Historical Society 1792*, Samuel Tenny writes: 'This gross darkness held till about one o'clock, although the moon had filled but the day before.'

Uriah Smith, writing of Tenny's statement says: 'This statement respecting the phase of the moon proves the impossibility of an eclipse of the sun at that time. Whenever on this memorable night *the moon* did appear, as at times it did, it *had ... the appearance of blood*.'[1]

Many of the scholars made much of the uniqueness of this event, pointing out that it was not a natural eclipse of the sun—but a sudden darkening of the sky, with the moon having the appearance of blood. The more conservative scholars explained that it did not matter whether the happening was a natural one or a mysterious one. The important thing was that *the sun was darkened* and *the moon turned into blood*. What caused it was of no importance, they said.

Many explanations were advanced for this phenomenon, but the millennial scholars were at least agreed that it was the fulfilment of the prophecy which was important, and not the manner in which it came to pass. Some protested that the 'dark day' was not seen by the whole world. Others replied that the 'Star of Bethlehem' was seen only in the Middle East, and that half the world is dark each day—how could all see it at once? The excitement and debates were vigorous. Excitement over Christs' return grew in ratio to the intensity of the disputes.

The *Massachusetts Spy* reported the following: 'Nor was the darkness of the night less uncommon and terrifying than that of the day; notwithstanding there was almost a full moon, no object was discernible, but by help of some artificial light. . . . Some considered it as the immediate harbinger of the last day, when "the sun shall be darkened, and the moon shall not give her light." '

Barber, in his *Connecticut Historical Collections* reports an amusing drama which took place in the Connecticut Legislature at Hartford. The body was in session when the day suddenly darkened. The general view soon prevailed that the Day of Judgement had come.

However, Colonel Davenport spoke against a motion for adjournment. He said: 'The Day of Judgement is either approaching or it is not. If it is not, there is no cause for adjournment; if it is, I choose to be found doing my duty. I wish therefore that candles be brought.'

The poet Whittier wrote of the awesome day, saying:

'. . . there fell . . .
Over the fresh earth and heaven of noon,
A horror of great darkness . . .
                        . . . all ears grew sharp
To hear the doom-blast of the trumpet shatter
The black sky . . .'[2]

Christ said:

'. . . shall the sun be darkened, and the moon shall not give her light. . . . And then . . . shall they see the Son of man coming . . .'[3]

Millennial scholars of that day were deeply moved by the event. Many of them were satisfied that the *Dark Day* which followed the *Great Earthquake* had fulfilled in succession *two* of the prophecies recorded in *Revelation*, events which would precede the appearance of the Messiah on earth.

Both had taken place in the Western world. Anxious eyes looked heavenward, awaiting with expectancy the fulfilment of the third prophecy when *The stars would fall from heaven.*

4. When Stars Fell Like Snowflakes

I admit that as the detective in charge of *The Case of the Missing Millennium*, I found the story fascinating. The third *clue* even more so. The *third* prophecy of *Revelation* said:

'And *the stars of heaven fell* unto the earth, even as a fig tree casteth her untimely figs, when she is shaken by a mighty wind.'

I had found just such an event. It was called:

THE STAR-FALL OF 1833

So exceptional was this event, that Clarke in his *History of Astronomy in the Nineteenth Century* writes: '. . . a tempest of falling stars broke over the earth.'

According to the millennial scholars of the 1840s, the *third* sign in the sixth chapter of *Revelation* came to pass on November 12th, 1833, the night of the unique star-fall.

Clarke wrote of that night, saying: 'Once and for all, then, as the result of the star-fall of 1833, the study of luminous meteors became an integral part of astronomy.' He goes on to say: 'North America bore the brunt of its pelting. From the Gulf of Mexico to Halifax, until daylight with some difficulties put an end to the display, the sky was scored in every direction with shining tracks and illuminated with majestic fireballs.'

Denison Olmsted, Professor of Mathematics at Yale University, wrote the following in the *American Journal of Science:*

186

'The morning of November 13th, 1833, was rendered memorable by an exhibition of the phenomenon called shooting stars, which was probably more extensive and magnificent than any similar one hitherto recorded. . . . Probably no celestial phenomenon has ever occurred in this country, since its first settlement, which was received with so much admiration and delight by one class of spectators, or with so much astonishment and fear by another class. For some time after the occurrence, the "meteoric phenomenon" was the principal topic of conversation.'

Simon Newcomb in *Astronomy for Everybody* called the display of falling stars 'the most remarkable one ever observed'.

The French astronomer, Flammarion, in *Popular Astronomy*, wrote: 'The Boston observer, Olmsted, compared them, at the moment of maximum, to half the number of flakes which are perceived in the air during an ordinary shower of snow.'

Professor Olmsted estimated 34,640 falling stars per hour. His estimate was made after the shower had diminished sufficiently for him to make some sort of a count.

Dr. Humphreys, President of St. John's College, Annapolis, Maryland, in his report in the *American Journal of Science*, said: 'In the words of most, they fell like flakes of snow.'

The *American Journal of Science* carried the following report: 'Though there was no moon, when we first observed them, their brilliancy was so great that we could, at times, read common-sized print without much difficulty, and the light which they afforded was much whiter than that of the moon, in the clearest and coldest night, when the ground is covered with snow.' (Vol. xxv, 1834, p. 372).

The *New York Journal of Commerce* wrote: 'No philosopher or scholar has told or recorded an event like that of yesterday morning. A prophet eighteen hundred years ago foretold it exactly, if we will be at the trouble of understanding stars falling to mean falling stars.' (Nov. 14, 1833).

Thomas Milner of Britain, writing in the *Gallery of Nature* in 1852, points out that not only America but all the world was aroused by the profound impression the display made. 'In many districts,' he said, 'the mass of the population was terror-struck, and the more enlightened were awed at contemplating so vivid a picture of the apocalyptic image—that of the stars of heaven falling to earth, even as a fig tree casting her untimely figs, when she is shaken of a mighty wind.'

Astronomers, after careful study, learned that this particular meteoric display occurs every thirty-three years. However, the display of 1833 was unique in its drama. The fall of 1866 did not rival it in any way, and that of 1899 was of even less interest.

In any event, as the millennial scholars said, it was not the cause behind the *sign*, but *the time of its arrival*, and *its sequence* with the *earthquake* and the *dark day* which were important. Many biblical scholars pointed to the exact fulfilment, and in the proper order of the prophecies concerning the heavens and the signs of the coming of Christ as given in the sixth chapter of *Revelation*

First: The appearance of the great earthquake in 1755.
Second: The sun darkened and the moon turned into blood on the Dark Day of 1780.
Third: The stars falling from the heavens in 1833.

In this same chapter it is foreseen that the Messiah shall come and topple the kings from their thrones, for the great day of the Lord will have come. Christ said:

'. . . and the stars shall fall from heaven. . . . And then . . . shall they see the Son of man coming . . .'[1]

The millennial scholars pointed to the great convergence of prophecies on the year 1844. Now that the three signs in the heavens, promised as a prelude in *Revelation*, had been fulfilled, it further strengthened their belief that the hour of the *return of Christ* was at hand.

The Rev. L. D. Fleming, in his *Synopsis of the Evidences of the Second Coming of Christ about A.D. 1843*, written in 1842, declares: 'Many distinguished students of prophecy have come to very similar conclusions.... How can that wonderful phenomenon of falling stars, or meteors, which astonished the world a few years since, be regarded but as a sign of the last times?' Fleming then reminds the people of the strange 'nocturnal light' which a few years before had 'hung over the earth'. He concludes, saying: 'May God help us to watch!'

It is interesting to note that the great star-fall came on the night of November 12th, which is the birthday of Bahá'u'lláh.

Could there possibly be any additional signs?

5. The Face of Heaven

There were! Many more!

In addition to these general wonders in the sky preceding the coming of the Faith of Bahá'u'lláh in 1844, I found other more specific happenings recorded during that period.

Margaret Fuller (Ossoli), friend of Emerson, made the following statement: 'One very marked *trait* of the period was that the agitation reached all circles.'[1]

Another account of those days says: 'Now it was about this time that strange signs appeared in the heavens with such frequency as to cause great uneasiness.'[2]

An article in the *Connecticut Observer* on November 25th, 1833, declared: 'We pronounce the raining of fire which we saw on Wednesday morning, last, an awful type, a sure forerunner—a merciful sign of the great and dreadful day which the inhabitants of the earth will witness when the Sixth Seal (of *Revelation*) shall be opened. The time is just at hand described, not only in the New Testament, but in the Old.'

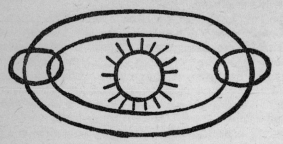

February 1843[3]

January 4th, 1843[4]

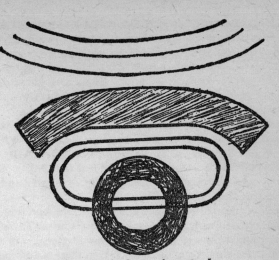

New York, September 1844[5]

After the star-fall of 1833, the interest in the prophecies concerning *the time of the end* grew by leaps and bounds, reaching a zenith in the 1843–4 period. The concern and zeal were greatly accelerated by the sight of the above parhelic circles or haloes which were seen around the sun in 1843–4, and were reported in the press.

The signs and prophecies became so overpowering to the Reverend Charles Fitch, pastor of the Marlborough Street Chapel in Boston, Massachusetts, that he 'took upon himself the duty of warning the public of the coming end. By so doing he lost all connection with his church.'

Fitch himself said: 'I became in part an ecclesiastical outcast. But I gained deliverance.'[6]

I was still not at the end of the signs in the heavens which heralded that hour. I had read Bahá'u'lláh's own words which said that whenever a Messiah appeared on earth, a star appeared in the heavens. In his *Book of Certitude*, Bahá'u'lláh said that there were in reality *two* stars which attended the appearance of a Messenger of God on earth. There was, he said, the human herald who was the symbolic star, and there was the actual physical star in the heavens.

Scripture confirms this truth, telling of the star which warned Nimrod of Abraham's coming, the star which the soothsayers pointed out to Pharaoh concerning Moses, the star of Bethlehem which made Herod fear the Christ. These same stories of stars have been told of Zoroaster and the other great Messengers of God.

Each of these Prophets had a human herald who prepared the way for him, as John the Baptist did for Christ. Therefore, if this were *the time of the end*, when *two* Messengers of God would come almost simultaneously, then there should be *two* heralds on earth, and *two* signs in the heavens. It was a fantastic thought, I felt, but if the formula of Scripture were to be followed, it should be so. Besides, by now I was prepared for anything.

In the history of Persia I found exactly this event. There were twin heralds who foretold the coming of both the Báb and Bahá'u'lláh. These two holy souls were called Shaykh Ahmad and Siyyid Kazím. This accounted for the two human (symbolic) stars on earth, but what about the two stars in the heavens?

Oddly enough, I found that the interest in the study of 'double'- or 'twin'-stars began at this very period. *Two* men, William Herschel and William Struve, were primarily responsible for 'the foundation of systematic measurement and study of double-stars'. Struve completed his work at Dorpat in 1835.[7]

At almost that exact hour, <u>Shaykh</u> Ahmad and Siyyid Kázim were proclaiming to the world the coming of the Twin Messengers of God for the last day. Siyyid Kázim, like <u>Shaykh</u> Ahmad before him, prophesied to the people of Persia concerning the Two Who were about to appear. He told them:

> 'Verily, I say that after the promised *Dawn*, the promised *Sun* will be made manifest. For when the light of the *Former* has set, the *Sun* of the *Latter* will rise and illuminate the whole world.'[8]

I learned another unusual thing about *double-stars* which happened at this same time. One of the brightest stars in the heavens is Sirius. The astronomer Bessel advanced a theory that Sirius was not a single star, but a *double-star*. He made his pronouncement in the year *1844*. Sirius has been called a *double-star* 'of exceptional historical interest'.

To the millennial scholar this was also true. Bessel made his announcement in 1844, the year of the announcement of the Báb, and the year of the beginning of Bahá'u'lláh's Faith.

Alvan Clark studied Sirius carefully, and then announced that Bessel's theory was correct. Sirius *was* a *double-star*. It had a companion. Clark made his statement in 1862, but a few months before Bahá'u'lláh made his declaration to the world that he was the one foretold by the Báb.[9]

This was fascinating, but it was only the beginning. As in almost every prophecy associated with the life and history of Bahá'u'lláh, I found that the prophecy was not only fulfilled, but the 'cup runneth over'.

I understood and sympathised with the words of the student of prophecy who said of these fulfilments: 'It is difficult for a seeker to find spring or a stream, or even a river, but who can fail to behold the ocean?'

6. The Night Visitor

The most important date to confirm by signs in the heavens was the date of the birth of the Faith of Bahá'u'lláh. It was also the easiest. The sign was a great comet.

The famous astronomer, Sir James Jeans, writes in his well-known book *Through Space and Time*: '. . . oddly enough many of the most conspicuous appearances of comets seem to have coincided with, or perhaps just anticipated, important events in history.'

The following headlines tell their own story:

SUDDEN APPEARANCE OF A GREAT AND FIERY
COMET IN THE SKIES AT NOONDAY

This comet appeared in 1843, the year before the birth of the Faith of Bahá'u'lláh, 'anticipating' this event. It was a giant comet with a tail 105 million miles long. It appeared at the time when a great parhelic circle around the sun was causing much wonder and speculation. (See above).

This appearance is reported in *Our First Century* as follows: 'The *Comet of 1843* is regarded as perhaps the most marvellous of the present age, having been observed in the daytime even before it was visible at night—passing very near the sun, exhibiting an enormous length of tail; and arousing interest in the public mind as universal and deep as it was unprecedented.'

The *New York Tribune*, and the *American Journal of Science* devoted special sections to this great comet of 1843, the *Journal of Science* identifying it in those very words: 'The Great Comet of 1843.'

I found an even more dramatic story told in the heavens during this same period. It was the story of still another comet. It was seen in the skies in 1845. It appeared to be quite an ordinary comet in a year in which some 300 comets had appeared. It had been studied many times in the past. In 1846, the comet was still visible.

However, at this period in its history, it became one of the rare comets of history. It was now entering what were to be the last dramatic moments of its life. It was called Biela's comet, after the original discoverer. The *Encyclopaedia Americana* (1944 ed.) gives the following account of this event: 'It was found again late in November 1845, and in the following month an observation was made of one of the most remarkable phenomena in astronomical records, the division of the comet. It put forth no tail while this alteration was going on. Professor Challis, using the Northumberland telescope at Cambridge, on January 15th, 1846, was inclined to distrust his eyes or his glass when he beheld two comets where but one had been before. He would call it, he said, a binary (twin) comet if such a thing had ever been heard of before. His observations were soon verified, however.'

Sir James Jeans has written of this same comet, saying: 'The most interesting story is that of Biela's comet which broke in two while under observation in 1846.'[1]

Professor Challis was wrong. It was not the only binary comet in history, just as Sirius was not the only double-star, nor the Star of Bethlehem the only bright star, or novae, or conjunction of planets in astronomical history. It was not the uniqueness of the event that made it important in prophecy, but its remarkable timing.

Biela's comet disappeared in 1846. It returned in August, 1852. This was the very month and year in which Bahá'u'lláh was cast into an underground prison in Teheran. It was the beginning of the *forty years* of his Mission which ended in Israel in 1892 with his death; the *forty years* foretold by Micah during which God would show to the Messiah 'wonderful things'.

This year 1852 was also the beginning of the year 1269 of the Persian calendar. It was the ninth year following the Báb's prophecy concerning the coming of Bahá'u'lláh. The Báb had written,

'In the year *nine* ye will attain unto all good . . . in the year *nine* ye will attain unto the presence of God.'[2]

When the single comet which had now become a twin-comet reappeared in August 1852, one half had receded far into the background. The other half now dominated the sky. So the Báb, the Herald of Bahá'u'lláh, had now passed into history through martyrdom, and the one whose coming he had foretold, Bahá'u'lláh, had now assumed his Mission.

An account of the reappearance of the comet states: 'Late in August 1852, the larger came into view and three weeks later the smaller one, now much fainter than its former companion.'[3]

Sir James Jeans confirms this, saying that in 1852, the two pieces were one and a half million miles apart.

Bahá'u'lláh has written of that hour when the twin-comets rode the skies. He lay chained in an underground prison. Of that moment, he has said:

'. . . lo, the breezes of the All-Glorious (God) were wafted over Me, and taught Me the knowledge of all that hath been. This thing is not from Me, but from One Who is Almighty and All-Knowing. And He bade Me lift up My voice between earth and heaven. . . .'[4]

In that very hour, just as the dove had descended upon Jesus in the river Jordan, and the Burning Bush had appeared to Moses, so did the Most Great Spirit appear to Bahá'u'lláh. He wrote of that experience, saying:

'By my life! Not of Mine own volition have I revealed

196

Myself, but God, of His own choosing, hath manifested Me . . . Whenever I chose to hold My peace and be still, lo, the Voice of the Holy Spirit, standing on My right hand, aroused Me . . . and the Spirit of Glory stirred within My bosom, bidding Me arise and break My silence.'[5]

The comet which announced this twin-event of the appearance of the Báb and Bahá'u'lláh, disappeared, never to return again. Sir James Jeans says: '. . . neither of them (the twin comets) has been seen in cometary form, but the place where they ought to be is occupied by a swarm of millions of meteors, known as the Andromedid meteors. Occasionally these meet the earth in its orbit, and make a grand meteoric display. . . .'[6]

Thus the two comets were no longer separate comets, but were mingled in *one* show of light, just as the Faith of Bahá'u'lláh and that of the Báb were no longer separate, but *one* in the light they shed upon the world.

There is yet another unique way in which this same oneness of the Faith of Bahá'u'lláh and the Báb is expressed. Even in the calendar of their native land, they are inseparably intertwined.

In the calendar of Persia where both Bahá'u'lláh and the Báb were born, their birthdays fall upon successive days in the exact order in which their Missions were declared.

In the calendar of the West, the Báb was born on October 20th, and Bahá'u'lláh on November 12th. But in the calendar of Persia, the Báb was born on the *first* day of the month of Muharram, and Bahá'u'lláh on the *second* day.

In Persia, these two birthdays are celebrated as *one* great *twin-festival*.

I was more than gratified by the list of events which I had found written in the skies concerning the coming of Bahá'u'lláh and his Faith. It made an arresting array:

1. The star-fall of 1833 and the periodic appearance of this shower of meteors always in November, the month of the birth of Bahá'u'lláh.
2. The beginning of the study of 'double-stars'.
3. The parhelic circles surrounding the sun in 1843.
4. The great comet of 1843.
5. The parhelic circles of 1844.
6. The comet of 1845, which split in two in 1846, and the mingling of the twin-comets into one single shower of light.
7. The belief that the brightest star Sirius had had a twin companion; a belief announced in 1844. It was proved to be true in 1862, on the eve of Bahá'u'lláh's declaration.

Although all these dramatic events, earthquakes, dark days, falling stars, comets and signs in the heavens concerned the appearance of Bahá'u'lláh, *the Glory of God*—indeed they seemed a further fulfilment of the words of the Psalm,

'The heavens declare *the glory of God*',⁷

I must make it clear that they are not in any way teachings of the Bahá'í Faith. They were physical signs which added fuel to the Messianic zeal of the 1800's, which was itself a Christian enthusiasm for the return of Christ. The Bahá'í Faith, I learned, gave far more weight to the symbolic fulfilment of 'falling stars' and all the other signs.

I now heartily agreed with the newspaper men who said that this story of *the return of Christ*, if it could be printed as a true story, would be the most dramatic tale it would be possible to tell mankind. I felt that it *was* now possible to tell this story.

Beneath the *proof*: The coming of the Messiah shall be told in the heavens as well as on the earth, I wrote: *Fulfilled*.

In fact, it was at this point that I closed my file on the *Prophecies*. That part of *The Case of the Missing Millennium* was complete.

There was only one more obstacle to overcome. This hurdle faced every person who sincerely followed Christ's command to:

> 'Watch therefore: for ye know not what hour your Lord doth come.'[8]

If I were successful in overcoming this next obstacle, I felt that I would have without doubt solved for all time this century-old mystery of *the return of Christ*.

The obstacle could be stated in four words: 'Beware of false prophets!'

PART FIVE

THE FINAL EVIDENCE

1. Beware of False Prophets

Christ warned His followers to beware of false prophets and not to be misled by them before the Day of His *return*. He said:

> 'Take heed that no man deceive you.
> For many shall come in my name, saying, I am Christ; and shall deceive many.'[1]

Again He said:

> 'Then if any man shall say unto you, Lo, here is Christ, or there; believe it not.'[2]

Jesus warned His followers that there would not be one, but *many* false Christs and false prophets who

> '... shall shew great signs and wonders; insomuch that, if it were possible, they shall deceive the very elect.'[3]

It was to protect His followers from error that Christ gave them His three great promises concerning the proof of his return: (1) The Gospel would be preached everywhere; (2) the times of the Gentiles would be fulfilled; and (3) the abomination of desolation spoken of by Daniel would come to pass. He warned them to 'watch!' with spiritual eyes and ears for these proofs, so that they would not be misled. Christ knew that only the pure in heart would recognise Him in the day of His return. He knew that every Prophet had been called false by His own generation. It had been true of Himself as well.

Christ was considered, by the great mass of the people of His day, to be a 'false prophet'. It is written:

> 'And there was much murmuring among the people concerning him: for some said, He is a good man; others said, Nay; but he *deceiveth the people*.'[4]

When the simple, humble people went to their religious leaders and asked about the truth of Christ's Mission, they were told that He was a false prophet. They were warned against Him. Even though Christ showed signs and wonders that attracted people, the leaders still denied Him. This is shown clearly in the words:

> 'The officers answered, Never man spake like this man. Then answered them the Pharisees, *Are ye also deceived?*'[5]

The great separation between the few who considered Him true and the vast majority who considered Him false is clear from the words of John:

> 'So there was a division among the people because of him.'[6]

The public was told that only the lowest class believed in Christ, and that the important and influential people who had knowledge, education, and wisdom *knew* Christ to be false. It was pointed out to those foolish ones who wanted to believe:

> 'Have any of the rulers or of the Pharisees believed on him?'[7]

It was repeatedly said that only those ignorant ones who didn't know the book of Moses believed in Christ. These people were misled, and as false as Christ, the leaders warned, saying:

> '... this people who knoweth not the law are cursed.'[8]

The great public of Palestine did not believe in Jesus of Nazareth because He had not fulfilled their understanding of the prophecies concerning the coming of the Messiah.

To the followers of Christ who tried to win over their allegiance, the people replied scornfully that He, Christ, was a false prophet. They proved it from the prophecies in their Scriptures.

'The Messiah will sit upon the throne of David,' they pointed out. 'Where is the throne of the Nazarene?'

'Mount Zion will dance in the day of the Messiah. Who has yet seen this wonder?'

'The Messiah will rule with a sword. This Jesus does not even have a staff, let alone a sword.'

'He will be a son of David, yet you say he is born of a virgin. He cannot fulfil this prophecy.'

'Daniel has promised that He will be a prince. This Jesus is but a carpenter, and not a prince of noble birth.'

'It is written that a holy one will not hang upon a tree, yet this Nazarene was nailed to a tree and hung.'

'In *Deuteronomy* it states plainly:

". . . he that is hanged is accursed of God." '[9]

The Jews pointed out all these things to the Christians, asking, 'How can we believe in one who is accursed according to the book?'

One of the most difficult questions for the Christians to explain to the Jews was the prophecy that the Messiah would bring together the dispersed sheep of Israel. The Jews said: 'It is written of the Messiah that He will gather us out of the nations where we are scattered, but we are *not* scattered, we are *here*. How can he be a true prophet? How can he gather us if we are not separated?'

Later, after the year 70 A.D., when Jerusalem was destroyed

and the Jews scattered, this question was even harder to answer. For the Jews would then reply: 'The Messiah is to gather us together when He comes. Christ has come and we are driven out of our homeland. This is the opposite of what the Messiah is to do. Therefore, we think Him to be false. How can you expect us to believe?'

Philip met his friend Nathanial and said to him, 'We have found him of whom Moses wrote in the Law. He is Jesus of Nazareth.'

Nathanial, quoting Scripture, replied: 'Can there any good come out of Nazareth?'

Nicodemus said to the Pharisees concerning Jesus: 'Doth our law judge any man before it hear him, and know what he doeth?'

The Pharisees answered him from Scripture, saying, 'Art thou also of Galilee? Search, and look: for out of Galilee ariseth no prophet.'

The people of Palestine said honestly to themselves:

'How then can this Jesus of Nazareth be the Messiah?'

The people of that day were sceptical of Messiahs, especially those from Galilee. Within the time of many of them, Judas the Gaulonite had claimed to be the Messiah, and had arisen to free the Jews from the yoke of Rome. Many thousands perished in Galilee in the ensuing war, until Josephus, a contemporary historian, concluded 'that God had given up the Galileans to the Romans. . . .' This Jesus of Galilee might well be another such false Christ, they reasoned. It would be wiser to ignore him.

The followers of Jesus explained to the people that these prophecies concerning Christ had been fulfilled 'inwardly' not 'outwardly'; that these prophecies were to be understood *symbolically* and not *literally*. The people, however, refused to accept such an explanation.

Some of Christ's own followers eventually thought Him false too, because they could not understand the symbolical meaning of His parables.

It was the *inward* truth not the *outward* form which they must understand, He told them:

'... the flesh profiteth nothing; the words that I speak unto you, they are spirit, and they are life.'[10]

They heard from His lips words which they felt were contrary to all the things they had been taught for generations; and we are told:

'From that time many of his disciples went back, and walked no more with him.'[11]

His Holiness Christ was considered to be a false prophet for hundreds of years by many. To the present day the followers of Moses do not accept Christ as the Messiah, nor does the majority of mankind.

The Roman historian Tacitus wrote that the Christians were condemned by Nero 'for their enmity to mankind'. They were 'criminal, and deserving of exemplary punishment ...' Again he wrote that the Christian religion was a 'pernicious superstition'.

Suetonius, another Roman philosopher and historian, labelled the Holy Faith of Christ 'a new and magical superstition'. Its followers, he said, 'were continually making disturbances ...'

Celsus, in the second century, compiled a large book filled with terrible libels and dreadful stories of the sacred person of Jesus. Celsus wrote that His Holiness Christ was born out of wedlock, that he was little, ill-favoured, and ignoble, that because of poverty he went to Egypt and worked as a hired labourer, learning magic while there, that he went about begging and gathered round him ten or eleven infamous men.

Porphyry, one of the Neo-Platonic philosophers, wrote similar books which were later burned and destroyed by order of two Christian emperors.

The Emperor Julian, whom the Christians called the Apostate, attacked Christianity and Christ in his writings.

Fronto, the tutor of one of the emperors, published an oration against Christianity.

According to Mírzá Abu'l-Fadl, just a list of the writings of those who denied Christ and His Faith through the centuries would make a volume in itself.

The Messiah, it appears, can only be recognised by those who have 'eyes to see.' These spiritual souls must find the truth in His Teaching and His life through personal investigation. No man of perception will accept the words of an enemy of the Messiah as his own appraisal.

Yet how could a sincere seeker be sure? Surely God must have given some guide upon which His children could depend.

2. Enemy of the People

Christ knew that this same disbelief would be repeated in the day of His return. He warned His followers not to be misled by outward, physical wonders which might be worked in His name, but to look for the Figure Who would have that humble, loving, in-dwelling Spirit.

Whenever a Messenger of God such as Jesus, Moses, Zoroaster, Buddha, Muhammad, the Báb, or Bahá'u'lláh appears, He is considered to be a 'false prophet' by those who are not spiritually awake.

This is not a new problem. It did not begin with Christ or with Bahá'u'lláh. It is as old as the human race.

In that same chapter of Matthew in which Christ so clearly

foretold the time of His return, He also gives His strongest warnings about the *false prophets* in the *last days*. He says:

'Wherefore if they shall say unto you, Behold, he is in the desert; go not forth: behold, he is in the secret chambers; believe it not.'[1]

It is said that in the fifty years following the crucifixion, many people arose and claimed to be the Messiah, and throughout the centuries many have made this false claim.

In spite of these false prophets and fake Messiahs, Durant, in his *The Age of Faith*, says that the Jewish thinker Maimonides 'accepted the Messianic hope as an indispensable support to the Jewish spirit in the Dispersion, and made it one of the thirteen principal tenets of the Jewish Faith.'

Although both Christianity and Judaism eagerly awaited the coming of the Messiah, the great mass of believers lost interest and became indifferent, even though in both Faiths the coming Kingdom was spoken of in prayer each day.

And so I asked myself if there were not some positive way in which I could test Bahá'u'lláh to make certain that He was a true prophet, and not a false prophet.

Fortunately, there was a way. It was given us by Christ Himself. He gave all Christians an infallible method by which they could test each prophet that came.

'Beware of false prophets,' Christ warned, 'which come to you in *sheep's* clothing, but inwardly they are ravening wolves.'[2]

Christ promised that if we looked for the 'inward' truth and not the 'outward' appearance, we would know the true from the false, for:

'He that entereth in by the door (Gate) is the shepherd

of the sheep . . . he goeth before them, and the sheep follow him: for *they know his voice.*'[3]

Christ was clearly speaking of the day of His return in this warning, for He said:

' And other sheep I have, which are not of this fold (Christianity): them also I must bring, and they shall hear my voice; and there shall be *one fold, and one shepherd.*
Therefore doth my Father love me, because I lay down my life, *that I* might take it up again.'[4]

In the very prophecy in which Christ warns His followers to 'beware of false prophets', He gives them the method by which they can judge the *true* from the *false.* He has provided humanity with an unerring standard by which every person can determine for himself whether a prophet is *true* or *false.*

I found this standard in the seventh chapter of *Matthew.* In this one chapter Christ gives the warning concerning false prophets, and gives the measuring rod by which to judge them.

I felt that there was no excuse for me, or any other follower of Christ not to know the truth, for it is taken from His famous Sermon on the Mount.

'Beware of false prophets,' He warns, 'which come to you in sheep's clothing, but inwardly they are ravening wolves.
Ye shall know them by their fruits. Do men gather grapes of thorns, or figs of thistles?
Even so every good tree bringeth forth good fruit; but a corrupt tree bringeth forth evil fruit.
A good tree cannot bring forth evil fruit, neither can a corrupt tree bring forth good fruit . . .
Wherefore by their fruits ye shall know them.'

Therefore, I intended to use this sound basis for judgment. I would do as Christ Himself advised. I would judge Bahá'u'lláh by His fruits. I would measure Bahá'u'lláh according to the standard which Christ had given, knowing that it would prove once and for all whether Bahá'u'lláh had the right to be called the Messiah.

If the *fruit* is good, the *tree* is good; and the prophet is *true*. That would be my test.

I decided to make this one of my most fundamental proofs, for I felt that the solution to *The Case of the Missing Millenium* depended upon this one proof perhaps more than on any other.

3. The Tree of Life

Christ foretold that the One Who came in His name at *the time of the end* would be the 'Spirit of Truth:'

'. . . he will guide you into all truth. . .'[1]

In another place, He said:

'. . . he shall teach you all things, and bring all things to your remembrance, whatsoever I have said unto you.'[2]

And yet again:

'. . . he shall receive of mine, and shall shew it unto you.'[3]

I was determined to seek for the *inward* truth behind the *outward* symbol in Christ's words, for I found written in yet another place:

' . . . the word that I have spoken, the same shall judge him (the believer) *in the last day*.'[4]

Bahá'u'lláh, I found, had written over a hundred volumes. Here it is possible for me to mention but a few of His teachings, and in only the briefest manner. It is like trying to catch the ocean in a cup.

The scholar Charles Baudouin, in his book *Contemporary*

Studies, writes of Bahá'u'lláh's Teachings, saying that this 'ethical code is dominated by the law of love taught by Jesus and by all the prophets. In the thousand and one details of practical life, this law is subject to manifold interpretations. That of Bahá'u'lláh is unquestionably one of the most comprehensive of these, one of the most exalted, one of the most satisfactory to the modern mind . . .'[5]

The former President of Czechoslovakia, Eduard Benes wrote of Bahá'u'lláh's Teachings, 'The Bahá'í Cause is one of the great moral and social forces in all the world today.'[6] Mr. Benes wrote on another occasion, 'The Bahá'í Teaching is one of the spiritual forces now absolutely necessary to put the spirit first in this battle against material forces. . . . The Bahá'í Teaching is one of the great instruments for the final victory of the spirit and of humanity.'[7]

The scientist, Dr. Glenn A. Shook, inventor of the colour-organ, and former head of the Physics Department at Wheaton College, Norton, Massachusetts, wrote of Bahá'u'lláh's Teachings: 'Here is a mighty river of knowledge. It appeals to the scientist as well as to the layman. Bahá'u'lláh's Teachings meet the challenge of our age head-on, and offer sound, reasonable solutions. They have been an invaluable discovery to me as a scientist, and a treasure and comfort to me as an individual human being.'[8]

Queen Marie of Rumania wrote in the *Daily Star* of Toronto, Canada, on May 4th, 1926: 'If ever the name of Bahá'u'lláh (or His son) comes to your attention, do not put their writings from you. Search out their Books, and let their glorious, peace-bringing, love-creating words and lessons sink into your hearts as they have into mine.'[9]

Eight years later, she wrote: 'These books have strengthened me beyond belief and I am now ready to die any day full of hope. . . . The Bahá'í Teaching brings peace and understanding. . . . It accepts all great prophets gone before, it destroys no other creeds and leaves all doors open. . . . To those in search of assurance, the words of the Father are as a fountain in the desert after long wandering.'[10]

The following words of Bahá'u'lláh, I felt, reflected the spirit of His entire Teaching:

'O ye children of men! The fundamental purpose animating the Faith of God and His Religion is to safeguard the interests and promote the unity of the human race, and to foster the spirit of love and fellowship amongst men.'[11]

At this point, I began systematically to examine the *fruits* from the *tree of Bahá'u'lláh*, so that I might determine whether He was a *true* or a *false* prophet.

I searched out Bahá'u'lláh's words upon those subjects which I felt were nearest to my heart and to the heart of every human being. These subjects I thought were most vital to every man's welfare:

1. His home and family.
2. His country.
3. His religion.
4. His individual self.

The first *fruit* I planned to test was that relating to man's home and family.

4. The First Fruit: Home and Family

Bahá'u'lláh declares that the home and the family are sacred. These precious possessions are of the utmost importance for a useful and worthwhile life. He calls upon all mankind to honour the sanctity of marriage.

He forbids His followers to live lives of monastic seclusion.

According to Bahá'u'lláh it is not sufficient in this day to be good in isolation. We must be good in a group. A wholesome family life, He tells us, is the basis of society.

Bahá'u'lláh says:

> 'Enter ye into wedlock, that one may rise in your stead, for We have gainsaid impurity and enjoined fidelity upon you.'[1]

Dr. J. E. Esslemont in his analysis of the Teachings of Bahá'u'lláh writes: 'Whatever justification there may have been for the monastic life in ancient times and bygone circumstances, Bahá'u'lláh declares that such justification no longer exists; and, indeed, it seems obvious that the withdrawal of a large number of the most pious and God-fearing of the population from association with their fellows, and from the duties and responsibilities of parenthood, must result in the spiritual impoverishment of the race.'[2]

The Teachings of Bahá'u'lláh say:

> 'The Bahá'í betrothal is the perfect agreement and entire consent of both parties. They must show forth the utmost attention and become informed of one another's character. The firm covenant between them must become an eternal binding and their intentions must be everlasting affinity, friendship, unity and life. . . .
>
> 'The marriage of Bahá'ís means that the man and woman must become spiritually and physically united, so that they may have eternal unity throughout all the divine worlds, and improve the spiritual life of each other. This is Bahá'í matrimony.'[3]

Bahá'u'lláh advises all men and women to marry so that children may be raised up who can honour the name of God and who can render service to mankind.

Bahá'u'lláh's followers have been given the following counsel about their homes and their families: 'Make your home a haven of rest and peace. Be hospitable, and let the doors of your home be open to the faces of friends and strangers. Welcome every guest with radiant grace and let each feel that it is his home.

'Nourish continually the tree of your union with love and affection so that it may remain ever green throughout all seasons, and when God gives you sweet and lovely children, consecrate yourselves to their instruction and guidance so that they may become the servants of the world of humanity.'[4]

The son of Bahá'u'lláh, 'Abdu'l-Bahá, spoke in Paris on November 6th, 1911. He said: 'This is in truth a Bahá'í house.' He told the people who were gathered in that home that every time such a house is established in a community it must become known for the 'intense spirituality and for the love it spreads among the people.'

He said:

'Oh, friends of God! If ye will trust in the Word of God and be strong; if ye will follow the precepts of Bahá'u'lláh to tend the sick, raise the fallen, care for the poor and needy, give shelter to the destitute, protect the oppressed, comfort the sorrowful and love the world of humanity with all your hearts, then I say unto you that ere long this meeting-place will see a wonderful harvest . . . but ye must have a firm foundation and your aims and ambitions must be clearly understood by each member.

They shall be as follows:

1. To show compassion and goodwill to all mankind.
2. To render service to humanity.
3. To endeavour to guide and enlighten those in darkness.
4. To be kind to everyone, and show forth affection to every living soul.
5. To be humble in your attitude towards God, to be

constant in prayer to Him, so as to grow daily nearer to God.

6. To be so faithful and sincere in all your actions that every member may be known as embodying the qualitities of honesty, love, faith, kindness, generosity, and courage. To be detached from all that is not of God.'[5]

The home and family that fulfilled these conditions, He said, would be true to the teachings of Bahá'u'lláh.

This is one of the *fruits* taken from the *tree of Bahá'u'lláh* by which you may judge Him.

5. The Second Fruit: Country

The Teachings of Bahá'u'lláh, I found, say specifically:

'According to the direct and sacred command of God, we are forbidden to utter slander, are commanded to show forth peace and amity, are exhorted to rectitude of conduct, straightforwardness and harmony with all the kindreds and peoples of the world.'[1]

It is, these Teachings state further, the duty of every one of His followers to demonstrate their unqualified loyalty and obedience to their respective governments.[2]

The followers of Bahá'u'lláh are instructed to consider disloyalty unto a just government as disloyalty to God Himself. It is the sacred obligation of each individual Bahá'í, Bahá'u'lláh's Teachings state,

'. . . to promote, in the most effective manner, the best interests of their government and people.'[3]

According to the written word of the Bahá'í Teachings it is the sincere desire of every true and loyal follower,

'. . . to serve, in an unselfish, unostentatious and patriotic fashion, the highest interests of the country to which he belongs.'[4]

These Bahá'ís are willing to give their energies, even their lives, to the just government which does not require them to be disloyal to their love for God, and to the spiritual teachings given by Christ and Bahá'u'lláh.

Although the essence of Bahá'u'lláh's Teaching is the establishment of the unity of all nations, His words neither condemn nor disparage or censure an intelligent patriotism; nor do they in any way try to alter the natural, warm love one feels for one's native land.

The Teachings of Bahá'u'lláh's Faith say specifically that His Message concerning world government and world unity does not,

'. . . seek to undermine the allegiance and loyalty of any individual to his country, nor does it conflict with the legitimate aspirations, rights, and duties of any individual state or nation. All it does imply and proclaim is the in-sufficiency of patriotism, in view of the fundamental changes effected in the economic life of society and the interdependence of the nations, and as the consequence of the contraction of the world, through the revolution in the means of transportation and communication, conditions that did not and could not exist either in the days of Jesus Christ. . . . It calls for a wider loyalty, which should not, and indeed does not, conflict with lesser loyalties. It in-stills a love which, in view of its scope, must include and not exclude the love of one's own country. It lays, through this loyalty which it inspires, and this love which it infuses, the only foundation on which the concept of world citizenship can thrive, and the structure of world unifica-tion can rest. It does insist, however, on the subordination of national considerations and particularistic interests to the imperative and paramount claims of humanity as a whole,

214

inasmuch as in the world of interdependent nations and peoples the advantage of the part is best to be reached by the advantage of the whole.'[5]

Bahá'u'lláh's Teachings not only demand that His followers be loyal to their government, but they are also specifically and firmly forbidden to take part in any subversive political or social movement.

Viscount Samuel, High Commissioner for Palestine under the British Mandate, wrote of the Faith of Bahá'u'lláh in August, 1959 that the Bahá'ís 'were generally regarded as a valuable element in the population, intelligent, orderly, well-educated, and above all, trustworthy. In Government service and in commercial employment they were much esteemed as being free from corruptibility . . . well-behaved, courteous to others . . .' The Bahá'í Faith, Samuel said, 'commands the respect and goodwill of its neighbours.'[6]

That the Bahá'í makes an honest, useful, and desirable citizen in every land, becomes apparent from these words of counsel which Bahá'u'lláh gives His followers:

1. 'It is incumbent upon every man, in this Day, to hold fast unto whatsoever will promote the interests, and exalt the station of all nations and just governments.'[7]
2. 'Let integrity and uprightness distinguish all thine acts.'[8]
3. 'That one indeed is a man who, today, dedicateth himself to the service of the entire human race.'[9]
4. 'Beautify your tongues, O people, with truthfulness, and adorn your souls with the ornament of honesty. Beware, O people, that ye deal not treacherously with anyone. Be ye the trustees of God amongst His creatures . . .'[10]

This is another *fruit* by which you may test the *tree of Bahá'u'lláh*.

215

6. The Third Fruit: Religion

Bahá'u'lláh has written:

'O ye people of the world! The Religion of God is for the sake of love and union; make it not the cause of enmity and conflict . . . by this one Word shall the diverse sects of the world attain unto the light of real union.'[1]

Bahá'u'lláh teaches that just as there is only *one God*, there is also only *one religion*. All the great Prophets have taught this same one religion. There is, Bahá'u'lláh tells us, no exclusive salvation for the Hindu, the Jew, the Zoroastrian, the Buddhist, the Christian, the Muslim, or the Bahá'í.

The Bahá'í Faith is not a sect, but an independent religion. The famous historian Arnold Toynbee was asked about Bahá'u'lláh's Faith. He replied: 'My opinion is that (1) Bahá'ísm is undoubtedly a religion, (2) Bahá'ísm is an independent religion, on a par with Islám, Christianity, and the other recognized world religions. Bahá'ísm is not a sect of some other religion; it is a separate religion, and it has the same status as other recognized religions.

'This opinion is based both on study and on personal acquaintance with Bahá'ís.'[2]

All these pure and holy Faiths are part of the one eternal religion of God which goes on for ever. No single religion is the one exclusive Faith, or the final outpouring of truth from Almighty God.

Each religion is true, is beautiful, is valid. It is the *one* Message from God for that age in which it appears. It is the *only* truth for that particular age, yet it is not final. It is but one part of a single, great, progressive, never-ending religion of God which has no beginning and will have no end.

Though the Word (Holy Spirit) of God is one, the Speakers

(Messengers) of this Word are many. It is the one light in many lamps.

The *golden rule* can be found in all the great religions of the world:

> *Hinduism :* The true rule is to do by the things of others as you do by your own.
>
> *Judaism :* Whatever you do not wish your neighbour to do to you do not to him.
>
> *Zoroastrianism :* As you do you will be done by.
>
> *Buddhism :* One should seek for others the happiness one desires for one's self.
>
> *Christianity :* Therefore, all things whatsoever you would that men should do to you, do ye even so to them.
>
> *Islám :* Let none of you treat a brother in a way he himself would dislike to be treated.
>
> *Bahá'í Faith :* If thou regardest Mercy, look not to that which benefits thyself; but hold to that which will benefit thy fellowmen. If thou regardest Justice, choose thou for others that which thou choosest for thyself.

The Teachings of Bahá'u'lláh liken religion to the growth of a plant. Dr. Esslemont who spent many years studying the Teachings of Bahá'u'lláh states it in this way: 'The religion of God is the One Religion, and all the Prophets have taught it, but it is a living and a growing thing, not lifeless and un-changing. In the teaching of Moses we see the bud; in that of Christ the flower; in that of Bahá'u'lláh the fruit. The flower does not destroy the bud, nor does the fruit destroy the flower. It destroys not, but fulfils. The bud-scales must fall in order that the flower may bloom, and the petals must fall that the fruit may grow and ripen. Were the bud-scales and the petals wrong or useless, then, that they had to be dis-carded? No, both in their time were right and necessary;

without them there could have been no fruit. So it is with the various prophetic teachings; their externals change from age to age, but each revelation is the fulfilment of its predecessors; they are not separate nor incongruous, but different stages in the life history of One Religion, which has in turn been revealed as seed, as bud, and as flower, and now enters on the stage of fruition.'[3]

Thus, one step is not greater than another. No step is exclusive. No stage is final. Not even the stage of the 'fruit'. The 'fruit' is the fulfilment of the 'seed'. It is the end of a cycle, but from that 'fruit' will come the 'seed' of another great cycle. The Religion of God is continuous and never-ending and like the rain, never ceases to shed its water of life upon mankind.

This oneness and progressive unfoldment of spiritual truth can be shown from the Bible. Moses, knowing that His followers could not understand all of His teachings, said:

> 'The Lord thy God will raise up unto thee a prophet from the midst of thee of thy brethren, like unto me; unto him ye shall hearken.'[4]

This foretold the coming of Christ. When He came, Christ reminded the people of His day about these words of Moses. Christ said:

> 'For had ye believed Moses, ye would have believed me, for he wrote of me.'[5]

Then Christ rebuked them for being blind. He said:

> 'But if ye believe not his writings, how shall ye believe my words?'[6]

At a later time, Christ spoke almost the same words to *His* followers that Moses had spoken to those who had followed

Him. Christ knew that His followers could not understand all that He had taught them. He was disappointed many times by their failure to perceive His meaning. He promised them that another would come and explain these hidden truths to mankind. He said:

'I have yet many things to say unto you, but ye cannot bear them now. Howbeit, when he, the Spirit of truth, is come, he will guide you into all truth. . . .'[7]

This foretold the coming of the Messiah. When Bahá'u'lláh came, He reminded the people of His day about these words of Christ. He said:

'Heard ye not the saying of Jesus, the Spirit of God. . . . He saith: "When He, the Spirit of Truth is come, He will guide you unto all truth." '[8]

Then Bahá'u'lláh rebuked them for being blind. He said:

'Wherefore, then, did ye fail . . . to draw nigh unto Him? . . . And yet . . . ye refused to turn your faces towards Him.'[9]

Bahá'u'lláh addressed special letters to the heads of Christianity. These letters can be studied. He urged them to lead their flocks into the sacred fold. Among His words are these:

'Come, O ye people. . . . Tarry not, even for an hour!'[10]

Bahá'u'lláh proclaims:

'Truly, I say, whatever lowers the lofty station of religion will increase heedlessness in the wicked.'[11]

Bahá'u'lláh also counsels the people of all religions to follow the precepts given by Christ in His famous Sermon:

'Show forth that which is declared by the Speaker of the Mount (Jesus the Christ), and . . . render justice in affairs.'[12]

219

Bahá'u'lláh upholds the oneness of religion and the Prophets throughout His Writings. In one instance He says:

'Know thou assuredly that the essence of all the Prophets of God is one and the same. Their unity is absolute. God, the Creator, saith: "There is no distinction whatsoever among the Bearers of My Message. They all have but one purpose; their secret is the same secret. To prefer one in honour to another, to exalt certain ones above the rest, is in no wise to be permitted. Every true Prophet hath regarded His Message as fundamentally the same as the Revelation of every other Prophet gone before Him'. If any man, therefore, should fail to comprehend this truth, and should consequently indulge in vain and unseemly language, no one whose sight is keen and whose understanding is enlightened would ever allow such idle talk to cause him to waver in his belief." '13

Bahá'u'lláh addresses the people of the religions of the world, saying:

'Blessed are they who hold fast to the rope of compassion and kindness and are detached from animosity and hatred.'14

The great tragedy of religion, Bahá'u'lláh tells us, is that mankind remembers the Messenger and forgets the Message. Sainte Beuve told the people of France that they would be members of sects long after they had ceased to be Christians, They were more interested in the lamp than in the light.

The Prophets are all mirrors in which the sun of God's truth shines. The mirror is not the truth. The light that shines in it is the truth. Christ emphasised this truth, saying it was God in Whom the people must believe, not in Him, Jesus. He said:

'He that believeth on me, believeth not on me, but on him that sent me.'15

Bahá'u'lláh speaks of the Founders of all the world's religions with great love, tenderness and beauty. He counsels His followers to look upon the people of all beliefs with radiance and friendliness. He reminds them:

'Ye are all the leaves of one tree and the drops of one ocean.'

In *The Coming World Teacher*, Pavri writes: '. . . among the Bahá'ís is that remarkable movement emphasising the Brotherhood of Religions, a brotherhood which the Teacher, alike of gods and men, alone can make possible.'

Bahá'u'lláh calls upon His followers to dedicate their lives to the well-being and happiness of the people of all religions and nations. To those who would follow Him, He says:

'Address yourselves to the promotion of the well-being and tranquillity of the children of men. Bend your minds and wills to the education of the peoples and kindreds of the earth, that haply the dissensions that divide it may, through the power of the Most Great Name (of God), be blotted out from its face, and all mankind become the upholders of one Order, and the inhabitants of one City. Illumine and hallow your hearts; let them not be profaned by the thorns of hate or the thistles of malice. Ye dwell in one world, and have been created through the operation of one Will. Blessed is he who mingleth with all men in a spirit of utmost kindliness and love.'[16]

This is another *fruit* by which you may test the *tree of Bahá'u'lláh* and judge His life.

7. The Fourth Fruit: Individual Life

Bahá'u'lláh has explained that the purpose of His own coming, and of the coming of Jesus the Christ, as well as that of all the other Prophets, is,

'To effect a transformation in the whole character of mankind, a transformation that shall manifest itself both outwardly and inwardly, that shall affect both its inner life and external conditions.'[1]

The underlying reason for which a Messenger of God appears, Bahá'u'lláh tells us, is,

'To educate the souls (and to) refine the character of every living man.'[2]

Bahá'u'lláh has repeatedly emphasised the absolute necessity of a pure and holy individual life. His Teachings stress:

'The most vital duty, in this day, is to purify your characters, to correct your manners, and improve your conduct.'[3]

The followers of His Faith,

'Must show forth such character and conduct among His creatures, that the fragrance of their holiness may be shed upon the whole world, and may quicken the (spiritually) dead.'[4]

Bahá'u'lláh wrote an entire book upon the subject of the individual life of the believers in God. It is called *The Hidden Words*.

George Townshend, former Archdeacon of Clonfert and Canon of St. Patrick's Cathedral in Dublin, wrote of this book: '*The Hidden Words* is not a digest, nor an ordered statement. It is a new creation. It is a distillation of Sacred Fragrances. It is a focus in which all the Great Lights of the past are joined into one Light, and all God's Yesterdays become Today.

'It is given us as a single spiritual force, instinct with the presence of all the Spiritual Monarchs of the past. . . . No book radiant with such intensity of light has ever been given or could have been given to mankind before. It contains the whole sum of all Revelations rounding to their completeness, renewed in power, and brought to the perfection of unity by the crowning words of Bahá'u'lláh.'[5]

Bahá'u'lláh Himself says of *The Hidden Words*:

'This is that which hath descended from the realm of glory, uttered by the tongue of power and might, and revealed unto the Prophets of old. We have taken the inner essence thereof and clothed it in the garment of brevity, as a token of grace unto the righteous, that they may stand faithful unto the Covenant of God, may fulfil in their lives His trust, and in the realm of spirit obtain the gem of Divine virtue.'

The Book begins:

'O SON OF SPIRIT!
The best beloved of all things in My sight is Justice; turn not away therefrom if thou desirest Me, and neglect it not that I may confide in thee. By its aid thou shalt see with thine own eyes and not through the eyes of others, and shalt know of thine own knowledge and not through the knowledge of thy neighbour. Ponder this in thy heart; how it behooveth thee to be. Verily justice is My gift to thee and the sign of My loving-kindness. Set it then before thine eyes.'

This spirit of justice and uprightness has been mentioned by Supreme Court Justice William O. Douglas in his book *West of the Indus*. He speaks of his visit to Iran, the land of the birth of Bahá'u'lláh and His Faith. Of the followers of Bahá'u'lláh in that land, Douglas says: 'The Bahá'ís have many business-men among their numbers. They enjoy a fine reputation as merchants. The reason is that they maintain a high ethical standard in all their dealings. Merchants in the bazaars are quick to take advantage; they will cheat and palm off false or inferior goods. Never the Bahá'ís. They are scrupulous in their dealings; and as a result, they grow in prestige.'

The following verses from *The Hidden Words* will convey the spirit of the Words of Bahá'u'lláh:

'O YE RICH ONES ON EARTH!
The poor in your midst are My trust; guard ye My trust, and be not intent only on your own ease.'

'O SON OF BEING!
How couldst thou forget thine own faults and busy thyself with the faults of others? Whoso doeth this is accursed of Me.'

'O SON OF MAN!
Breathe not the sins of others so long as thou art thyself a sinner.'

'O MY SERVANT!
Free thyself from the fetters of this world, and loose thy soul from the prison of self. Seize thy chance for it will come to thee no more.'

Throughout His Writings Bahá'u'lláh expresses such thoughts as these:

'The essence of faith is fewness of words and abundance of deeds. . . . Beware lest ye walk in the ways of them whose words differ from their deeds. . . . Men must show forth fruits. A fruitless man, in the words of His Holiness the Spirit (Jesus the Christ), is like a fruitless tree, and is fit for the fire. . . . Let your acts be a guide to all mankind. It is through your deeds that ye can distinguish yourselves from others. Through them the brightness of your light can be shed upon the whole earth.'

The Teachings of Bahá'u'lláh offer such counsels on individual behaviour as follows:

'Do not be content with showing friendship in words alone, let your heart burn with loving-kindness for all who may cross your path.'[6]

'Show the utmost kindness and compassion to the sick and suffering. This has greater effect than the remedy itself. You must always have this love . . . and affection when you visit the ailing and afflicted.'[7]

After examining the writings of the Bahá'í Faith, the great Tolstoy, author of *War and Peace*, said that the Teachings of Bahá'u'lláh, 'Now present us with the highest and purest form of religious teaching.'[8]

Anyone who becomes a follower of Bahá'u'lláh accepts as binding upon his own individual and inner life, the following words:

'O ye beloved of the Lord! In this sacred Dispensation, conflict and contention are in no wise permitted. Every aggressor deprives himself of God's grace. It is incumbent upon everyone to show the utmost love, rectitude of conduct, straightforwardness and sincere kindliness unto all the peoples and kindreds of the world, be they friends or strangers.

'So intense must be the spirit of love and loving-kindness, that the stranger may find himself a friend, the enemy a true brother, no difference whatsoever existing between them. For universality is of God and all limitations earthly. . . . In like manner, the affections and loving-kindness of the servants of the One True God must be bountifully and universally extended to all mankind. Regarding this, restrictions and limitations are in no wise permitted.

'Wherefore, O my loving friends! Consort with all the peoples, kindreds, and religions of the world with the utmost truthfulness, uprightness, faithfulness, kindliness, good-will and friendliness; that all the world . . . may be filled with the holy ecstasy of the grace of Bahá, that ignorance, enmity, hate and rancour may vanish from the world and the darkness of estrangement amidst the peoples and kindreds of the world may give way to the Light of Unity. Should other peoples and nations be unfaithful to you show your fidelity to them, should they be unjust toward you show justice towards them, should they keep aloof from you attract them to yourself, . . . should they poison your lives sweeten their souls, should they inflict a wound upon you be a salve to their sores. Such are the attributes of the sincere! Such are the attributes of the truthful.'[9]

The Reverend J. Tyssul Davis in his book *A League of Religions* has spoken of the pattern of individual life set by Bahá'u'lláh. He writes: 'The Bahá'í religion has made its way . . . because it meets the needs of its day. It fits the larger outlook of our time better than the rigid exclusive older faiths. A characteristic is its unexpected liberality and toleration. It accepts all the great religions as true and their scriptures as inspired. . . . Their ethical ideal is very high and is of the type we Westerners have learnt to designate "Christlike". "What does he do to his enemies that he makes them his friends?" was asked concerning the late leader. What astonishes the student is not anything in the ethics or philosophy of this movement, but the extraordinary response its ideal has awakened in such numbers of people, the powerful influence this standard actually exerts on conduct. . . . "By their fruits shall ye know them!" We cannot but address to this youthful religion an All Hail! of welcome. We cannot fail to see in its activity another proof of the living witness in our own day of the working of the sleepless spirit of God in the hearts of men. . . .'[10]

Bahá'u'lláh has given the following standard of personal conduct for each of His followers to observe:

'Be generous in prosperity, and thankful in adversity. Be worthy of the trust of thy neighbour, and look upon him with a bright and friendly face. Be a treasure to the poor, . . . an answerer of the cry of the needy. . . . Be unjust to no man. . . . Be as . . . a joy to the sorrowful, a sea for the thirsty, a haven for the distressed, an upholder and defender of the victim of oppression. . . . Be a home for the stranger, a balm to the suffering, a tower of strength for the fugitive. Be eyes to the blind, and a guiding light unto the feet of the erring, . . . a breath of life to the body of mankind. . . .'[11]

This is another *fruit* taken from the *tree of Bahá'u'lláh*. Christ said: "By their fruits ye shall know them." This is one of the *fruits* by which I was able to judge whether or not Bahá'u'lláh was a true or a false prophet.

8. A Searching Eye

The Irish scholar George Townshend, sometime Archdeacon of Clonfert, states that when modern thinkers speak of world government, social security, an international language, world courts and human rights, they are merely 'ringing the changes' on themes which were set down in everlasting language by Bahá'u'lláh nearly one hundred years ago.

The following sections give but a small selection of other *fruits* I have gathered from this living tree which Bahá'u'lláh has planted in the world.

Each individual shall make his own independent search after truth.

Bahá'u'lláh not only approves of, but strongly encourages, the use of scientific methods in approaching a solution to our problems. To quote Dr. J. E. Esslemont: 'Bahá'u'lláh asked no one to accept His statements and His tokens blindly. On the contrary, He put in the very forefront of His Teachings emphatic warnings against blind acceptance of authority, and urged all to open their eyes and ears, and to use their own judgment, independently and fearlessly, in order to ascertain the truth. He enjoined the fullest investigation and never concealed Himself, offering, as the supreme proofs of His Prophethood, His words and works and their effects in transforming the lives and characters of men.'[1]

Bahá'u'lláh Himself said:

'Look into everything with a searching eye.'

Each individual human being should investigate spiritual truth for himself. His relationship to Almighty God is the responsibility of no one but himself. He can, and should, learn from the knowledge and experience of others, but he should not accept their findings as the final truth for himself without a careful personal investigation.

That this search for spiritual truth would require constant effort we are told in the Bible. *Deuteronomy* says:

'If from thence thou shalt seek the Lord thy God, thou shalt find him, if thou seek him with all thy heart and with all thy soul.'[2]

The prophet Jeremiah echoes this, saying:

'And ye shall seek me, and find me, when ye shall search for me with all your heart.'[3]

In the very chapter in which Christ warned about false prophets and said 'By their fruits ye shall know them', He told his followers to search earnestly:

'Seek, and ye shall find; knock, and it shall be opened unto you . . . and he that seeketh findeth; and to him that knocketh it shall be opened.'[4]

Bahá'u'lláh has written:

'Arise, therefore, and with the whole enthusiasm of your hearts, with all the eagerness of your souls, the full fervour of your will, and the concentrated efforts of your entire being, strive to attain the paradise of His presence.'[5]

Bahá'u'lláh, like Christ, warned that it would not be easy, for 'many are called but few are chosen'. He said:

'Only when the lamp of search, of earnest striving, of longing desire, of passionate devotion . . . is kindled within the seeker's heart . . . will the darkness of error be dispelled, the mists of doubts and misgivings be dissipated, and the lights of knowledge and certitude envelop his being.'[6]

This search after truth, Bahá'u'lláh taught, was not the entire aim of life. Once the truth was found, it should not be put aside. It must take root in the heart of the seeker and bear fruit in his life, or he would not benefit therefrom. Bahá'u'lláh says that He desires:

'The freedom of man from superstition and imitation, so that he may discern the Manifestations (Messengers) of God with the eye of Oneness, and consider all affairs with a keen sight.'[7]

The Teachings of Bahá'u'lláh's Faith say plainly: 'The greatest gift of God to man is his intelligence.'
He must use it to the full to discover the truth.
This is another *fruit* from the *tree of Bahá'u'lláh*.

9. The Bird with Two Wings
Men and women should enjoy equal rights, privileges, education, and opportunities throughout the world.

Bahá'u'lláh attached great importance to this principle. His Teachings emphasise the fact that since the mother is the first teacher of the child during its early and formative years, it is most necessary that the mother should have a good education.

The universal education which Bahá'u'lláh advocates would give an equal position to boys and girls.

The Bahá'í Teachings say that when the station of woman is elevated until it is equal to that of man everywhere in the entire world, the stability and wholesomeness of social affairs throughout the world will be greatly improved.

The Teachings of Bahá'u'lláh also say:

'If the mother is educated, then her children will be well taught. When the mother is wise, then will the children be led into the path of wisdom. If the mother be religious she will show her children how they should love God. If the mother is moral she guides her little ones into the ways of uprightness.'[1]

This raising of the status of women is one of the fundamental principles of Bahá'u'lláh.

It is written in His Teachings:

'Humanity is like a bird with its two wings—the one is male, the other female. Unless both wings are strong and impelled by some common force, the bird cannot fly heavenwards. According to the spirit of this age, women must advance and fulfil their mission in all departments of life, becoming equal to men. They must ... enjoy equal rights.'[2]

These Teachings of Bahá'u'lláh were given in an age when the station of women was very low in all parts of the world, and in some parts she was considered to be only slightly higher than the animals.

One of the great early teachers of this Faith was a woman. Her name was Táhirih, which means 'the pure one'. She was martyred for her belief. Before her death she worked earnestly for her Faith and for the advancement of women. She was called the first woman suffrage martyr. Bravely and defiantly she cried out to her captors: 'You can kill me as soon as you like, but you cannot stop the emancipation of women.'[3]

Professor E. G. Browne said that if this Faith had no other claim to greatness, it would be sufficient that it had produced a heroine such as Táhirih. Sir Valentine Chirol wrote that 'No memory is more deeply venerated or kindles greater enthusiasm than hers, and the influence which she wielded in her lifetime still inures to her sex.'[4]

This is another *fruit* taken from the *tree of Bahá'u'lláh*.

10. The Real Treasury

Education must be made available to all.

Education is the real treasury of mankind, Bahá'u'lláh tells us, and the teacher is the most potent factor in civilisation. His or her work is one of the highest to which mankind can aspire.

Education has been the supreme aim of all the holy Prophets since the world began, and in the Faith of Bahá'u'lláh, the fundamental importance and limitless possibilities of education are proclaimed in the clearest terms. When education on the right lines becomes general, humanity will be transformed, and the world will become a paradise.

Bahá'u'lláh has written the following 'concerning sciences, crafts and arts':

'Knowledge is like unto wings for the being, and is as a ladder for ascending. To acquire knowledge is incumbent on all, but of those sciences which may profit the earth, and not such sciences as begin in mere words and end in

231

mere words. The possessors of sciences and arts have a great right among the people of the world. . . . Indeed, the real treasure of man is his knowledge. Knowledge is the means of honour, prosperity, joy, gladness, happiness and exultation.'[1]

It is not sufficient to gain mere knowledge. It is equally important to know how to make right decisions. Therefore, education in character training is of vital importance. Knowledge alone does not guarantee wisdom.

'Filling the memory with facts about grammar, geography, languages, arithmetic, etc., has comparatively little effect in producing noble and useful lives' unless it is accompanied by moral education as well.

Dr. Esslemont, writing of Bahá'u'lláh's Teachings, says: 'At present a really well-educated man is the rarest of phenomena, for nearly everyone has false prejudices, wrong ideals, erroneous conceptions and bad habits drilled into him from babyhood. How few are taught from their earliest childhood to love God with all their hearts and dedicate their lives to Him; to regard service to humanity as the highest aim of life; to develop their powers to the best advantage for the general good of all! Yet surely these are the essential elements of a good education.'[2]

Nearly a century ago Bahá'u'lláh declared the vital necessity of compulsory education for the children of the world. If the parents are unable to assume this responsibility, He said, then the community must do so. Children are like green and tender branches, and if the early training is right, they will grow straight and strong. If it is wrong, the children will grow crooked and weak. They will be affected to the very end of their lives by the education they receive in their earliest and all important years.

Bahá'u'lláh

'Enjoins upon all to instruct and educate the children. . . .
He who educates his son, or any other's children, it is as
though he hath educated one of My children.'[3]

This is another *fruit* by which you may test the *tree of
Bahá'u'lláh*.

11. No Man is a Stranger

*An international (auxiliary) language must be taught throughout
the world in addition to the mother tongue of each nation.*

Bahá'u'lláh has instructed that a universal language must be
either adopted from one of the existing languages, or fashioned
as a new language. This will greatly aid in breaking down the
barriers of misunderstanding that exist between the nations
and peoples and will benefit the flow of commerce throughout
the world.

This international language would be an *auxiliary* one. Each
land would keep the beauty and charm of its own mother
tongue, but would learn in addition the international *auxiliary*
language.

Bahá'u'lláh pointed out that this universal language was
essential to the establishment of a lasting world peace. It was
another step which He had taken to bring the nations of the
earth together in harmony and cooperation in this *last day*.
This world language was also prophesied in the Scriptures
for that *great and dreadful day of the Lord* when the nations would
be gathered together.

The *Old Testament* prophesies:

'My determination is to gather the nations. . . . For then
will I turn to the people a *pure language*, that they may all call
upon the name of the Lord, to serve Him with one consent.'[1]

Bahá'u'lláh's Teachings say:

'It will make the whole world one home and become the strongest impulse for human advancement. It will upraise the standard of the oneness of humanity. It will make the earth one universal commonwealth.'[2]

The name of Bahá'u'lláh is never translated into any other than this one form. Moses is sometimes called Moise; Jesus is known as Jesu or Jeshua, but Bahá'u'lláh is always written and pronounced Bahá'u'lláh.

Thus the meaning behind the words of the prophet Zechariah were fulfilled:

'And the Lord shall be King over all the earth: *in that day* shall there be one Lord, and his name one.'[3]

To those national leaders who hold the welfare of the world in their hands, Bahá'u'lláh issued a commandment:

'To choose one of the existing tongues, or to originate a new one, and in like manner to adopt a common script, teaching these to the children in all the schools of the world, that the world may become even as one land and one home.'[4]

If this single principle of Bahá'u'lláh were to be adopted by the nations of the world, the differences of language, and the misunderstandings that arise from these differences, would be erased in one generation.

Bahá'u'lláh wrote 'concerning union and harmony among mankind':

'The greatest means is that the peoples should be familiar with each other's writing and language. . . . The most splendid fruit of the tree of Knowledge is this exalted Word: "Ye are all fruits of one tree and leaves of one branch." '[5]

This is yet another *fruit* from the *tree of Bahá'u'lláh* by which we may judge Him.

12. Partners in Progress

Religion must agree with science and reason, or it is mere superstition.

The Teachings of Bahá'u'lláh's Faith say plainly:

'Whatever the intelligence of man cannot understand, religion ought not to accept. Religion and science walk hand in hand, and any religion contrary to science is not the truth.'[1]

To quote again from Dr. J. E. Esslemont's analysis of Bahá'u'lláh's Teachings: 'One of the fundamental teachings of Bahá'u'lláh is that true science and true religion must always be in harmony. Truth is one and whenever conflict appears it is due, not to truth, but to error. Between so-called science and so-called religion there have been fierce conflicts all down the ages, but looking back on these conflicts in the light of fuller truth (as given by Bahá'u'lláh) we can trace them every time to ignorance, prejudice, vanity, greed, narrow-mindedness, intolerance, obstinacy, or something of the kind—something foreign to the true spirit of both science and religion, for the spirit of both is one.'[2]

The point is expressed in the words of Thomas Huxley: 'The great deeds of philosophers have been less the fruit of their intellect than the direction of that intellect by an eminently religious tone of mind. Truth has yielded herself rather to their patience, their love, their single-heartedness and self-denial than to their logical acumen.'[3]

The famous mathematician, Boole, states: 'Geometric induction is essentially a process of prayer—an appeal from the finite mind to the Infinite for light on finite concerns.'[4]

The Bahá'í Teachings, speaking of the day of the 'one fold and one shepherd' foretold in all the Holy Books of the past,

235

say: 'In such a world society, *science and religion*, the two most potent forces in human life, will be reconciled, will cooperate, and will harmoniously develop.'[5]

The word 'science' itself comes from the root infinitive 'scire', *to know*. There is no room for prejudice or privilege in the same room with true knowledge. Man must set his preconceived ideas aside when he searches for truth, be it material or spiritual. The harmony between science and religion is evident throughout the Teachings of Bahá'u'lláh. The manner in which His followers are instructed to seek the truth makes this principle crystal clear:

'In order to find truth we must give up our prejudices, our own small trivial notions; an open receptive mind is essential. If our chalice is full of self, there is no room in it for the water of life. The fact that we imagine ourselves to be right and everybody else (to be) wrong is the greatest of all obstacles in the path towards unity, and unity is essential if we would reach the Truth, for Truth is one . . . No one truth can contradict another truth. Light is good in whatsoever lamp it is burning! A rose is beautiful in whatsoever garden it may bloom. . . . When we are free from all these bonds, seeking with liberated minds, th shall we be able to arrive at our goal.'[6]

Perfect harmony between science and religion is essent for the happy, peaceful life of society. If religion dominates science, the world falls into superstition and bigotry. If science dominates religion, we fall into excessive materialism and corruption.

We need a high moral quality in our religious life in order to give the powers of *science* the proper direction so that its tremendous force may be used for the welfare of mankind and not for its destruction.

The Teachings of Bahá'u'lláh say:

'When religion, shorn of its superstitions, traditions and unintelligent dogmas, shows its conformity with science, then there will be a great unifying, cleansing force in the world, which will sweep before it all wars, disagreements, discords, and struggles, and then will mankind be united in the power of the love of God.'[7]

This is another of the *fruits* from the *tree of Bahá'u'lláh's Teaching*.

13. The Beauty of the Rainbow

All men are the children of one Father, God, and are the brothers and sisters of one human family.

The followers of the Faith of Bahá'u'lláh are given the following commandment:

'You will be the servants of God, who are dwelling near to Him, His divine helpers in the service, ministering to all humanity. ALL humanity! Every human being! Never forget this!'[1]

Bahá'u'lláh has written:

'Blessed is he who prefers his brother before himself.'[2]

However great the conqueror may be, he is finally entombed possessionless. He keeps but one small plot of earth for his bones. Thus every warrior is interred. The earth, Bahá'u'lláh tells us, belongs to God, and man is tenant here for but a brief span. His greatest possession, next to love of God, is love for his fellow-man.

Bahá'u'lláh insists that devotion to God implies a life that is devoted to the service of our fellow human beings. We cannot serve God unless we serve humanity. If we turn our backs upon our fellow-man, we are turning our backs upon God. Christ said:

> 'Inasmuch as ye did it not to one of the least of these, ye did it not to me.'[3]

In the Teachings of Bahá'u'lláh we can hear the echo of the words of Christ, Who said of the One who would come after Him: 'He shall take of mine and shew it unto you.'

Bahá'u'lláh tells us that the solution to the problem of racial prejudice is the elimination of racial consciousness. We should look upon our fellowmen, not as yellow, red, brown, black, white, but as children of our common Father, God.

The differences in colour among human beings are really factors of pleasing variety and beauty, and should not be causes of prejudice and division. They should be regarded as the many different colours of a garden whose variety adds to the beauty of the whole.

The problem of brotherhood varies with different areas of the world. In some there is a class problem, in others that of caste, in others of religion, in still others that of race. The corrosion of these prejudices has eaten into the fabric of human society.

It is not sufficient merely to believe that these things are wrong, and to accept the fact that they are wrong intellectually. We must *behave* as though we knew they were wrong, and we must correct them. Every man has the power to remove these prejudices from his own life.

The Bahá'í Teachings say plainly that:

> 'To discriminate against any race, on the ground of its being socially backward, politically immature, and numerically in a minority, is a flagrant violation of the spirit that animates the Faith of Bahá'u'lláh. The consciousness of any division or cleavage in its ranks is alien to its very purpose,

principles, and ideals . . . every differentiation of class, creed, or colour must automatically be obliterated, and never be allowed, under any pretext, and however great the pressure of events or of public opinion, to reassert itself. . . . Unlike the nations and peoples of the earth, be they of the East or of the West, democratic or authoritarian, communist or capitalist, whether belonging to the Old World or the New, who either ignore, trample upon, or extirpate, the racial, religious, or political minorities within the sphere of their jurisdiction, every organised community, enlisted under the banner of Bahá'u'lláh should feel it to be its first and inescapable obligation to nurture, encourage, and safeguard every minority belonging to any faith, race, class or nation within it.'[4]

When love of God and love of one's fellow-man die out in any land, the followers of prejudice and hate have their hour. They dethrone God from the human heart and exalt gods of their own making. These false gods are: the superiority of Nation, Race, Class and Creed. These are unsound and destructive beliefs. They would have one nation dominate all others. They would subordinate the many-hued peoples of the world to one of the shades of face among them. They would discriminate between the black and the white, yellow and brown, white and yellow, etc. They would tolerate the domination of one privileged class over all others. They would tamper with a man's right to believe and worship as he chooses. These are dark, crooked and false doctrines. The man, the people, and the nation which believes in them and acts upon them must sooner or later incur the wrath and chastisement of God.[5]

Bahá'u'lláh has written:

'This handful of dust, the earth, is one home: let it be in unity.'[6]

Freedom from racial prejudice, in any of its forms, should be adopted as the watchword of society in this day. The banishment of all prejudice is one of the basic Teachings of Bahá'u'lláh's Faith.

'God maketh no distinction between the white and the black. If the hearts are pure both are acceptable unto Him. God is no respecter of persons on account of either colour or race . . . all men are equal. There is no distinction or preference for any soul. . . . Colour is not important: the heart is all-important.'[6]

'The lovers of mankind, these are the superior men, of whatever nation, creed, or colour they may be.'[7]

This is still another *fruit* taken from the *tree of Bahá'u'lláh* by which you may judge whether He is a true or false prophet.

14. The Worlds Beyond

The soul is the essential part of every human being.

Bahá'u'lláh teaches that the soul is immortal. It will last as long as the dominion of God lasts, and therefore it is eternal. Bahá'u'lláh says:

'Know thou of a truth that the soul, after its separation from the body, will continue to progress until it attaineth the presence of God, in a state and condition which neither the revolution of ages and centuries . . . can alter. It will endure as long as the Kingdom of God. . . . The movement of my Pen is stilled when it attempteth to befittingly describe the loftiness and glory of so exalted a station.'[1]

The true purpose of the countless ages of evolution was to produce and develop a being capable of reflecting 'the image of God'.

The end of creation was not to develop a perfect physical being culminating in man. The true end of all creation was to develop a channel for the 'spirit'. Man represents the end of physical evolution and the beginning of spiritual evolution. This is explained in greater detail in the book, *The Wine of Astonishment*.

When the perfect physical creation, man, evolved, he was capable of being a channel for the 'spirit'. He was the first being that was both self-conscious and God-conscious.

Concerning this truth of evolution, Bahá'u'lláh has written:

'Having created the world and all that liveth and moveth therein, He, through the direct operation of His unconstrained and sovereign Will, chose to confer upon man the unique distinction and capacity to know Him and to love Him—a capacity that must needs be regarded as the generating impulse and the primary purpose underlying the whole of creation.'[2]

The body of man became the temple in which the 'spirit' or soul developed. The body was the lamp and his soul the light thereof. The soul of man was able to develop in the most perfect form of physical creation, the human body, but it does not perish with the death of the body, any more than the sun perishes when the mirror in which it is reflected is broken.

This factor of life, the immortality of the soul, with its 'freedom of choice', is the most potent cause of morality and order in the world. It is the basis of all morality.

In every man there is a powerful inherent demand for something which is of more importance than this physical life. He instinctively longs for a life in which he is free to choose his own way. This inner insistence upon a spiritual life has been so strong that down through the ages, it has risen up and overthrown those materialistic schools which have tried to deprive man of this basic belief.

Leucippus and Democritus raised up the school of 'Atomists', a mechanistic concept that 'only the atoms and the void are real'. But Socrates and Plato gave a new direction to Greek philosophy, and the mind, rather than atoms, became 'the central fact of the cosmos' for a considerable time.

In a later age, mechanistic determinism came into being and man's 'choice' was again taken away from him. Science, in revolt against the appalling orthodox teachings of an 'unseeing' religious leadership, again established a form of fatalism which left no room for the free-will of the soul. This time, the defeat of 'choice' seemed to be a permanent one.

Then, suddenly, in the last half-century, a new spirit came into the scientific world. The old 'classical physics' of Newton was gone, and a 'nuclear' physics replaced it. Determinism was replaced by indeterminism. The studies in the experimental behaviour of the electron led to a new principle of 'indeterminacy'.

Fatalism and atheism are being pushed into a corner. They have, as one scientist put it, 'lost out'. It is a comfort to the sincere seeker after truth to know that true science and true religion can, at last, in this day, walk hand in hand, and that the resources of research and science are gradually coming to his rescue in defence of that inward longing toward God. Dean Inge has written, 'Science has become an ally of religion.'

Bahá'u'lláh has urged His followers never to doubt that inner prompting which tells man that he has an immortal soul. All the forces of life, both spiritual and material, His followers are assured, will sooner or later confirm this unquestioned truth.

Many of the great scientific minds of our day already support this truth from their own research. They point out that 'matter' itself is indestructible. It never 'dies'. It merely assumes a new shape. It, too, has a form of immortality; therefore, how can the 'spirit' or soul, which is not composed, be mortal?

It is the 'non-believer', the doubter, the atheist, who is old-fashioned in this day of nuclear physics. The stream of truth and life is passing by the sceptical, the sophisticated, and worldly wise. They have become 'a barren coast without a harbour or a lighthouse'.

The eminent biologist C. C. Hurst writes: 'Recent genetical research leads us to the inevitable conclusion that, in general, living genes are relatively immortal.'[3]

A. H. Compton, Nobel Prize winner for his work in physics, says: '... it is only fair to point out also that science has found no cogent reason for supposing that what is of importance in a man can be buried in a grave.'[4]

Dr. Compton says in yet another place: 'Biologically speaking, life, whether it be an apple seed or the germ cell of a man, is essentially continuous and eternal. ... May we not also logically say that continuity of consciousness, mind or soul may be presumed from the essential eternality of the germ cell?'[5]

Bahá'u'lláh has written:

'The Prophets and Messengers of God have been sent down for the sole purpose of guiding mankind to the straight Path of Truth. The purpose underlying their revelation hath been to educate all men, that they may, at the hour of death, ascend, in the utmost purity and sanctity and with absolute detachment, to the throne of the Most High.'[6]

Christ instructed each man among His followers to:

'... take up his cross and follow me. ... For what shall it profit a man, if he shall gain the whole world, and lose his own soul?'[7]

To believe in Him, Christ, was the way for a man to save his soul, Jesus told them. If they had pure hearts and remained faithful, He would be proud of them; but if they were unfaithful, and ashamed of His teachings, then in the day when He came 'in the Glory of the Father', He, Christ, would be ashamed of *them*.

Jesus was asked by His disciples:

'Who then can be saved?'

He replied:

'Verily, I say unto you, That ye which have followed me in the regeneration (day of return and renewal) when the Son of man shall sit in the throne of his glory . . shall inherit everlasting life.'[8]

Then Christ cautions them to have spiritual eyes to see for many who are leaders and do not believe, will be replaced by the humble people who *do* believe. He warns:

'But many that are first shall be last; and the last shall be first.'[9]

Bahá'u'lláh's Teachings tell us that to believe in the Messenger of God when He comes is to have *life*, not to believe is to be *dead*.

All things are alive from the stone to the human being. The mineral, vegetable, animal and human kingdoms are all alive. In the atoms of the stone, the electrons spin and revolve around the central proton in a wondrous form of life but compared to the life of a human being, the stone is dead. So is the difference between the believer and the non-believer in the world to come. While all souls have immortality, and live forever, the difference in their stations can be as great as the difference between a stone and a human being. The believer is at the apex of spiritual life and *alive*. The non-believer, while not dead, has what is equivalent to a form of death, like unto a stone.

Of the soul, Bahá'u'lláh has written:

'It is the first among all created things to declare the excellence of its Creator, the first to recognize His glory, to cleave to His truth, and to bow down in adoration before Him. If it be faithful to God, it will reflect His light, and will, eventually, return unto Him.'[10]

This is a *fruit* from *the tree of Bahá'u'lláh*.

15. Food for the Soul

Prayer is both a blessing and an obligation.

According to the Bahá'í Teachings, prayer brings healing to the soul. It brings joy and happiness, and protects man from tests and difficulties. Prayer is essential to the life of the spirit.

Just as the physical body must have food each day, so does the soul need food each day. Prayer is the spiritual food of the soul. A physical body which is not fed regularly becomes emaciated from malnutrition. It sickens and dies. The same is true of the soul of man. This spirit must be fed regularly and well, or it will suffer the same loss of power. It, too, will sicken. While it never dies, it becomes helpless.

Dr. Alexis Carrel states that there is a therapy in prayer which Science cannot explain but knows it exists, performing miracles of cures which Carrel himself has witnessed, as have many other noted scientists.

For example, if a man lets his arm hang at his side without ever using it, soon the power to move the arm vanishes. The arm has become atrophied and useless. A man's soul without

245

the nourishment of regular prayer also becomes useless and atrophied.

Bahá'u'lláh has left a rich legacy of beautiful, uplifting prayers. However, He instructs man to remember that prayer is by no means limited to the use of these prayers.

Work itself, Bahá'u'lláh tells us, is worship. He says:

'We have made this, your occupation, identical with the worship of God.'[1]

His teachings say in yet another place:

'Arts, sciences and all crafts are (counted as) worship. The man who makes a piece of notepaper to the best of his ability, conscientiously, concentrating all his forces on perfecting it, is giving praise to God. Briefly, all effort and exertion put forth by man from the fullness of his heart is worship, if it is prompted by the highest motives and the will to do service to humanity.'[2]

It is also written:

'A physician ministering to the sick, gently, tenderly, free from prejudice and believing in the solidarity of the human race, he is giving praise.'[3]

Behá'u'lláh's Faith teaches that a man's entire life should be a prayer. Every thought, word or deed which he devotes to the good of his fellow-man is prayer in the truest sense of the word.

This also is a *fruit* from *the tree of Bahá'u'lláh*.

16. Each Soul is King

A child cannot inherit the faith of his father or mother. He must decide about God for himself.

246

Bahá'u'lláh teaches that no one should become a believer in any Faith merely because his parents or his family were believers.

Each human being must be given the privilege of investigating and deciding for himself whether he wishes to believe or not.

For this reason, no child is born a Bahá'í. The decision to become a Bahá'í can be made only after the child reaches the age of fifteen, which Bahá'u'lláh calls the age of 'spiritual maturity'.

It is the duty of the parents to give the child a spiritual as well as a material education. The child should be told about the history and teachings of all the great and holy Messengers of God. This will remove religious prejudice at an early age, and will be a foundation upon which a future decision about his own belief may be based.

Parents, by the example of their own lives, and by living according to the teachings of God, may attract their children to their own belief. However, there must be no compulsion. It must be done by love. Each soul is free to choose his own path, and each soul is king of his own spiritual destiny.

This is another *fruit* of *the tree of Bahá'u'lláh*.

17. One Fold and One Shepherd

A world commonwealth of all the nations of the earth must protect the rights of men.

Nearly a century ago, Bahá'u'lláh addressed the rulers of the earth, saying:

'Be united, O kings of the earth, for thereby will the tempest of discord be stilled amongst you, and your peoples find rest...'[1]

247

On another occasion, He wrote concerning the method by which the world could obtain peace and tranquillity. He said:

'The time must come when the imperative necessity for the holding of a vast, an all-embracing assemblage of men will be universally realised. The rulers and kings of the earth must needs attend it, and, participating in its deliberations, must ... lay the foundations of the world's *Great Peace* amongst men. Such a peace demandeth that the Great Powers should resolve, for the sake of the tranquillity of the peoples of the earth, to be fully reconciled among themselves.'[2]

The consequence of their failure to consider the welfare of the children of God on earth is told in part six of this book, *The Challenge.*

Throughout His Writings, Bahá'u'lláh has laid the foundation for a united world so that the prophecies of the Scripture might be fulfilled, and so that mankind might enjoy that peaceful promised day of the 'one fold and the one shepherd'.

Bahá'u'lláh prophesies that mankind can 'woo' this great day of unity through peaceful methods. If he fails, then he will be beaten to his knees time after time by circumstances until he does choose to make the effort. Bahá'u'lláh has given man the steps by which such a united world can be brought about, but the responsibility for achieving it remains with mankind.

Bahá'u'lláh proclaimed the need for a great universal body which would be dedicated to assuring and preserving the welfare of all men upon the planet. It would protect both great and small nations. It would guarantee the rights of individuals.

Bahá'u'lláh addressed the rulers and kings of the earth, including the Presidents of the United States and the other republics of the West. He warned them of the dire consequences of failing to raise up such a structure. Without it,

He told them, disaster after disaster, would come upon the world.

This world organisation envisioned by Bahá'u'lláh would have a world parliament which would be freely elected by the peoples of the world. It would have a world metropolis, an international police force, and a world tribunal or court.

This world union of nations would not be dedicated to the West or to the East. It would not favour the light or the dark skin. It would not offer special privileges to the rich or the poor. It would not prefer the Gentile or the Jew. This world gathering of nations would be dedicated to one purpose only: the welfare of the entire human race, the rights and privileges of each individual human being.

Bahá'u'lláh not only foresaw the need for such a universal institution, but He provided the structure, laws, and principles upon which it could be raised.

This great universal body would establish a common system of weights and measures and a common currency. It would utilise and develop all natural resources and regulate all markets on a world scale so that 'have not' nations would no longer have a grievance.

It would eliminate extremes of poverty and wealth without destroying the natural degrees of difference which talent and initiative create and to which they are entitled.

It would harmonise capital and labour, protecting the rights of the labourer as well as those of the investor, to the advantage of both.

It would foster an international auxiliary language.

In short, it would take all the steps necessary to bring about a peace-loving, progressive, prosperous, spiritually-directed human family. It would be the family of nations foretold by Moses, Christ, and all the Prophets of the past, the day of the 'one fold and one shepherd'.

This is the final *fruit* I have taken from *the still heavily laden tree of Bahá'u'lláh* by which you may judge Him.

Christ said:

'Beware of false prophets . . . ye shall know them by their fruits . . . A good tree cannot bring forth evil fruit, neither can a corrupt tree bring forth good fruit . . . Wherefore by their fruits ye shall know them.'[3]

These *fruits* are but a handful from the great harvest of Bahá'u'lláh's Faith, but they will be sufficient for you to judge the spirit of His Teaching. Bahá'u'lláh Himself (in His greatest Book, which contains His Laws and fundamental ordinances) calls these Teachings the '*fruits*' of His '*tree*'.[4]

By these *fruits*, using the standard given by Christ, you can judge whether or not Bahá'u'lláh is a true or a false prophet.

Thus after long years of search and study, I brought to a close *The Case of the Missing Millennium*. The final proofs were in, and could now be turned over to the public for judgment. My work was finished.

When, later, I embraced the Faith of Bahá'u'lláh, I discovered there was far less emphasis on prophecy than on logic and reason. Yet so remarkable were these events, and so astonishing their undeniable fulfilment of prophecy, that I felt it would be wrong to deprive the public of the facts. It would seem clear that in this day of the coming of the 'one fold and one shepherd' there was both an outward and an inward fulfilment of the prophetic vision.

You will have to decide for yourself whether I have solved the century-old mystery. That is your problem. I still had my own personal problem to face. The most difficult choice ever to face a man. Sometime in life it faces each man or woman.

I called it: *The Challenge*.

PART SIX

THE CHALLENGE

1. Except These Days be Shortened

I had solved the case to my own complete satisfaction. Was it possible for me to set it aside? What would I do about it now? Forget it?

My years of study and search had taught me one bitter truth. Religious movements, like man, pass through the progressive stages of childhood, adolescence, maturity, and old age, and eventually die. Since the life span of great religions is measured in thousands of years, the period of old age often endures for centuries. Death comes so slowly that whole generations may not notice it. If the words of Christ Himself were correct, religious institutions maintained themselves long after the creative spirit which gave them birth had departed.

I recalled the three stages of religion spoken of by an educator and philosopher.

Stage One: God is real to man. He is intimate. His spirit is among the people in every walk of life. It is a living Faith.

Stage Two: Culture now becomes more important than God to man. Theology takes over the conduct of the Faith. There is an intellectual acceptance rather than a deep inner conviction of truth. The pilgrims and the holy men are pushed aside and are replaced by artisans and adventurers who spend their time in search of beauty and romance rather than spiritual truth.

Stage Three: In this last stage, material power and physical pleasures become the determining factor, neither God nor culture dominate any longer. Of the once live and active religion only the outward form remains. The faith and teachings of the Messenger have crystallised as do the blood vessels of an old man. Religion then falls behind the times. It cannot understand nor interpret what is happening in the world. It lives in its past and, for this reason, appeals only to the old and the conservative in man. The highways which were once frequented by pilgrims and artisans are now travelled by tourists who neither contemplate nor seek beauty, but crave only pleasure and gratification of the outward senses.

Certainly our Western Civilisation has reached, and is immersed in, stage number three. No wonder religion has been abandoned. Man attends his church, synagogue, mosque or temple as a social convention with an unbelieving heart.

Under almost any other circumstances, this part of the story of *The Case of the Missing Millennium* is something which I would share only with my intimate friends. I would not offer it to the world. I know what can happen to the teller of such a story. Yet, because of the danger that is slowly but surely engulfing our society, I feel that it is a story which every one should hear. What they do about it rests with them.

It is not a case of now it *can* be told, but rather, I feel, of now it *must* be told. At least once, in clear, straight-forward terms. If a man is riding with a friend on a winding mountainous road, and sees him asleep at the wheel, he has no choice but to awaken him—for the sake of both the driver and himself. If a neighbour lies asleep in a burning house, it is the duty of the one who sees the fire to do everything in his power to arouse the victim.

I was a Christian when I first began my investigation into this century-old riddle of the Messiah. I had no idea where it would lead me. Now that it is ended, I am still a Christian, but in a fuller, richer sense than I ever dreamed could be possible.

I have also become a follower of Bahá'u'lláh. I have become a Bahá'í. I had no choice. I had to accept Bahá'u'lláh or deny Christ.

There are four methods by which we can prove a thing:

1. By Reason (logic and experiment).
2. By the Senses (experience).
3. By tradition or prophecy (fulfilment of promises).
4. By inspiration or intuition (inward conviction above the senses or logic).

I had tested Bahá'u'lláh by all four. My self-importance had gradually diminished until I became like an ant which has come out to look at the sun.

With the exactness of the stars, Bahá'u'lláh had fulfilled all of the prophecies required. He had exalted reason to its proper throne. He had urged scientific method and experiment in seeking truth. His life, which is told in another book called *The King of Glory*, was filled with such beauty and inspiration that a Christian clergyman, and famous Bible scholar, declared: 'If there has been any prophet in recent times, it is to Bahá'u'lláh we must go'.[1]

I discovered the reason why the Bahá'ís have such a tender love and reverence for Christ and for Moses. To deny Moses and Christ would be to deny Bahá'u'lláh. They are one in the Holy Spirit they bring. God is like the sun, and Moses, Christ and Bahá'u'lláh, as well as the other prophets, are like mirrors. They all reflect the same truth. They merely come at different ages in history. For example:

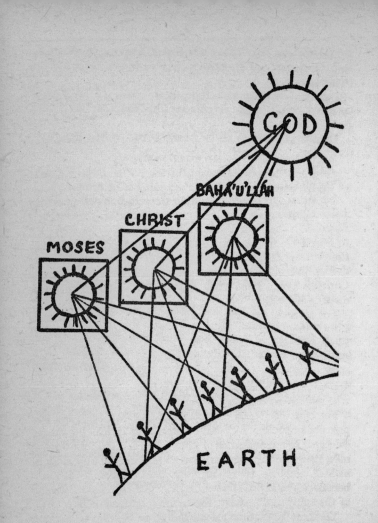

I could not refuse to accept Bahá'u'lláh, or I would be denying Christ Himself, *and* Moses; for, in reality they were one.
The same light of God shines in each mirror. The name
Bahá'í became familiar, simple and filled with warmth and
love. It meant: follower of Bahá'u'lláh. For example:

CHRIST—IAN (of)
BAHÁ —Í   (of)

A Christian is a follower of Christ, and a Bahá'í is a follower
of Bahá'u'lláh.

Now that I have become a follower of Bahá'u'lláh, perhaps
I would write this book in a different manner. However, it
was not written as a Bahá'í, but as a Christian who was led
to search for the missing Messiah. I only know that my love
for Christ is far greater now than ever before, and infinitely
deeper and more precious than at any time when I was a
Christian only. Bahá'u'lláh has taught me the beauty and
majesty of Christ.

For all these reasons, I finally decided to share the entire
story with you. It was impossible for me to remain silent when
I learned these astonishing things. What a pity that the world
still knows so little of them. The responsibility to tell the
story weighed as heavily on my heart as did the story of the
first coming of Christ on the heart of the Apostle of Jesus
who said: 'Yea, woe is unto me, if I preach not the Gospel!'[2]

For over one hundred years, mankind has neglected this
precious opportunity. From 1844 until today, man has turned
a deaf ear to the entreaties of Bahá'u'lláh and His followers. It
may, therefore, be too late now to prevent the final clash of
nations intent on destroying themselves. Unless great numbers flock quickly to His banner, and give a mass transfusion
of the spirit to humanity, the future looms ominous.

Yet there is still time for the individual believer to respond to this call of the Messenger of God for this day. Each ear that 'hears' and eye that 'sees' can still arise to serve Almighty God. He can be numbered among the *elect* who were promised spiritual guidance in the last days when 'two would be taken and one remain'. Christ said:

'And except those (last) days should be shortened, there should no flesh be saved; but for the *elects'* sake those days *shall* be shortened.'[3]

In the chapter in which Isaiah prophesies that the followers of God in *the last day* will be called by *a new name*, he promises also that God will be merciful to His *elect* in *the time of the end*, so that

'I may not destroy them all.'[4]

If there is no God, and man is but a creature that comes up out of the earth for a few brief years in the sun, then nothing matters. Yet if, as the overwhelming evidence proclaims, he is a spiritual being with a soul, then the relationship of that soul to God is the most important and precious knowledge and possession he has in all the earth.

The following chapters present the two alternatives which, following my study, I feel face every single human being in the days immediately ahead. The sands are running out. The die is cast. The battle lines are being formed. Who will be of the elect?

2. Nuclear Giants and Ethical Midgets

We have been called a race of 'nuclear giants and ethical midgets'. We are material monsters and moral dwarfs.

We can arrest cancer, cure tuberculosis, prevent disease, fly faster than sound, split the atom, conquer space—but we are unable to control the emotions of a single man.

We are helpless before those prejudices of flag, complexion, pocket-book and prayer. We cannot create a political penicillin that will reduce the fever of suspicion and hate. There is no antibiotic for protection against bribery and corruption. We cannot isolate the bacillus of indifference. We cannot innoculate against these evils in our lands. We cannot operate.

We are thus the victims of our own genius in dealing with matter, and of our own stupidity in dealing with men. We are in truth nuclear giants and ethical midgets.

Technical development has shrivelled our globe into a marble. Every part of the planet is now within range of the hawk. When the shadow of the bird falls upon a land, none can tell whether it is friend or foe. The nation one applauds and praises in the newsreels one year, is the nation that is hissed and booed the next.

Inside this shrunken arena of the world, a frightened mankind watches as in the story book of old. Glances of worry and terror are turned upon the doors of the world's council chambers: Who will come out—the lady or the tiger?

Men everywhere are beginning to wonder if perhaps they have not paid too dearly for these great material gains which one moment's caprice on the part of the world's leaders could sweep away.

Where can man turn? Where is the hope?

Bahá'u'lláh has written that man is a spiritual being, not an animal. If his heart is turned toward God and the things of the spirit, he will be both a nuclear and ethical giant, 'little less than an angel'. If his heart is turned toward himself and the material pleasures of the body, he will become a moral dwarf that is more like an animal than a man. He will be so addicted to the pleasures of the flesh, that he will not even recognize the spirit. He will instead, ridicule it as fanatic and out of date, when in reality he himself is a dead thing.

The one possession that truly belongs to each individual human being, Bahá'u'lláh tells us, and the only one which no one else can take from him, is his spirit, his soul. Bahá'u'lláh echoes the words spoken by Christ so long ago:

> 'But lay up for yourselves treasures in heaven, where neither moth nor rust doth corrupt, and where thieves do not break through nor steal: *For where your treasure is, there will your heart be also.*'[1]

Man has set his heart 'on that which perishes'. Even the most brief glance at the state of our society will reveal this bitter truth:

1. We spend billions more each year on liquor than we spend on education.
2. We spend billions more each year on cosmetics than we do on education.
3. We spend billions more each year on entertainment than we do on education.
4. We spend billions more each year on all forms of pleasure than we do on education.
5. We have stream-lined cars in multicolours standing empty on our used-car lots, while thousands of people are without proper housing.
6. We have an endless variety of alcoholic and carbonated beverages for which we spend countless pounds while there are many families who do not have enough milk for their children.

Suicide has become, not a daily, not an hourly, but a minute-by-minute catastrophe. These deaths by self-destruction are not among the old and feeble and helpless. They are among the young people of the world who supposedly have their lives before them. They can see no future, no way out. They have become disillusioned with the 'thing that perishes'.

The author, while in Detroit, Michigan, in May 1959, watched a television programme which reported that the national mental institutions were more crowded than ever before in history. Mental hospitals were filled to overflowing. There was no room for the patients that needed help. They had to be released before they were cured. They had to be sent back, still mentally warped, into the world that took away their lives.

Another report stated that there were now more mental patients in the hospitals than all other patients combined. Still another declared that alcoholism had surpassed mental disease as a critical problem. So prevalent was this sickness that there were far more in need of treatment from alcoholism than from all the mental diseases combined. There were so many that it was not possible to give them all proper care. They had to be turned away, untreated.

We have become a pleasure-seeking, not a truth-seeking people. We should be both. We should be balanced, mature human beings extracting the wonder, joy, and awe out of life, living a full, rich useful life of happiness surrounded by the warming love of our families.

We are a profit-making rather than a welfare-producing civilisation. We should be both. We have turned our back upon God, and, as a consequence, upon our fellow-man. We are dying of the drug of materialism in the West, and have become 'pushers' for the rest of the world. We can no longer get enough of it. We have become numbed to the simple pleasures and joys of God, home, family and the loving friendship of our neighbours.

3. The Chariots Shall Rage in the Streets

We are the people, and these are the days, promised for the terrible *time of the end*. This is the hour spoken of in such strong language in the New Testament:

> 'This know also that *in the last days* perilous times shall come. For men shall be lovers of their own selves, covetous, boasters, proud, blasphemers ... unthankful, unholy, lovers of pleasures more than lovers of God; Having a form of godliness, but denying the power thereof ... '[1]

It is also prophesied that we shall be 'untrustworthy' and 'truce-breakers'.

We slay and injure more people on our highways than we do in battle. We have more traffic fatality reports than we have 'missing in action' reports from all our war-fronts. This, too, is foreshadowed in the Scriptures for the *last days*. It would be a day we are told when mankind, living in the presence of the Messiah, would turn a deaf and mocking ear to His healing words. It is prophesied:

> 'The chariots shall be with flaming torches *in the day of His preparation* ... The chariots shall rage in the streets, they shall jostle one against another in the broad ways; they shall seem like torches, they shall run like lightnings.'[2]

Anyone who has tried to return home by automobile on the evening of a national holiday has witnessed this scene. We have left the slain upon the highways beneath the torchlike beam of our rushing chariots, unaware that *the day of His preparation* has passed, and the day of His judgment is upon us.

The Messiah has come that there may be the day of 'one fold and one shepherd', but the Lord is no longer the shepherd of mankind. The sheep can no longer hear His voice. Their ears are tuned to a different song.

Bahá'u'lláh has written:

'The vitality of men's belief in God is dying out in every land; nothing short of His wholesome medicine can ever restore it. The corrosion of ungodliness is eating into the vitals of human society; what else but the Elixir of His potent Revelation can cleanse and revive it?'[3]

Christ spoke to the individual conscience, preparing mankind for this great day of His return. He said:

'Come ye after me, and I will make you to become fishers of men.'[4]

Bahá'u'lláh spoke to collective society saying:

'Come ye after Me, that We may make you to become quickeners of mankind.'[5]

Christ spoke to the individual consciences of men, concerning the personal relationship of one man to another saying:

'Whosoever shall smite thee on thy right cheek, turn to him the other also.'[6]

Bahá'u'lláh spoke to the collective conscience of men, addressing them through their rulers and kings, saying:

'Be united, O kings of the earth, for thereby will the tempest of discord be stilled amongst you, and your peoples find rest, if ye be of them that comprehend. Should any one among you take up arms against another, rise ye all against him, for this is naught but manifest justice.'[7]

Christ spoke to the individual conscience in the Sermon on the Mount, saying:

'Repent: for the Kingdom of heaven is at hand.'[8]

He promised that at the *time of the end,* in the *last days,* the same spiritual kingdom which He was establishing in the *individual* hearts, would be raised up throughout the earth among *all* men. He gave this teaching in His *Lord's Prayer.* These words of Christ are both a prayer and a prophecy.

'*Thy kingdom come.* Thy will be done *in earth* as it is *in heaven.*' 9

Bahá'u'lláh has written:

'Followers of the Gospel, behold the gates of heaven are flung open. He that had ascended unto it is now come. Give ear to His voice calling aloud over land and sea, announcing to all mankind. . . . "Lo, the sacred Pledge hath been fulfilled, for He, the Promised One, is come!" '10

In yet another place, Bahá'u'lláh warns mankind that nothing but a fresh outpouring of the divine love which Christ offered on the Mount of Olives can ever revive humanity and turn it away from material things back to spiritual things.

Society faces the same challenge in this day as it faced in the days of Jonah, the prophet. Almighty God sent Jonah to cry against the wicked city of Nineveh, a city of worldliness, and pleasure devoid of the spirit and the love of God. The materialism of the West has made *it* a modern Nineveh.

The words which God put into the mouth of Jonah could well be directed against us all in this day:

'Arise, go to Nineveh, that great city, and cry against it; for their wickedness is come up before me.'11

Jonah cried out: 'Repent, or be destroyed!' Nineveh repented of its past, turned unto God, and was delivered from its destruction.

We are the Nineveh of today. We must either repent of our

evil ways, or be destroyed by the forces we have ourselves put into operation. Bahá'u'lláh has cried out to us the warning.

There is no place for us to hide.

Bahá'u'lláh repeatedly warned mankind that nothing would save it from self-destruction except the unity of all the peoples of the world. It must be, He said, a unity based upon love for each other and not upon fear. This unity could not be established by any human agency. It would come only when humanity turned to the Messenger of God Who had been sent for the specific purpose of bringing mankind together. All other remedies were temporary and sectional. They would end, Bahá'u'lláh said, in further division and war. He wrote:

'It beseemeth all men in this Day . . . to establish the unity of all mankind. There is no place to flee to, no refuge that anyone can seek, except Him.'[12]

And again:

'That which the Lord hath ordained as *the sovereign remedy* and mightiest instrument for the healing of all the world is the union of all its peoples in *one universal Cause, one common Faith*.'[13]

There is but one God, He proclaimed, and therefore but one religion. There is no exclusive salvation for the Jew, the Christian, the Muslim, the Hindu, the Buddhist, or the Bahá'í, or for the people of any of the great religions of the world. God is not in competition with Himself. His religion is one. He is the Father of all, and we are all children of this one human family. That He (God) should compete for the souls of His children on separate corners of great city streets is a man-made invention.

263

Sectarian beliefs have no value in an age where unity is essential for our very survival.

This unity can be brought about, Bahá'u'lláh tells us, only through the agency of a Messenger of God. This is the *Master* allegiance before which we must lay down our lesser allegiances of nation, race, class, and creed.

Bahá'u'lláh has written:

'This (union of mankind) can in no wise be achieved except through the power of a skilled, an all-powerful and inspired Physician.'[14]

Bahá'u'lláh directed His Message to all the peoples of the world, but He laid special emphasis on the responsibility of the people of the West who had been prepared for this very day by Jesus, the Christ. The Christians, He said, were now facing the great day foretold by Christ, the day of 'judgment', when they would have to decide for or against the Messenger of God. Bahá'u'lláh wrote, calling their attention to the promise of Christ:

'The *Comforter* Whose advent all the scriptures have promised is now come that He may reveal unto you all knowledge and wisdom. Seek Him over the entire surface of the earth . . . '[15]

In yet another place, Bahá'u'lláh addressed the whole of Christendom, reminding them of the Son of man who was promised for the *last day* by Daniel, Isaiah, and by Christ Himself. The Day had come at last, Bahá'u'lláh assured them, and the hour for waiting was over. The Father foretold by Jesus had appeared. The hope of humanity lay in turning to His face. He declared:

'The voice of the Son of man is calling aloud from the sacred vale: "Here am I, here am I" . . . the Father hath come.

That which ye were promised in *the Kingdom of God* is ful-filled.'[16]

4. Terror in the Sky

What will be the fate of humanity if it refuses to 'repent' and to turn back to God?

Bahá'u'lláh has written:

'Know ye that the world and its vanities and its embellish-ments shall pass away. Nothing will endure except God's Kingdom.... The days of your life shall roll away, and all the things with which ye are occupied and of which ye boast yourselves shall perish, and ye shall, most certainly, be summoned . . . to appear at the spot where the limbs of the entire creation shall be made to tremble, and the flesh of every oppressor to creep . . . and shall be repaid for your doings. This is the day that shall inevitably come upon you, the hour that none can put back.'[1]

The world must unite or perish, Bahá'u'lláh declares. It is already one in spirit, even though it is blind to this truth. It must become united both inwardly and outwardly. It must have a world conscience and live according to that conscience.

The discoveries in medicine and other sciences, made by men and women of all races, are for all members of the human race. From the moment we are born until the hour we die, we are surrounded by the fruit of the spirits of men who never thought in terms of flags or boundaries or special prayer-books or pigmentation of skin. These men never served a lesser loyalty than the welfare of mankind.

The Bahá'í Teachings state:

'Anything which affects any one of the children of men, affects all. Whatever happens in one part of the world will have a great affect on the affairs of men in another part of the world, for they are all members of one great human family.'

Nearly one hundred years ago, Bahá'u'lláh wrote:

'This handful of dust, the earth, is one country, let it be in unity. . . . Address yourselves to the promotion of the well-being and tranquillity of the children of men. Bend your minds and wills to the education of the peoples and kindreds of the earth, that haply the dissensions that divide it may . . . be blotted out from its face. . . . Ye dwell in one world, and have been created through the operation of one Will. Blessed is he who mingleth with all men in a spirit of utmost kindliness and love.'[2]

Any plan which ignores Almighty God has no future, however powerful its immediate present may appear. Any plan which does not include all nations, colours, classes, and faiths has failed before it begins. The same night darkens and cools all men, and the same sun lights and heats their lives. Even this devastating power of destruction imprisoned so long in the atom and now released, this power which the world holds so much in awe, did not come about through the efforts of any one group. It was not the fruit of the labours of any one nation, race, religion or class. For example, among some of its perfectors are the following:

1. Mendelief, a *Russian*, discovered the periodic law of elements.
2. Thomson, an *Englishman*, developed the electron theory.
3. The theory of relativity came from a *German*, Einstein.
4. The radio-activity of radium was discovered by Mme. Curie, a *Pole*.
5. A *New Zealander*, Rutherford, discovered the atomic nucleus, by experimenting with radium.

266

6. Fermi, an *Italian*, accomplished the first transmutation of uranium.

7. The mesotron theory was first developed by Yukawa, a *Japanese*.

8. Barium was first derived from uranium by Hahn, a *German*.

9. The atomic structure was analysed by Niels Bohr, a *Dane*.

10. Anderson of the *United States* discovered the positron.

11. Chadwick of *Great Britain* discovered the neutron.

12. Meitner of *Austria* succeeded in splitting the atom.

And so on, and on, and on: right down to Los Alamos, Hiroshima, Nagasaki, Bikini, Siberia, Sputnik, Vanguard, Jupiter, rockets to the moon, rockets circling the sun—and *ad infinitum*. No one mind, no individual man, no single nation, nor particular people brought this power into a reality. But it now exists!

Science has become a warm putty that we can shape with our fingers into any form we choose: an article of beauty or an instrument of death.

Where can we flee to safety? Either we turn back to God and become spiritual and moral in our motives, either our hearts catch up with our heads, or we shall all be engulfed in a disaster. It is not sufficient for a few individuals to recognize this truth, the mass of humanity must respond. Otherwise: total eclipse.

It was not a clergyman, nor a statesman, nor an educator, but the victorious general, MacArthur, who warned the world in a broadcast from the deck of the battleship *Missouri*, following the last war: 'We have had our last chance. The only thing that can save humanity now is a spiritual resurgence.'

Wherever there are television sets, cinema screens, or radios, humanity has looked upon and heard the dreadful sight and sound of that 'mushroom' cloud, which a picturesque press has labelled: *The Toadstool of Terror.* There is no place on earth where you can rest at ease, without knowing that suddenly, even now as you read this, a guided missile may be on the way to turn all your hopes to ashes in one fiery blast.

As far back as the spring of 1954 an H-bomb was dropped in Namu, Bikini Atoll. It is already totally obsolete. Yet, is it possible to imagine man, a creation of God, not being satisfied with the following statistics of destruction:

1. That one bomb represented the equivalent of 12 to 14 *million* tons of TNT.
2. One such bomb is equal to all the bombs dropped by all the nations in the last great war.
3. The resultant explosion rose to a height of 100,000 ft.—nearly 20 miles.
4. Its cloud of poison spread over 100 miles in radius.
5. Strategically dropped, it could destroy immediately 35 million people, or twice the number of people slain by all means in both of the last great world wars.

That bomb is now outdated. Something more lethal may soon be speeding on its way by jet-propelled long-range bombers, or on the wings of inter-continental missiles and rockets. Like 'fingers of death' they sit silent on their launching pads. Who knows what city-labels they carry, or toward whose homeland they are pointed, or whose mistake or fear may trigger their firing? No one will have the time to ask himself later: Are these not the days promised in the Bible when 'He shall come like a thief in the night' and the 'fire will rain down from heaven'?

Even before the year 1844, a poet wrote:

'The time will come when thou shalt lift thine eyes
To watch a long drawn battle in the skies.
While aged peasants, too amazed for words,
Stare at the fleets of wondrous flying birds.'

The 'birds' have come before, striking with terror, darkening the cities, loosing the shriek of the sirens, driving the people like ants into the bowels of the earth. This time there is no hiding place. Never before have the flying birds come to pour out that destruction foretold by Christ and Zechariah when two would be taken and one would remain.

Nearly a century ago the famous Hebrew scholar, Albert Barnes, maintained that the most exact and proper translation of the prophecy in *Daniel* ix. 27 about the dreadful 'last days' is this:

'Something resembling the wings of a bird spread out, pouring down desolation upon the people in the manner of a storm.'

Are these metal-eggs the 'hailstones' promised in yet another Book of the Scriptures?

Are the radar instruments in your home town already seeking out the coming of the shadow of the bird upon its screens? Are the sonar instruments listening for the sound of the rustle of its wings?

The late Albert Einstein, in a television interview in 1950, warned the world in these words: 'The hysterical race between the United States and Russia to unfold the secret of the H-bomb could bring about the destruction of the world as we know it. It could result in the poisoning of the atmosphere of the earth.'

These words were but an echo of those spoken by Bahá'u'lláh Himself nearly a century before:

'A strange and wonderful instrument (force) exists in the

269

earth. It . . . has the power to change the atmosphere . . .
and its infection causes destruction.'³

In 1912 when 'Abdu'l-Bahá, the son of Bahá'u'lláh, was in
Paris on His journey to the West to awaken the world to His
Father's message, to try and bring mankind to its senses, he
spoke of this statement of Bahá'u'lláh's. 'Abdu'l-Bahá later
made it clear that this power would not be exercised in the
Great War of 1914–18. He prophesied that this First World
War would not be the last war, but that unhappily a greater
and more terrible conflict would break out. Mankind, He said,
was still motivated by hate and not by love. It still had refused
to heed the counsels of Bahá'u'lláh, counsels which were its
only safeguard.

In 1912 He repeated the words of Bahá'u'lláh:

'There is a powerful force in the earth. Pray God that it
may remain undiscovered until mankind has perfected his
spiritual qualities so that it may be used for man's welfare
and not destruction. It can poison the atmosphere of the
earth. Its flames can devour the cities.'⁴

These last words were also a quotation from Bahá'u'lláh,
Himself, Who had warned humanity in His writings:

'If carried to excess, civilisation will prove as prolific a
source of evil as it had been of goodness when kept
within the restraints of moderation . . . its flame will
devour the cities. . . .'⁵

Was it an ironic coincidence, or was it a warning from God,
that 'Abdu'l-Bahá spoke these words concerning the 'force
that could poison the atmosphere' to Viscount Arawaka, an
Ambassador from Japan, a man from the very country where
the first atomic bomb was to be exploded, in that 'greater and
more terrible war to come!'

The Second War is past. Will mankind *en masse* turn to God and avert a third? The summit conferences proceed slowly while the missile parts roll rapidly off assembly lines. For every rocket that goes into space for research, a dozen fall with temporarily empty nose cones on predetermined targets.

Can the meaning of the words 'He (Christ) shall come like a thief in the night' be misunderstood any longer? Can the words of John the Baptist, in their social sense, 'Repent for the Kingdom of God is at hand' be any longer neglected? Are there no 'eyes to see' and 'ears to hear?'

Isaiah prophesies that:

'. . . it shall come to pass in that (last) day, that the Lord shall punish the hosts of the high ones that are on high, and the kings of the earth upon the earth.'[6]

'. . . therefore shall all hands be faint, and every man's heart shall melt.'[7]

It is no longer for a far distant time. It is upon us. Isaiah says:

'Therefore, I will shake the heavens, and the earth shall remove out of her place . . . and the foundations of the earth do shake . . . the inhabitants of the earth are burned and few men left . . . the earth shall reel to and fro like a drunkard . . .'[8]

It is not an attractive alternative. Atomic power can illuminate a city or evaporate it. It depends upon the moral conscience that motivates its use.

5. The Hour Hath Come

For over one hundred years mankind has ignored the message of Bahá'u'lláh. Man has made no effort to investigate

271

His Teachings, in spite of the promises in all the Holy Books from the beginning of time concerning the day of His coming; in spite of Christ's explicit warning: 'Watch! For ye know not what hour your Lord doth come!'

Bahá'u'lláh wrote these words to the entire company of the monarchs of East and West:

> 'Examine our Cause, inquire into the things that have befallen Us and decide justly between Us and Our enemies. . . . Your people are your treasures. Beware lest your rule violate the commandments of God, and ye deliver your wards (the people) to the hands of the robber. By them ye rule, by their means ye subsist, by their aid ye conquer. Yet, how disdainfully ye look upon them! How strange, how very strange!'[1]

When Bahá'u'lláh was cast into the Most Great Prison at 'Akká, He warned the king who had thus sentenced Him that such persecutions could never silence Him. He was merely uttering the words that Almighty God had instructed Him to speak, in the hope that perhaps one sovereign, one ruler, one nation, one people might arise to defend and spread the Word of God amongst men, so that the sufferings of man might come to an end.

Bahá'u'lláh's letters to the rulers of the world were emphatic and clear. He told them that unless the bonds of affection and unity among all men were increased, unless the nations united in loving cooperation to bring peace to the world, unless the rights of all men and especially the poor and lowly were secured and safeguarded, unless all men and especially the leaders lived their lives according to what would be pleasing to God rather than what would be pleasing to themselves and other men, their kingdoms, their possessions, their privileges, their pleasures would all be taken from them by the

Lord of the Vineyard (the Messiah) who would then give the vineyard (earth) out to those worthy souls among the elect who would be left after the great affliction which mankind would have brought upon itself.

'It is not Our wish to lay hands on your kingdoms,' Bahá'u'lláh told them. 'Our Mission is to seize and possess the hearts of men. . . . How great the blessedness that awaiteth the king who will arise to aid my Cause. . . .'[2]

Bahá'u'lláh waited patiently for some sign that the world had heard His voice. At last He broke His silence:

'Twenty years have passed, O kings!' He warned them. '. . . Ye, nevertheless, have failed to stay the hand of the aggressor. For is it not your clear duty to restrain the tyranny of the oppressor, and to deal equitably with your subjects, that your high sense of justice may be fully demonstrated to all mankind?'[3]

In yet another place He warned them:

'Withdraw your hands from tyranny, for I have pledged Myself not to forgive any man's injustice.'[4]

Again recognizing the shortness of the time, He entreated the rulers:

'Summon the nations unto God!'[5]

The dominion of the earth belongs to God, Bahá'u'lláh told them, and the kings are but the custodians thereof. The hearts of the people, He said, are jewels. Be faithful to the trust of God and do not permit the thieves and the ungodly to steal away the treasures from their rightful owner, God.

In His great love for the underprivileged, Bahá'u'lláh had tried to impress upon their leaders the need to become the example and to show the way. Now that the rulers had refused to heed His summons, Bahá'u'lláh turned with that same great compassion to the simple and lowly. He told them that unless they turned their hearts to God, they too would find themselves involved in increasing difficulties and problems. The material civilisation which they so highly prized would be turned against them. Instead of a blessing, it would become a scourge. It would fashion instruments of warfare which would batter humanity to its knees. This, in turn, would purify them so that their hearts might become more receptive to the message of God.

It was a God of love and not a God of fear which bade Him speak out this way, Bahá'u'lláh informed them. It was not Almighty God Who would inflict this disaster upon mankind, but man himself. Man would make it inevitable by his neglect of the laws of God. Humanity could choose the easy way or the hard way. The choice was man's. God's Kingdom on earth could be hastened or delayed depending upon man's response, but it could not be prevented. It would be established sooner or later. If not by the present people of earth, then by those who survived another man-imposed disaster.

Bahá'u'lláh was greatly saddened when the kings and rulers of the earth failed to respond to His message. He knew only too well the sorrow it would bring upon the world.

'Witness how the world is being afflicted with a fresh calamity every day,' He sighed. 'Its tribulation is continually deepening. From the moment the Tablet (letter—to Ra'ís) was revealed, until the present day, neither hath the world been tranquillized, nor have the hearts of its peoples been at rest. At one time it hath been agitated by contentions and disputes, at another it hath been convulsed by wars, and fallen a victim to inveterate diseases. *Its sickness is approaching the stage of utter hopelessness, inasmuch as the true Physician is debarred from administering the remedy,* whilst unskilled practitioners are regarded with favour, and are accorded full freedom to act. . . . Ere long, they will perceive the consequences of what their hands have wrought in the Day of God. Thus warneth you He Who is the All-Informed, as bidden by . . . the Almighty.'[6]

Until the present day mankind has not heeded the warning.

6. The Day of the Lord

Having failed to arouse mankind by love and kindness, Bahá'u'lláh, like a stern but responsible Father pointed out the consequences of man's continued neglect. He said that if man did not forsake his past ways and show a sincere love for God and for his fellowmen, he would suddenly find himself 'in the shadow of a black smoke.' The following are but a few of Bahá'u'lláh's warnings to mankind of the vision of things that they will bring upon themselves if they neglect God:

1. '"The Hour" hath come upon them, while they are disporting themselves. They have been seized by their forelock, and yet know it not.'[1]
2. 'The thing that must come hath come suddenly; behold how they flee from it! The inevitable hath come to pass; . . . Say: by God! The blast hath been blown on the trumpet, and lo, mankind hath swooned away before us!'[2]
3. 'This is the Day on which all eyes shall stare up with terror, the Day in which the hearts of them that dwell on earth shall tremble, save them whom thy Lord . . . pleaseth to deliver.'[3]
4. 'How long will ye sleep? . . . Will ye not recognise how the mountains have become like flocks of wool, how the people are sore vexed at the awful majesty of the Cause of God? Witness how their houses are empty ruins, and they themselves a drowned host.'[4]
5. 'Bestir yourselves, that the brief moments that are still

275

yours may not be dissipated and lost. Even as the swiftness of lightning your days shall pass, and your bodies shall be laid to rest beneath a canopy of dust. What can ye then achieve? How can ye atone for your past failure?'[5]

6. 'Appreciate the value of the days in which you live.'
7. 'Turn back while there is yet time!'[6]
8. 'Whither do ye flee? The mountains have passed away, and the heavens have been folded together, and the whole earth is held within His grasp. . . . Who is it that can protect you? . . . None, except God, the Almighty . . .'[7]

These words of awe and majesty had been written by the same Pen which for nearly half a century had poured out such gentle love on humanity. Bahá'u'lláh loved His family, His children, the countryside, green fields, meadows, mountains, streams, and all living creatures; yet, for almost fifty years He had been subjected to the rigours of persecution and imprisonment. Through it all there streamed from His Pen such forgiving words of love, such a deep affection for mankind. His same Pen had written:

'Now is the time to cheer and refresh the down-cast through the invigorating breeze of love and fellowship, and the living waters of friendliness and charity.'[8]

The same Pen that shook the heavens, had also written:

'They who are the beloved of God, in whatever place they gather, and whomsoever they may meet, must evince, in their attitude towards God, and in the manner of their celebration of His praise and glory, such humility and submissiveness that every atom of the dust beneath their feet may attest the depth of their devotion. The conversation carried by these holy souls should be informed with such power that these same atoms of dust will be thrilled by its influence.'[9]

The Pen of warning was once a pen of tenderness:

'Show forbearance and benevolence and love to one another. Should any one among you be incapable of grasping a certain truth, or be striving to comprehend it, show forth, when conversing with him, a spirit of extreme kindliness and good will. Help him to see and recognise the truth without esteeming yourself to be, in the least, superior to him, or to be possessed of greater endowments.'[10]

The song of the nightingale became the cry of the eagle only when humanity, immersed in its pursuit of pleasure, failed to hear His sweet music. Then, as a protection for a negligent society, Bahá'u'lláh changed the lute for the trumpet. He sounded an alarm, so that the spiritually sleeping might be awakened.

He called out to mankind to have 'eyes that would see' and 'ears that would hear'. He implored Almighty God to bear witness that He had not failed in His Mission to awaken a sleeping humanity:

'Have the verses been sent down?' He asks. 'Say: "Yea, by Him Who is the Lord of the heavens!" Hath the hour come? "Nay, more; it hath passed. . . . He, the True One, hath appeared with proof and testimony." '[11]

In the closing days of His life, Bahá'u'lláh wrote from the Holy Land, Israel:

'We, verily, have not fallen short of Our duty to exhort men, and to deliver that whereunto I was bidden by God, the Almighty, the All-praised. . . . Is there any excuse left for anyone? . . . No, by God, the Lord of the Mighty Throne! My signs have encompassed the earth, and my power enveloped all mankind.'[12]

He leaves this final thought:

'The Lord is come in His great glory! He verily, is the One Whom ye were promised in the Books of God. . . . Let it now be seen what your endeavours in the path of detachment will be.'

The responsibility therefore rests squarely upon the shoulders of each individual human being. He can listen to the word of God and repent as the city of Nineveh had done to the pleading of Jonah, and thus be saved; or he can ignore, ridicule, and oppose as he has done for more than one hundred years, thus bringing down more pain and purification upon himself. If he chooses this course, then the most terrible suffering of all is yet to come, as warned in both the *Old* and the *New Testaments*.

The Book of the followers of Moses says:

'The fishes of the sea, and the fowls of the heaven, and the beasts of the field, and all creeping things that creep upon the face of the earth, and all the men that are upon the face of the earth, shall shake at my presence, and the mountains shall be thrown down, and the steep places shall fall, and every wall shall fall to the ground.'[13]

This same Book, and the very Prophet who foretold that the 'Glory of God' would come *from the East* to Israel in *the last days*, prophesied that the destruction would be so great that:

'. . . *seven months* shall the house of Israel be burying of them, that they may cleanse the land. Yea, all the people of the land shall bury them, and it shall be to them a renown, the day that I shall be glorified, saith the Lord God.'[14]

The *Book of Enoch* declares:

'And all will fear and the watchers will tremble, and great fear and terror will seize them to the end of the earth.'[15]

The Book of the followers of Christ said:

1. 'By these (disasters) was the third part of men killed.'[16]
2. '. . . it rained fire and brimstone from heaven and destroyed them all.

   Even thus shall it be in the day when the Son of man is revealed.

   In that day, he which shall be upon the housetop, and his stuff in the house, let him not come down to take it away: and he that is in the field, let him likewise not return back . . .

   I tell you, in that night there shall be two men in one bed; the one shall be taken, and the other shall be left.

   Two women shall be grinding together; the one shall be taken, the other left.'[17]

And perhaps the most awesome of all:

'But the day of the Lord will come as a *thief in the night*; in the which the heavens shall pass away with a great noise, and the elements shall melt with fervent heat, the earth also and the works that are therein shall be burnt up.'[18]

Was there ever a more graphic description of the rising of that terrifying mushroom cloud than in the words: 'The heavens shall pass away with a great noise, and the elements shall melt with fervent heat?'

7. The Dawn of a New Day

Is there no escape from the awesome threat of this Armageddon? Must the world undergo another such disaster as the Deluge or Flood?

Whether our future will be one of 'fulfilment' or a reversion once again to 'Genesis' depends upon the response of mankind to the Message of God which has now been delivered into their midst by Bahá'u'lláh, and has been carried to every corner of the earth by His followers. There is no excuse for man to say that he hasn't heard. Only the spiritually deaf and blind are shut out. These words are not mine, they are to be found in the Teachings of Bahá'u'lláh.

He has written the following words to those who respond to His call:

'O My servant, who hast sought the good-pleasure of God and clung to His love on the Day when all except a few who were endued with insight have broken away from Him! May God, through His Grace, recompense thee with . . . an everlasting reward, inasmuch as thou hast sought Him on the Day when eyes were blinded.'[1]

Bahá'u'lláh cautioned the lovers of God to escape from the perilous trap of materialism:

'Beware, O men, lest ye be tempted to part with Him (the Messiah) in exchange for the gold and silver ye possess. Let His love be a storehouse of treasure for your souls, on the Day . . . when every pillar shall tremble, when the very skins of men shall creep, when all eyes shall stare up with terror . . .'[2]

Men, Bahá'u'lláh declared, were like black metal, but once they were placed in the fire of the love of God, they would glow with its heat and colour. They would take on the characteristics of this fire, and could be moulded by God into an instrument of value. He told His followers:

'Let thy soul glow with the flame of this undying Fire that burneth in the midmost heart of the world, in such wise that the waters of the universe shall be powerless to cool down its ardour . . .'[3]

'Soon will the present-day order be rolled up,' Bahá'u'lláh declared, 'and a new one spread out in its stead.'[4]

Even though a man may be alive, Bahá'u'lláh said, if he is without the knowledge of the coming of the Messiah, he is as one dead. Even though he may walk about, converse with his neighbour and eat his food, he still is as one dead.

Christ said:

'Let the dead bury their dead: but go thou and preach the kingdom of God.'[5]

He added:

'No man, having put his hand to the plough, and looking back, is fit for the kingdom of God.'[6]

His meaning was clear: let those who are spiritually dead to the Messiah's truth, bury the physically dead, but let those who believe in Him put their hand to the plough and never turn back until the victory is won.

Christ warned:

'Take heed to yourselves, lest at anytime your hearts be overcharged with surfeiting and drunkenness, and the cares of this life, and so *that day come upon you unawares.* . . .
For as a snare shall it come on all them that dwell on the face of the whole earth.
Watch ye, therefore, and pray always, that ye may be accounted worthy to escape all these things that shall come to pass, and to stand before the *Son of man.*'[7]

Bahá'u'lláh appealed to the followers of Christ:

'Beware lest celebration hinder you from (recognising) . . . the Worshipped One! Behold the Lord! . . . Are ye learned in the Gospel, and yet are unable to see the Lord of Glory?'[8]

Tomorrow morning when the sun comes up, each human being will awaken from sleep. He will rise and put on his clothes and begin the work of a new day.

All but those who are dead.

In like manner, now that the sun of the new Day of Christ and Bahá'u'lláh has dawned, all will awaken, arise, and put on their working clothes to serve God and their fellowmen; to do all they can to turn back the onrushing calamity.

All but those who are spiritually dead.

Whether a man is numbered among the living or among the dead is a hidden secret between himself and God. My responsibility has ended with the telling of the story. Each soul must choose his own path. The Books are unsealed, the ears are unstopped, the eyes are opened. It remains up to each individual human being.

Let us look to the future, remembering the words of St. Paul:

'How shall we escape, if we neglect so great salvation.'[9]

A man may see nothing but despair and destruction ahead. Or he may see *the Kingdom of God on earth*. It depends upon his vision, and whether he has spiritual eyes and ears. He can be like either the *son* or the *father* in the fable of the mountain-top. It depends on whether he turns to Bahá'u'lláh or does not. The choice belongs to man. The fable says:

'Once upon a time, a father and his young son journeyed into a far land, and climbing to the mountain-top, they rested for the night. At dawn, the sun banished the darkness and painted the snowcapped peaks with brilliant orange.

'The son awoke. He saw the glowing sky and the flame-coloured mountain-tips. He was a small boy, and could only see through the top of the window above him. He did not understand the brilliance. It alarmed him. He longed for the comfort of yesterday when he was at home with his mother. He wished he had never set out on the journey. He was sure there was only disaster and fire in the strange new heavens.

'The rising sun warmed the winter snow which had lain cold and barren for so long upon the mountainside. It loosened the drifts and sent cascades thundering down into the valley below.

'The dreadful roaring sound terrified the young son even more than the flaming sky. He rushed to his father and shook him. He roused him, crying:

' "Father! Father! Wake up! Wake up! It is the end of the world!"

'The father opened his eyes. He could see everything clearly through the window which was still too high for the vision of his son.

'He saw the sun-painted peaks with their morning fire. He heard the avalanche of snow released by the warming rays of the Spring sun. He knew that soon it would bring fresh water to the parched land below, restoring life. He understood these things. He took his son by the hand to comfort him.

' "No, my son,' he said. "It is not the end of the world. It is the dawn of a new day." '

REFERENCES

Foreword

1. E. G. Browne, quoted preface to *The Chosen Highway*, Lady Blomfield, 1940, pp. v–vi
2. E. G. Browne, letter to Mírzá 'Alí 'Aka Shírazí, from Cambridge University, April 9th, 1889
3. *Bahá'í World, The*, Vol. XII, p. 625

PART ONE

1

1. *The Story of Prophecy*, Henry James Forman, 1936, pp. 310–311
2. *Star of the West Magazine*, Vol. XIV, p. 304
3. *The Story of Prophecy*, Forman, pp. 310–311
4. *Days of Delusion*, Clara E. Sears, 1924, pp. 259–260
5. *The Present Crisis*, James Russell Lowell
6. *Job* 38 : 35
7. *Job* 19 : 25
8. *Numbers* 23 : 23

2

1. *Bahá'í World, The*, Vol. V, p. 604
2. *Our Day in the Light of Prophecy*, W. A. Spicer, 1925, p. 241
3. *The Penetralia*, Andrew Jackson Davis, Boston, 1846
4. *The Story of Prophecy*, Forman, pp. 309–310
5. ibid, p. 310
6. *New York Tribune*, November 20th, 1878
7. ibid.

3

1. *Matthew* 24 : 3
2. ibid. 24 : 13–14
3. *Year Book and Guide to East Africa*, Ed. by Robert Hale Ltd., London, 1953, p. 44
4. *Our Day in the Light of Prophecy*, Spicer, p. 308

5. *Mark* 13 : 10
6. ibid. 13 : 33
7. ibid. 13 : 26

4
1. *Luke* 21 : 7
2. ibid. 21 : 24–27
3. *God Passes By*, Shoghi Effendi, 1944 (Introduction by G. Townshend), iv

5
1. *Matthew* 24 : 3
2. ibid. 24 : 15
3. *Matthew* 24 : 30
4. *Daniel* 8 : 13–14
5. *Bible Reading*, Ed. Review and Herald Pub. Co. (Battle Creek, Mich.), p. 94

6
1. *Revelation* 9 : 15

7
1. *The Dawnbreakers*, Nabíl, 1932, p. 49
2. ibid. p. 50
3. *Leviticus* 26 : 28–33
4. *Daniel* 4 : 13–16

8
1. *Luke* 21 : 28

9
1. *Isaiah* 62 : 2
2. ibid. 65 : 15
3. *Revelation* 2 : 17
4. *Isaiah* 62 : 12
5. *Revelation* 3 : 12
6. ibid. 3 : 5
7. ibid.
8. ibid. 3 : 7–8

9. ibid. 3 : 22

10
1. *Revelation* 3 : 2, 3
2. ibid. 3 : 1
3. ibid. 2 : 2
4. ibid. 16 : 15
5. ibid.
6. *Revelation* 2 : 5, 7, 10, 11, 16, 17, 25, 29
   ibid. 3 : 2, 3, 5, 6, 10, 11, 12, 13, 15, 16, 17, 19, 20, 22
7. ibid. 3 : 12

11
1. *Isaiah* 35 : 2
2. ibid. 40 : 5
3. ibid. 42 : 18
4. *Revelation* 21 : 2, 23
5. *Matthew* 16 : 27
6. *Ezekiel* 1 : 28
7. *Daniel* 10 : 15
8. *Matthew* 24 : 30
   Luke 21 : 27
9. *Daniel* 7 : 13
10. ibid. 7 : 25
11. *Isaiah* 58 : 8
12. ibid. 60 : 1, 16

12
1. *Matthew* 24 : 42
2. *Mark* 13 : 33
3. ibid. 13 : 35–36
4. *Luke* 12 : 39–40
5. *Mark* 13 : 37
6. *Daniel* 12 : 4
7. ibid. 12 : 8
8. ibid. 12 : 9
9. *Isaiah* 29 : 11
10. ibid.
11. I *Corinthians* 4 : 5
12. II *Peter* 1 : 19–20

13. ibid. 1 : 21
14. *John* 16 : 25
15. ibid. 14 : 26

13

1. *Daniel* 12 : 4
2. *Isaiah* 29 : 11
3. ibid. 29 : 18, 24
4. *Daniel* 12 : 9
5. ibid. 7 : 9, 10
6. *Revelation* 22 : 10
7. ibid. 14 : 14
8. ibid. 19 : 13
9. ibid. 5 : 9

14

1. *Matthew* 8 : 22
2. *Jeremiah* 5 : 21
3. *Matthew* 13 : 11, 15, 16
4. ibid. 11 : 14
5. ibid. 11 : 15
6. *John* 1 : 21
7. *Luke* 1 : 15, 17
8. *Matthew* 17 : 10
9. ibid. 17 : 11, 12, 13
10. *Matthew* 24 : 15
11. I *Peter* 1 : 11
12. *Testament of the Twelve Patriarchs*, Asher 7 : 3
13. *The Dialogue with Trypho*, Justin Martyr, Chapter 49
14. *Beyond the Gospels*, Roderic Dunkerley, Pelican Books, 1957, p. 133
15. *Matthew* 17 : 12

15

1. *John* 14 : 18
2. ibid. 14 : 28
3. ibid. 16 : 16
4. ibid. 14 : 3
5. ibid. 16 : 7
6. ibid. 16 : 7–8

7. ibid. 16 : 12, 13
8. ibid. 15 : 26
9. ibid. 14 : 24
10. ibid. 14 : 10
11. ibid. 16 : 13
12. ibid. 14 : 26
13. *Matthew* 23 : 39
14. *John* 4 : 24

17

1. *Matthew* 24 : 14
2. ibid. 24 : 27
3. ibid. 24 : 30
4. ibid.
5. ibid. 24 : 33
6. ibid. 24 : 37
7. ibid. 24 : 39
8. ibid. 24 : 42
9. ibid. 24 : 44
10. ibid. 24 : 46
11. ibid. 24 : 50
12. *Luke* 21 : 27
13. ibid. 21 : 28
14. ibid. 21 : 31
15. ibid. 21 : 34
16. ibid. 21 : 36
17. *John* 14 : 18
18. ibid. 14 : 28
19. ibid. 14 : 3
20. *Matthew* 16 : 27
21. *Revelation* 22 : 20
22. *James* 5 : 7
23. *II Thessalonians* 2 : 1–3
24. *II Peter* 2 : 1–2

18

1. *Micah* 5 : 2
2. ibid. 7 : 7, 12
3. *Ezekiel* 43 : 2
4. *Isaiah* 41 : 2

5. *Matthew* 24 : 27
6. *The Messianic Idea in Israel*,
   J. G. Klausner, 1956, p. 376
7. *Daniel* 8 : 2
8. *Jeremiah* 49 : 38
9. *The Dawnbreakers*, Nabíl,
   p. 49

19

1. *II Peter* 3 : 10
2. *Joel* 2 : 31
3. *Matthew* 24 : 29–30
4. *Joel* 2 : 2
5. *Matthew* 24 : 21, 29–30
6. *Revelation* 6 : 12
7. ibid. 6 : 15, 17
8. *Daniel* 12 : 1
9. ibid.
10. *The Book of the Secrets of
    Enoch*, trans. Charles, p. 48
11. *Daniel* 10 : 13
12. ibid. 10 : 14
13. ibid. 10 : 21
14. ibid.
15. ibid. 10 : 15
16. ibid. 12 : 1
17. ibid. 10 : 14
18. ibid. 8 : 17
19. ibid. 12 : 9
20. ibid. 12 : 4
21. ibid. 7 : 10
22. ibid. 7 : 13
23. ibid. 7 : 22
24. ibid. 7 : 25
25. ibid. 12 : 7

20

1. *Behold He Cometh*, Pankhurst,
   cit. *Star of the West Magazine*,
   Vol. XIV, p. 303
2. *Matthew* 24 : 33

PART TWO

1

1. *The Dawnbreakers*, Nabíl, pp. 512-513
2. *La religion de Bab*, Clément Huart, 1889, pp. 3-4
3. ibid.
4. *Seyyèd Ali Mohammed dit le Bâb*, A.-L.-M. Nicolas, 1905, p. 375
5. E. G. Browne, cited in preface to *The Chosen Highway*, Blomfield, pp. v-vi

2

1. *God Passes By*, Shoghi Effendi, p. 56
2. *The Dawnbreakers*, Nabíl, p. 92
3. ibid. pp. 93-94
4. *Bahá'í World, The*, Vol. XII, p. 625

3

1. *John* 10 : 2-16
2. *The Dawnbreakers*, Nabíl, p. 41
3. *Zechariah* 4 : 14
4. *Malachi* 4 : 5
5. *Daniel* 7 : 13
6. *Malachi* 3 : 1

4

1. *Days of Delusion*, Sears, Introduction, p. xxiv
2. *The Dawnbreakers*, Nabíl, pp. 61-62
3. ibid. p. 69
4. ibid. pp. 62-65 (paraphrase)
5. cited *God Passes By*, Shoghi Effendi, p. 80
6. *The Dawnbreakers*, Nabíl, p. 65
7. *Seyyèd Ali Mohammed dit le Bâb*, Nicolas, p. 203
8. ibid. p. 376
9. *Journal of the Royal Asiatic Society*, 1889, p. 933
10. cited *God Passes By*, Shoghi Effendi, p. 56
11. *The Gleam*, Sir Francis Younghusband, 1923, pp. 183-184
12. *The Reconciliation of Races and Religions*, T. K. Cheyne, 1914, pp. 70, 8
13. *Matthew* 3 : 11

14. *The Covenant of Bahá'u'lláh*, Manchester, 1950, p. 20
15. *Epistle to the Son of the Wolf*, Bahá'u'lláh, 1941, p. 154
16. *The Covenant of Bahá'u'lláh*, p. 23
17. *Epistle to the Son of the Wolf*, pp. 157, 156

5

1. *The Covenant of Bahá'u'lláh*, p. 21
2. *Epistle to the Son of the Wolf*, p. 141
3. ibid. p. 141
4. *The Dawnbreakers*, Nabíl, p. 86
5. ibid. p. 96
6. ibid. p. 521
7. ibid. p. 50
8. *Bahá'u'lláh and the New Era*, Esslemont, Ch. III
9. ibid.
10. ibid.
11. ibid.
12. *Epistle to the Son of the Wolf*, Bahá'u'lláh, p. 142
13. ibid. p. 160
14. ibid. p. 152

6

1. *The Dawnbreakers*, Nabíl, pp. 104–106 (paraphrase)
2. *Daniel* 12 : 1
3. *Star of the West Magazine*, Vol. xiv, p. 291
4. Cheyne, cited *Appreciations of the Bahá'í Faith*, 1947, p. 18
5. *The Dawnbreakers*, Nabíl, pp. 607–608 (paraphrase)

PART THREE

1

1. *Star of the West Magazine*, Vol. xiv, p. 291
2. cited *God Passes By*, Shoghi Effendi, p. 95
3. *The Great Tribulation*, John Cumming, 1859, p. 246
4. *Enoch* 56 : 5
5. cited *The Messianic Idea in Israel*, p. 376
6. *Ezekiel* 43 : 2
7. ibid. 43 : 4

2

1. *Micah* 4 : 9
2. ibid. 4 : 10
3. ibid. 4 : 1
4. *Ezekiel* 1 : 1
5. ibid. 1 : 28
6. ibid. 3 : 12, 23
7. *The Chosen Highway*, Blomfield, p. 242

3

1. *God Passes By*, Shoghi Effendi, p. 110
2. ibid. *op cit.*
3. *Isaiah* 45 : 22
4. ibid. 46 : 3–4
5. ibid. 47 : 4
6. ibid. 48 : 14
7. ibid. 48 : 15
8. ibid. 48 : 16
9. ibid. 48 : 17
10. ibid. 48 : 20
11. ibid. 46 : 11, 13
12. *Zechariah* 4
13. ibid. 4 : 8–9
14. ibid. 4 : 6
15. ibid. 4 : 14

4

1. *Micah* 1 : 3
2. *Gleanings from The Writings of Bahá'u'lláh*, Section XI
3. *Micah* 2 : 12
4. *The Reconstructionist*, Vol. XXI, April 20, 1955
5. *Micah* 4 : 1
6. ibid. 3 : 12
7. ibid. 5 : 3
8. ibid. 4 : 10
9. ibid. 5 : 4
10. ibid. 4 : 3
11. *'Our God Shall Come'*, *Addresses on the Second Coming of the Lord*, Horatius Bonar, 1878

12. *Micah* 7 : 2–4
13. ibid. 7 : 4

5

1. *Micah* 7 : 10
2. ibid. 7 : 7
3. ibid. 7 : 12
4. ibid.
5. ibid.
6. ibid.
7. ibid. 7 : 13
8. *The Chosen Highway*, Blomfield, p. 64
9. cited *God Passes By*, Shoghi Effendi, p. 186
10. *Micah* 7 : 14
11. *The Promised Day Is Come*, Shoghi Effendi, 1941, p. 118
12. *Gleanings from The Writings of Bahá'u'lláh*, Section XI
13. *Micah* 7 : 15
14. *Psalms* 95 : 10
15. *The Great Tribulation*, Cumming, p. 246
16. *Bahá'í World Faith*, 1943, p. 55

6

1. *Isaiah* 58 : 8, 12
2. ibid. 59 : 20
3. ibid. 59 : 21
4. ibid. 60 : 1
5. ibid. 35 : 4, 2
6. ibid. 40 : 10–11
7. ibid. 40 : 5
8. *Ezekiel* 43 : 2
9. ibid. 43 : 4
10. *John* 10 : 2
11. *Matthew* 16 : 27
12. *Revelation* 21 : 1–2, 23
13. *John* 4 : 20
14. ibid. 4 : 21
15. *Revelation* 21 : 10–11
16. *Enoch* 69 : 26
17. ibid. 69 : 14
18. ibid. 69 : 15

19. *Gleanings from The Writings of Bahá'u'lláh*, Section XI
20. ibid.
21. *Habakkuk* 2 : 14
22. ibid. 2 : 2–3
23. ibid. 1 : 5

7

1. *God Passes By*, p. 94 (italics are author's)
2. *Ezekiel* 38 : 13
3. ibid. 38 : 22
4. *Genesis* 25 : 1–3
5. *Ezekiel* 38 : 8
6. ibid. 37 : 21, 22
7. ibid. 37 : 26
8. *Isaiah* 60 : 4
9. ibid. 60 : 1
10. ibid. 35 : 10
11. ibid. 35 : 2
12. ibid. 40 : 11
13. ibid. 40 : 5
14. *Ezekiel* 37 : 27–28
15. *Appreciations of the Bahá'í Faith*, p. 60

8

1. *Isaiah* 11 : 12
2. ibid.
3. ibid. 11 : 1
4. *Zechariah* 3 : 8
5. ibid. 1 : 16
6. ibid. 8 : 3
7. *Genesis* 15 : 4–7, 18
8. ibid. 15 : 9
9. *God Passes By*, Shoghi Effendi, p. 351
10. *Appreciations of the Bahá'í Faith*, p. 57
11. *Christian Century*, April 10th, 1957, Marcus Bach; *Bahá'í : A Second Look*
12. *Isaiah* 18 : 3
13. ibid. 30 : 18–20
14. *Psalms* 102 : 16

15. *Isaiah* 60 : 10
16. ibid. 60 : 1

9

1. *Hosea* 2 : 15
2. ibid. 2 : 23
3. ibid. 3 : 5
4. *Isaiah* 65 : 9–10
5. ibid. 65 : 15
6. ibid. 62 : 2
7. ibid. 62 : 12
8. *Ezekiel* 48 : 35
9. *Joshua* 7 : 24–26
10. *God Passes By,* Shoghi Effendi, p. 185
11. ibid. p. 187
12. ibid. p. 183
13. *Psalms* 24 : 9–10
14. *Isaiah* 9 : 1
15. ibid. 9 : 6–7
16. *Matthew* 22 : 21
17. *John* 18 : 36
18. *Mark* 10 : 18
19. *John* 10 : 29
20. ibid. 5 : 19
21. *Matthew* 10 : 34
22. *Luke* 12 : 51
23. ibid. 12 : 52
24. *A Traveller's Narrative,* E. G. Browne, 1891, p. xl
25. *Psalms* 50 : 2–3
26. ibid. 48 : 1–2

10

1. *The Jewish Encyclopedia,* Funk and Wagnalls, 1902, Vol. III,
   p. 579
2. ibid.
3. ibid.
4. ibid.
5. ibid.
6. ibid.
7. ibid.

8. *History*, Tacitus, Book II, lxxviii
9. *The Jewish Encyclopedia*, Vol. III, p. 579
10. ibid.
11. *A History of Messianic Speculation in Israel*, A. H. Silver, 1927, p. 42
12. *God Passes By*, Shoghi Effendi, p. 184
13. ibid.
14. ibid.
15. ibid.
16. ibid.
17. ibid.
18. ibid.
19. *A Traveller's Narrative*, Introduction, Browne
20. ibid.
21. *Isaiah* 53 : 3
22. ibid.
23. ibid. 53 : 4
24. *The Promised Day is Come*, Shoghi Effendi, pp. 42-3
25. *Isaiah* 53 : 5
26. ibid. 53 : 8
27. *God Passes By*, Shoghi Effendi, pp. 190–191
28. *Isaiah* 53 : 9
29. ibid. 53 : 10
30. *Psalms* 89 : 27, 28
31. *A Traveller's Narrative*, Browne, p. xxxvi
32. *Appreciations of the Bahá'í Faith*, p. 18
33. *Isaiah* 53 : 10
34. *Psalms* 142 : 7
35. *God Passes By*, Shoghi Effendi, p. 230

II

1. *Isaiah* 35 : 1
2. *The Chosen Highway*, Blomfield, p. 96
3. *Haifa, or Life in Modern Palestine*, Laurence Oliphant, 1887, pp. 103–104
4. ibid. p. 104
5. *Isaiah* 35 : 8, 10
6. ibid. 11 : 10
7. ibid. 60 : 1, 13
8. ibid. 41 : 18–20

9. *Zionism in Prophecy*, F. Hudgings, 1936, pp. 55–56
10. *Joel* 2 : 23
11. *Zechariah* 8 : 3, 11–12
12. *Isaiah* 35 : 6–7
13. *Haifa*, Oliphant, p. 104

12

1. *God Passes By*, Shoghi Effendi, p. 139
2. ibid. p. 138 (quotation from Shoghi Effendi)
3. ibid.
4. *Enoch* 46 : 3
5. *The Promised Day Is Come*, Shoghi Effendi, p. 26
6. ibid. pp. 21–22
7. ibid. p. 22
8. ibid. p. 34
9. *Appreciations of the Bahá'í Faith*, pp. 12–13
10. *Psalms* 76 : 12
11. *Job* 34 : 24
12. *Isaiah* 14 : 5
13. ibid. 24 : 21
14. *Daniel* 7 : 13
15. *Daniel* 7 : 9
16. *Enoch* 46 : 4–5
17. ibid. 56 : 5
18. *The Promised Day Is Come*, Shoghi Effendi, p. 22
19. *God Passes By*, Shoghi Effendi, p. 224

13

1. *Bahá'í World Faith*, p. 60
2. *The Bahá'í Revelation*, 1955, p. 58
3. ibid. p. 14
4. ibid. p. 148
5. ibid. pp. 235–236
6. *Star of the West Magazine*, Vol. XII, p. 188
7. *The Bahá'í Revelation*, p. 59
8. ibid. (The passage refers to several Prophets.)
9. ibid.
10. ibid. p. 58
11. ibid. p. 59
12. *The Promulgation of Universal Peace*, 'Abdu'l-Bahá, 1922, Vol. I

PART FOUR

1

1. *Revelation* 6 : 12
2. ibid.
3. ibid. 6 : 13
4. *Our Day in the Light of Prophecy*, Spicer, p. 77

2

1. *Our Day in the Light of Prophecy*, Spicer, p. 80
2. *The Life of Voltaire*, S. G. Tallentyre, 1903, Vol. II, p. 30
3. *Matthew* 24 : 7–8, 30

3

1. *Daniel and the Revelation*, Uriah Smith, 1904, p. 445
2. J. G. Whittier, *Abraham Davenport*
3. *Matthew* 24 : 29–30

4

1. *Matthew* 24 : 29–30

5

1. *Days of Delusion*, Sears, Introduction, p. xxiv
2. ibid. p. 37
3. *Days of Delusion*, facing p. 52
4. ibid. facing p. 56
5. ibid. facing p. 56
6. ibid. p. 68
7. *Encyclopaedia Britannica*, 1962, Vol. XI, p. 520; Vol. XXI, pp. 319–321, 480
8. *The Dawnbreakers*, Nabíl, pp. 41–42 (paraphrase)
9. *Encyclopaedia Britannica*, Vol. XX, p. 724

6

1. *Through Space and Time*, Sir James Jeans, 1934, p. 154
2. *Epistle to the Son of the Wolf*, p. 141
3. *Encyclopedia Americana*, 1944 ed., Vol. III, p. 690
4. *God Passes By*, p. 102
5. ibid.

6. *Through Space and Time*, Jeans, p. 154
7. *Psalms* 19 : 1
8. *Matthew* 24 : 42

PART FIVE

1

1. *Matthew* 24 : 4–5
2. ibid. 24 : 23
3. ibid. 24 : 24
4. *John* 7 : 12
5. *John* 7 : 46–47
6. ibid. 7 : 43
7. ibid. 7 : 48
8. ibid. 7 : 49
9. *Deuteronomy* 21 : 23
10. *John* 6 : 63
11. *John* 6 : 66

2

1. *Matthew* 24 : 26
2. *Matthew* 7 : 15
3. *John* 10 : 2, 4
4. ibid. 10 : 16–17

3

1. *John* 16 : 13
2. ibid. 14 : 26
3. ibid. 16 : 14
4. ibid. 12 : 48
5. *Appreciations of the Bahá'í Faith*, pp. 25–26
6. ibid. p. 62
7. ibid.
8. Glenn A. Shook, letter, July 1946
9. *Appreciations of the Bahá'í Faith*, p. 10
10. ibid. p. 13
11. *Gleanings from The Writings of Bahá'u'lláh*, Section CX

4

1. *Bahá'u'lláh and the New Era,* cited, Esslemont, Ch. xi
2. ibid. cited
3. ibid.
4. *Bahá'í Prayers,* London, 1951, pp. 47–49 (paraphrase)
5. *Paris Talks,* 'Abdu'l-Bahá, Lecture given at a studio, November 6th

5

1. *The Bahá'í Revelation,* p. 308
2. *The World Order of Bahá'u'lláh,* 1938, p. 64
3. ibid. p. 65
4. ibid.
5. *The Promised Day Is Come,* Shoghi Effendi, p. 127
6. *Bahá'í Journal,* British Isles, November, 1959
7. *Gleanings from The Writings of Bahá'u'lláh,* Section xliii
8. ibid. Section cxxx
9. ibid. Section cxvii
10. *The Bahá'í Revelation,* p. 89

6

1. *Bahá'u'lláh and the New Era,* Esslemont, Ch. viii
2. *Bahá'í Journal,* November, 1959
3. *Bahá'u'lláh and the New Era,* Esslemont, Ch. viii
4. *Deuteronomy* 18 : 15
5. *John* 5 : 46
6. ibid. 5 : 47
7. ibid. 16 : 12, 13
8. *The Promised Day Is Come,* Shoghi Effendi, pp. 26–27
9. ibid.
10. *Bahá'u'lláh and the New Era,* Esslemont, Ch. viii
11. *Bahá'í World Faith,* p. 180
12. ibid. p. 168
13. *Gleanings from The Writings of Bahá'u'lláh,* pp. 78–79
14. *Bahá'í World Faith,* p. 168
15. *John* 12 : 44
16. *Gleanings from The Writings of Bahá'u'lláh,* Section clvi

7

1. *Bahá'u'lláh and the New Era,* Esslemont, Ch. viii
2. *The Advent of Divine Justice,* Shoghi Effendi, 1939, p. 22

3. ibid. p. 21
4. ibid. pp. 21–22
5. *The Hidden Words*, Bahá'u'lláh, Introduction by George Townshend
6. *Paris Talks*, 'Abdu'l-Bahá. First talk
7. *The Promulgation of Universal Peace*, p. 199
8. *Appreciations of the Bahá'í Faith*, p. 36
9. *Bahá'í Administration*, Shoghi Effendi, 1928, pp. 9–10 (from 'Abdu'l-Bahá)
10. *Appreciations of the Bahá'í Faith*, pp. 33–34
11. *Gleanings from The Writings of Bahá'u'lláh*, Section CXXX

8

1. *Bahá'u'lláh and the New Era*, Esslemont, Ch. I
2. *Deuteronomy* 4 : 29
3. *Jeremiah* 29 : 13
4. *Matthew* 7 : 7–8
5. *Gleanings from The Writings of Bahá'u'lláh*, Section CLI
6. ibid. p. 267
7. *Bahá'u'lláh and the New Era*, Esslemont, Ch. V

9

1. *Paris Talks*, 'Abdu'l-Bahá, Tenth Principle
2. *Bahá'u'lláh and the New Era*, Esslemont, Ch. IX
3. *God Passes By*, Shoghi Effendi, p. 75
4. ibid. p. 76

10

1. *Bahá'u'lláh and the New Era*, Esslemont, Ch. IX (paraphrase)
2. ibid.
3. *Bahá'í World Faith*, p. 200

11

1. *Zephaniah* 3 : 8–9
2. *Bahá'u'lláh and the New Era*, Esslemont, Ch. X
3. *Zechariah* 14 : 9
4. *Bahá'u'lláh and the New Era*, Esslemont, Ch. X
5. *Bahá'í World Faith*, p. 199

12

1. *Bahá'u'lláh and the New Era*, Esslemont, Ch. XII
2. ibid.
3. ibid.
4. ibid.
5. *The World Order of Bahá'u'lláh*, pp. 203–204
6. *Bahá'u'lláh and the New Era*, Esslemont, Ch. XII
7. ibid.

13

1. *Paris Talks*, 'Abdu'l-Bahá, 'The Universal Love'
2. *Bahá'u'lláh and the New Era*, Esslemont, Ch. V
3. *Matthew* 25 : 45
4. *The Advent of Divine Justice*, Shoghi Effendi, p. 29
5. *The Promised Day Is Come*, Shoghi Effendi, pp. 117–118 (paraphrase)
6. *The Advent of Divine Justice*, Shoghi Effendi, p. 31
7. *Bahá'u'lláh and the New Era*, Esslemont, Ch. X

14

1. *Gleanings from The Writings of Bahá'u'lláh*, Section LXXXI
2. ibid. Section XXVII
3. *Heredity and the Ascent of Man*, C. C. Hurst, 1935, p. 131
4. *The Freedom of Man*, A. H. Compton, 1935, p. 121
5. *Washington Star*, April 12th, 1936
6. *Gleanings from The Writings of Bahá'u'lláh*, Section LXXXI
7. *Mark* 8 : 34, 36
8. *Matthew* 19 : 25–29
9. ibid. 19 : 30
10. *Gleanings from The Writings of Bahá'u'lláh*, Section LXXXII

15

1. *Bahá'í World Faith*, p. 195
2. *Paris Talks*, 'Prayer as Service'
3. ibid.

17

1. *Bahá'í Revelation*, p. 11

2. ibid. p. 76
3. *Matthew* 7 : 15–20
4. *God Passes By*, Shoghi Effendi, p. 215

PART SIX

1

1. Dr. T. K. Cheyne, cited, *Appreciations of the Bahá'í Faith*, p. 18
2. I *Corinthians* 9 : 16
3. *Matthew* 24 : 22
4. *Isaiah* 65 : 8–9

2

1. *Matthew* 6 : 20, 21

3

1. II *Timothy* 3 : 1–5
2. *Nahum* 2 : 3–4
3. *Gleanings from The Writings of Bahá'u'lláh*, Section XCIX
4. *Mark* 1 : 17
5. cited *The Promised Day Is Come*, Shoghi Effendi, p. 110
6. *Matthew* 5 : 39
7. *Gleanings from The Writings of Bahá'u'lláh*, Section CXIX
8. *Matthew* 4 : 17
9. ibid. 6 : 10
10. cited *The World Order of Bahá'u'lláh*, Shoghi Effendi, p. 104
11. *Jonah* 1 : 2
12. cited *The World Order of Bahá'u'lláh*, Shoghi Effendi, p. 163
13. ibid.
14. ibid.
15. ibid. pp. 104–105
16. ibid. p. 104

4

1. *Gleanings from The Writings of Bahá'u'lláh*, Section LXV
2. ibid. Section CLVI
3. *Bahá'í World Faith*, p. 183

4. *The Chosen Highway*, Blomfield, p. 184 (paraphrase)
5. *Gleanings from The Writings of Bahá'u'lláh*, Section CLXIII
6. *Isaiah* 24 : 21
7. ibid. 13 : 7
8. ibid. 13 : 13; 24 : 18, 6, 20

5

1. *Gleanings from The Writings of Bahá'u'lláh*, Section CXVIII/CXIX
2. ibid. Section CV
3. ibid. Section CXVI
4. *The Hidden Words*, Persian, No. 64
5. Tablet to the Czar, cited *God Passes By*, p. 226
6. *Gleanings from The Writings of Bahá'u'lláh*, Section XVI

6

1. *Gleanings from The Writings of Bahá'u'lláh*, Section XVIII
2. ibid.
3. ibid.
4. ibid.
5. ibid. Section CLI
6. *The Hidden Words*, Persian, No. 21 (paraphrase)
7. *Gleanings from The Writings of Bahá'u'lláh*, Section XVIII
8. ibid. Section V
9. ibid.
10. ibid.
11. *Epistle to the Son of the Wolf*, p. 131
12. *God Passes By*, p. 220
13. *Ezekiel* 38 : 20
14. ibid. 39 : 12–13
15. *Enoch* 1 : 5
16. *Revelation* 9 : 18
17. *Luke* 17 : 29–37
18. II *Peter* 3 : 10

7

1. *Gleanings from The Writings of Bahá'u'lláh*, Section XV
2. ibid.
3. ibid.
4. ibid. Section IV

5. *Luke* 9 : 60
6. ibid. 9 : 62
7. ibid. 21 : 34–36
8. *Bahá'u'lláh and the New Era*, Esslemont, Ch. VIII
9. *Hebrews* 2 : 3

PRESCRIPTION FOR LIVING

by Ruhiyyih Rabbani

A sympathetic and timely presentation of the rules of spiritual living which make for individual happiness and fulfilment.

THE HEART OF THE GOSPEL

by George Townshend

A brilliant exposition of the central theme of Christ's Message (which Christianity has forgotten) by a former dignitary of the Church.

THE RENEWAL OF CIVILISATION

by David Hofman

A brief introduction to the history and teachings of the Bahá'í Faith.

THE PROMISE OF ALL AGES

by George Townshend

A scholarly presentation of the Bahá'í Faith as the fulfilment of the age-old promise of God's Kingdom on earth.

CHRIST AND BAHÁ'U'LLÁH

by George Townshend

A profound and challenging book, written with clarity and reverence by a dignitary of the Church who resigned his orders to proclaim the truth that Christ has come again to an unheeding world.

THE FLAME

by William Sears and Robert Quigley

The story of Lua Getsinger, one of the first Bahá'ís of the West (1894), whose heroic travels in four continents to herald the Faith of Bahá'u'lláh are legendary.

RELIGION FOR MANKIND

by Horace Holley

A selection from the works of one of the most eminent Bahá'ís. The special relationship of the Bahá'í Faith to present-day problems and the evolution of world order is brilliantly discussed.

THE WINE OF ASTONISHMENT

by William Sears

A clear and straight-forward consideration of many puzzling and controversial Christian doctrines, such as the Trinity, Baptism, Resurrection, Miracles, and others, with conclusions simple and satisfying to the modern mind.

Our current list available on request:

George Ronald
46 High Street, Kidlington, Oxford,
England